How To Care For Your Typewriter

√ Dust every day the exterior parts of your typewriter that can be easily reached. Use a brush or a lint-free dry cloth.

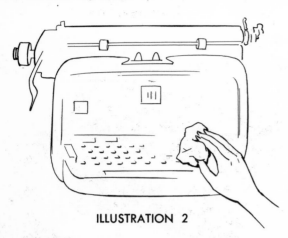

ILLUSTRATION 2

√ Keep the carriage rail clean. Move the carriage to the extreme left. Wipe the exposed surface of the carriage rail with a dry cloth. Move the carriage to the extreme right and wipe.

√ Clean the type with a dry bristle brush. Every second or third day use a small amount of cleaning fluid. Brush dust and erasure dirt from the type bars. Brush *toward* you.

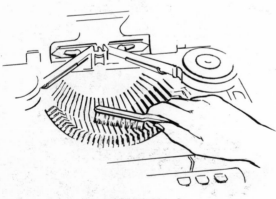

ILLUSTRATION 3

√ When you erase, move the carriage to the extreme left or extreme right to prevent gritty particles from dropping into the machine.

√ About once a week clean the cylinder and the paper feed rolls. Use a cloth slightly moistened with cleaning fluid. Rotate the cylinder to make sure that you clean the entire surface.

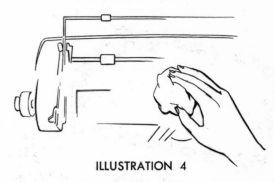

ILLUSTRATION 4

√ Make it a practice to use a backing sheet inserted behind the paper on which you are to type. The use of a backing sheet will reduce wear on the surface of the cylinder.

√ Always cover your typewriter when the machine is not in use.

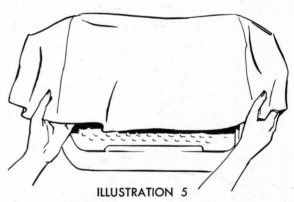

ILLUSTRATION 5

Changing A Ribbon

1. Put the ribbon indicator on red, lock the shift, and then press down any two central keys until they lock. You will thus raise the ribbon guide into full view.

2. Wind the used ribbon on one spool.

3. Fix the route of the ribbon in your mind. Then detach the used ribbon from the empty spool and lift out the ribbon.

4. Unroll about ten inches of the new ribbon and fasten it to the empty spool.

5. Fix both spools in position and check to see that the ribbon is straight. Then thread the new ribbon through the guide.

6. After you have inserted the new ribbon, move the ribbon indicator to blue and unlock the keys and the shift.

Electric Typewriters

ILLUSTRATION 6
IBM

ILLUSTRATION 7
Olivetti Underwood

ILLUSTRATION 8
Royal

ILLUSTRATION 9
Remington

Rowe
COLLEGE TYPING

Second Edition
Revised

BY

CHARLES G. REIGNER, Ed. D.

THE H. M. ROWE COMPANY

Baltimore • **Chicago**

Acknowledgment

Grateful acknowledgment is made to the many teachers who have taught ROWE COLLEGE TYPING and whose wide and successful experience is reflected in the simplified presentation of this Second Edition.

Index

REFERENCE LIST OF OPERATING PARTS

Parts Used for Inserting the Paper (Page 6)

Cylinder (Platen)—the roller around which the paper is fed and held in position for typing.

Cylinder (Platen) Knob—the knob at each end of the cylinder; used to feed the paper into the typewriter and to turn the cylinder by hand.

Bail—used with the paper bail rolls to hold the paper firmly against the cylinder.

Paper Rest—the wide metal plate which supports the paper after it is fed into the machine (also called paper table).

Parts Used in Setting Margin Stops (Page 7)

Margin Stops—the metal catches used to set the length of the writing line and the width of the side margins.

Automatic Margin Stop Set—the mechanism used for setting the margin stops.

Line Scale—the scale at the front of the typewriter that shows the spaces in the line.

Paper Guide—the movable metal strip on the left side of the paper rest; used to guide the left edge of the paper.

Paper Guide Scale—the scale on the paper rest that marks the edge of the paper.

Paper Bail Scale—the scale along the paper bail to help check writing position.

Parts Used in the Preliminary Lesson and in Division One (Pages 8-36)

Line Space Regulator—the device used to adjust the typewriter for single spacing, double spacing, or triple spacing.

Carriage Return Lever—used to return the carriage and to space to the next line of writing.

Carriage Return Bar or Key—the bar or key on an electric typewriter to return the carriage and to space to the next line of writing.

Space Bar—the long bar just below the bottom row of keys; operated by the right thumb and used for spacing. Each time the bar is struck, the carriage moves one space. Additional pressure on the bar will cause some electric typewriters to continue to space until the bar is released. Other electric typewriters are equipped with a separate key for repeat forward spacing.

Paper Release—the lever which releases the pressure on the paper; used when straightening or removing the paper.

Shift Keys—used in writing capitals and shift-key characters.

Shift Lock—used to lock the shift keys in position.

Tab Clear Key—the key used to clear the tabulator stops.

Tab Set Key—the key used to set a tabulator stop.

Tab Key or Bar—used to indent for paragraphs or to set up tabulations. When this key or bar is depressed, the carriage jumps to the next tabulator setting.

Other Operating Parts

Carriage Release Lever—the lever at each end of the cylinder which releases the carriage and enables the operator to move it quickly to any point.

Card Holders—the metal fingers in front of the cylinder used to hold envelopes, cards, or small pieces of paper against the cylinder.

Backspace Key—used to move the carriage backward one space at a time.

Ribbon Color and Stencil Control—the lever on the front of the machine used to raise, lower, or disengage the ribbon.

Touch Control—used to adjust the key tension to the individual touch.

Variable Line Spacer—used to reset the line of writing.

Ratchet Release (Line Finder)—permits typing above or below the regular line of writing.

Margin Release Key—permits writing in the margins without moving the margin stops.

Cylinder Scale—the scale showing the spaces across the machine; used as a guide in setting the margin stops and in locating the printing point.

Ribbon Reverse—the device used for reversing the movement of the ribbon by hand.

Contents

Typing Pointers

Before you start work on the Preliminary Lesson, page 8, your instructor will show you how to form correct habits in typewriting and will explain the proper operation of those parts of your typewriter that you will be using. The following paragraphs provide a summary of typing pointers to which you can refer if necessary.

Correct Position Of Book

Always place this book—or any other copy from which you type—at the *right* of your typewriter. Lay the book in a slanting position with the lower part closer to you than the upper part. You want your book to be in the position that will enable you to read the pages easily. You are going to keep your *eyes on the book*—not on the typewriter.

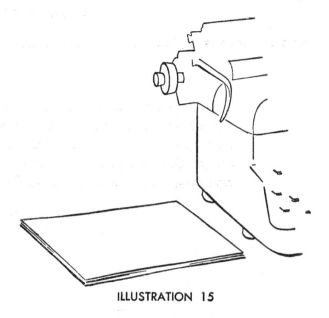

ILLUSTRATION 15

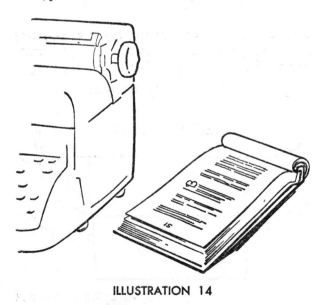

ILLUSTRATION 14

Correct Place For Paper

Lay the paper on which you are to type at the *left* side of your typewriter, with the 8½-inch edge endwise to the left side.

Inserting The Paper

Always pick up the paper with your *left* hand about midway along the 11-inch side—thumb under the sheet and fingers on top. Push up the bail with your right hand. Insert the paper between the paper rest and the cylinder (platen). At the same time grasp the right cylinder knob firmly with the thumb and the first two fingers of your right hand. Give the knob a quick twist or twirl so that the paper will feed into the machine in one movement. Drop the bail on the sheet.

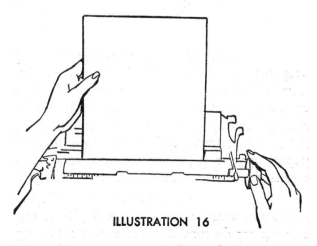

ILLUSTRATION 16

Straightening The Paper

If you notice, when you turn up the sheet, that the top edge is not straight, turn the sheet back (down) until the top edge is lined up more or less with the line scale. Now, loosen the paper by using the paper release; then straighten the paper by hand. Flip the paper release back into position. Turn up the sheet to the place where you are to begin typing.

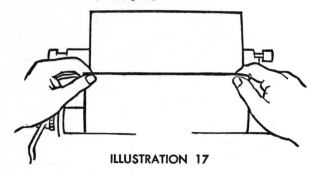

ILLUSTRATION 17

Moving The Carriage

To move the carriage, use the carriage release lever. Most machines have two carriage release levers—one at the left and the other at the right.

Returning The Carriage

If you have an electric typewriter, you return the carriage by simply touching lightly the *Re-* *turn* key with the little finger of your left hand. The carriage automatically turns up for the next line of typing and at the same time returns the carriage to the starting point.

If you are using a manual typewriter with a downsweep lever, hold your left hand in vertical position with your fingers extended and strike the lever with the inside of your fingers. If your typewriter has an upsweep lever, hold the palm of your left hand down—with the fingers close together—and strike the lever with your forefinger supported by the other fingers.

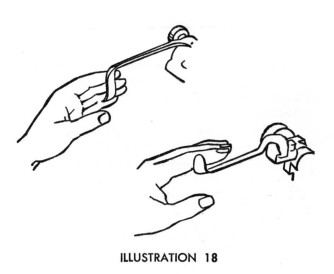

ILLUSTRATION 18

Spacing For Lines Of Typing

Near the left cylinder knob of your typewriter there is a small lever with settings marked 1 2 3. When you are to type with single spacing, set the lever at 1; with double spacing, at 2; with triple spacing, at 3. With the 1 setting you turn up the paper one line at a time when you return the carriage; with the 2 setting, two lines at a time; with the 3 setting, three lines at a time.

```
For single-spaced typing,     For double-spaced typing.     For triple-spaced typing,
use the setting marked 1.                                    use the setting marked 3.
                              use the setting marked 2.
```

ILLUSTRATION 19

Pica And Elite Type

Determine right now whether your typewriter has pica or elite type. Some manual typewriters and some electrics have pica type; others have elite type. Pica type, the larger of the two sizes, provides for ten (10) spaces to the inch across the page. Elite type, the smaller of the two sizes, provides for twelve (12) spaces to the inch across the page. Study this comparison.

```
Pica    You have fifty characters and spaces in this line.
Elite     This five-inch line has exactly sixty characters and spaces.
```

Setting The Left Margin Stop

In your work on Divisions One and Two you won't have to bother about the right margin stop. Just slide it over to the extreme right. You will use only the left margin stop, and you will begin each line at the point where you set that stop.

Your instructor may want you to center your lines on the paper, so that you will have the same width of white space in the right margin as in the left margin.

Different makes and models of typewriters have different devices for setting the margin stops. You can easily determine the point at which to set the left stop when you know that you must have one-half of your typed line to the left of the center point of your *paper* and the other half to the right of that center point.

Pica: The total number of spaces across the sheet is 85. The center point of the sheet is one-half of 85, or space 43. One-half of 50 (number of spaces in the line) is 25. Subtract 25 from 43. The result is 18. If you have the left edge of your paper at 0 on the line scale, set the left margin stop at 18. Set the paper guide in such

a way that when you insert the paper, it will be against the paper guide.

Elite: The total number of spaces across the sheet is 102. The center point of the sheet is one-half of 102, or space 51. One-half of 50 (number of spaces in the line) is 25. Subtract 25 from 51. The result is 26. If you have the left edge of your paper at 0 on the line scale, set the left margin stop at 26. Set the paper guide in such a way that when you insert the paper, it will be against the paper guide.

Vertical Spacing

There are six lines to the inch down the paper, no matter whether you are using a machine with pica type or one with elite type. Standard-size paper is 11 inches deep; hence there are 66 (6 $\times$ 11) lines available down the paper.

```
XXXXXXXXXX    XXXXXXXXXXXX
XXXXXXXXXX    XXXXXXXXXXXX
XXXXXXXXXX    XXXXXXXXXXXX
XXXXXXXXXX    XXXXXXXXXXXX
XXXXXXXXXX    XXXXXXXXXXXX
XXXXXXXXXX    XXXXXXXXXXXX
```

ILLUSTRATION 20

Preliminary Lesson

1. Insert a sheet of paper into your typewriter. Practice the operation until you can perform it easily and naturally.

2. Check the straightness of the paper. Make sure that the top edge is even with the line scale.

3. Set the line space regulator at 1 for single spacing.

4. Space down one inch from the top of the sheet; that is, strike the carriage return lever six times if you are using a manual typewriter; touch lightly the *Return* key six times if you are using an electric.

5. Disengage any margin stops that may have been set; then set the left margin stop for a line of 50 spaces.

You will note that the arrangement of the data in a bibliography is quite similar to the arrangement of the information in bibliographic footnotes. The chief difference is in the arrangement of the author's name. In a bibliography the author's surname appears first.

Problem 8. Type this bibliography for the manuscript, *The Story Of Paper.* Center the word *Bibliography* two inches from the top edge. Double-space. Set margin stops for a 6½-inch line.

Bibliography

Cole, Thomas F. (ed.) *Paper-Making through the Ages,* Rev. ed., New York, H. N. Young & Sons, 1952

Davidson, Herbert S., *A Brief History of Paper-Making,* Chicago, Watts Publishing Company, 1952

Garson, William F., "The Romance of Printing," *Graphic Arts Monthly,* February, 1952, pp. 67 ff.

Kent, George F., "French Industry during the Eighteenth Century," *Historical Review,* November, 1951, p. 132

Lewis, William F., *The American Revolution,* Boston, Parker Press, 1951

Patterson, John D., *Early European Paper-Makers,* St. Louis, Reese Publishing House, 1950

Robinson, Homer S., "From Pulp to Paper," *Science Today,* January, 1952, p. 27

Wainwright, Frank S., *American Pioneers,* Cleveland, Howard Publishing Company, 1951

West, Daniel R. and others, *Report of America's Forest Resources,* New York, American Lumber Association, 1952

Index. The final section of a manuscript is usually the index. When the manuscript is to be set in type and printed as a book, the author postpones the preparation of the index until the material is in page proof form. An index for a typewritten or a mimeographed manuscript may be prepared as soon as the body of the article has been typed.

The index is arranged alphabetically according to the first letter of the first word in each entry or subentry. The subdivisions of an entry should be indented. Capitalize the first word of each major entry. Use a small letter for the first word of each subentry. A comma separates the entry or subentry from the page number. Study Illustration 111.

Index, 8-15
    capitals in, 9
    cross references in,
    indention in, 10
    of names, 8
    preparation of, 9
    punctuation in, 11

ILLUSTRATION 111
Index

Problem 9. Type the following. It is the beginning of the index for the business law book for which you prepared a Contents page in Problem 7. Double-space after each entry or subentry.

INDEX

Absolute defenses, 203

Abstract of title, 557

Acceptance, bankers', 167
    general, 215
    presentment for, 214
    qualified, 215
    supra protest, 215
    trade, 167

Accommodation indorser, 194

Accord and satisfaction, 121

Acts of bankruptcy, 597

Administrator, contracts of, 88

Adverse possession, 549

6. Look at the keyboard, Illustration 21. Place the tips of the fingers of your left hand over (but not on) the keys lettered A S D F. Next, place the tips of the fingers of your right hand over the keys lettered J K L ; as shown in Illustration 22. These eight keys are called the *guide keys.* The row of keys (across the keyboard) of which they are a part is called the *home row.* See that your fingers are well curved and that your hands slope with the slope of the keyboard.

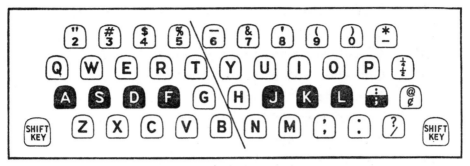

ILLUSTRATION 21

7. When you type, always strike each key with one continuous motion of the finger toward the palm of your hand. Never push down on the key, but strike it sharply and then quickly release it. When you have struck a key, always return your finger immediately to the guide key on the home row.

8. To operate the space bar, use your right thumb. Strike the space bar in the center with a quick downward and inward motion. Raise the thumb quickly after striking the space bar.

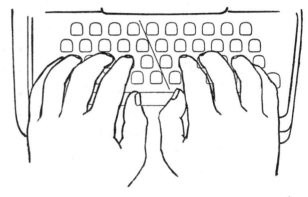

ILLUSTRATION 22

You will now type. First, type f d s a twice. Space after each letter. Your typing will look like this:

f d s a f d s a

Second, type j k l ; twice. Space after each letter. Your typing will now look like this:

f d s a f d s a j k l ; j k l ;

Third, type fdsa and space. Type fdsa again and space. Your typed line will look like this:

f d s a f d s a j k l ; j k l ; fdsa fdsa

Finally, type jkl; and space. Type jkl and return the carriage.

You have typed a line of 50 characters and spaces, and your completed line looks like this:

f d s a f d s a j k l ; j k l ; fdsa fdsa jkl; jkl

Turn the page and start typing Lesson One.

9

Problem 7. Prepare the following Contents page for a textbook in business law. Follow the style shown in Illustration 110.

CONTENTS

Bibliography. At the end of the manuscript the author usually includes a list of all the books, articles, and reports to which he referred while he was preparing the material. Occasionally a brief bibliography appears at the end of each chapter. Such a bibliography will list only references that are related to the subject-matter of the chapter.

When reference is made to a book, the following information should be included:

1. Author's name (last name first)
2. Title of the book
3. Edition
4. Place where the book was published
5. Name of the publisher
6. Date of publication

Robinson, Thomas R., Corporation Finance, Third Edition, Philadelphia, Davis Publishing Company, 1952

A bibliographic reference to an article should consist of the following:

1. Author's name (last name first)
2. Title of the article (enclosed in quotation marks)
3. Periodical in which the article appeared (name underscored)
4. Date of the periodical
5. Page number on which the article begins

Wilson, Harold S., "How To Increase Mail Returns," Direct Advertising, March, 1952, p. 63

Division One—The Letter Keys

Lesson 1

a s d f   j k l ;

Line of 50 spaces. Set left margin stop.
Type each line twice with single spacing.
Space twice after each 2-line group.

LEFT HAND

First finger strikes f.

Second finger strikes d.

Third finger strikes s.

Little finger strikes a.

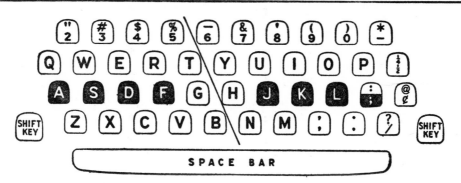

ILLUSTRATION 23

RIGHT HAND

First finger strikes j.

Second finger strikes k.

Third finger strikes l.

Little finger strikes semicolon (;).

Guide Keys

Curve the fingers over the keys.

```
fff faf faf faf aaa jjj j;j j;j j;j ;;; faf j;j fj
fff fdf fdf fdf ddd jjj jkj jkj jkj kkk fdf jkj dk
fff fsf fsf fsf sss jjj jlj jlj jlj lll fsf jlj sl
fja kd; sla als jf; kds ls; fla ja; dks f;s jkd a;
```

Strike the space bar with the right thumb.

Control Drill

Keep your eyes on the copy.

```
fjdk fsjl faj; fj;a fdka js;a faj; fsld fkda fa j;
fal fal kaj kaj lak lak flak flak kal kal lajf fja
skal laks jalk klaj jaks skaj kald dlak slak ka ls
lad ask lass fall fad all flask add ask a lad; sad
```

Strike the keys sharply.

Skill Building

Space once after the semicolon.

```
a fad; a lad; a dad; a sad fall; a lass; flask all
all dads ask lads; as a flask falls; all fads fall
a lass asks a dad; a salad; as a fad; add a salad;
a sad lad asks dad; dad asks a lass; as fads fall;
a sad lass; a lad asks; a salad falls; a dad asks;
```

Use paper release for removing the paper.

When you wish to spread the letters in a heading, leave one space after each letter and three spaces after each word. Note the first three styles in each of the groups shown above.

The title page may be prepared either with or without a border. Here are some suggestions to show how letters and characters may be arranged to make attractive border designs.

```
X X X X X        . . . . .        : : : : :        * * * * *        " " " " "
X                .                :                *                "
X                .                :                *                "
X                .                :                *                "
X                .                :                *                "
X                .                :                *                "
X                .                :                *                "
X                .                :                *                "
X                .                :                *                "
```

Problem 4. On plain paper, size 8½ x 11, prepare a title page for the article entitled *The Story Of Paper*. You may type the title in any style you select. Use your own name as the name of the author. Type the name of your city or town and the current year at the bottom of the sheet. If your instructor directs you to do so, you may type a border design of your own selection.

From the information given in Problems 5 and 6, prepare two additional title pages. Use your own judgment in arranging the data and in preparing a border design. Include the current year.

Problem 5. YOUR JOB AND YOUR COMPANY   A Booklet About The Personnel Policies Of Your Company Empire Products Company   New York New York   10015

Problem 6. HOW TO DO PRACTICAL TYPEWRITING   A Handbook for Office Typists   By Louise B. Peyton Director, Business Education Department Northern States University   Western Textbook Company   San Francisco

The Contents Page. Ordinarily a short manuscript, such as the one which you have just typed, does not require a contents page. For a long manuscript or for a book, a contents page should be included.

There are several styles that may be followed in preparing the contents page. Study Illustration 110. Note that the word CONTENTS has been typed in ALL CAPS and centered. Two line spaces have been left between this heading and the column headings *Chapter* and *Page*. Throughout the remainder of the copy the lines have been double spaced. A leader line, consisting of periods separated by spaces, has been typed from the chapter title to the page number. Line up the periods vertically by typing them all on odd or all on even spaces.

CONTENTS

Chapter		Page
I	Nature and Development of Law	1
II	The Substance of the Law	10
III	The Creation of Contracts	16

ILLUSTRATION 110

Contents Page

Lesson 2
r u   g i

Line of 50 spaces. Set left margin stop. Type each line twice with single spacing. Space twice after each 2-line group.

Review

Is your paper guide in the right position?

```
fjdk sla; lakd fjkd lajf ajf; skdl jals ksla a; sl
ala ala alas alas fla fla flask flask sal salad sa
as a sad fall; as a lass asks; all salads; flasks;
```

Is your paper in the machine straight?

LEFT HAND

F-finger reaches up to strike r.

F-finger reaches to the right to strike g.

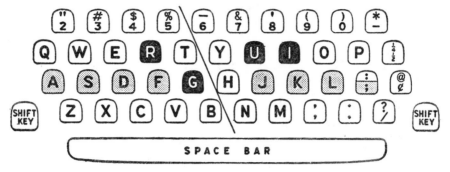

ILLUSTRATION 24

RIGHT HAND

J-finger reaches up to strike u.

K-finger reaches up to strike i.

New Stroke Drill

r u

g i

```
frf frf frf rrr juj juj juj uuu fur ruf jur ruj ru
fgf fgf fgf ggg kik kik kik iii gur rug fir rif gi
irk kri lau ual url lru jau uaj lrk krl sud dus ri
aid aid sir sir fur fur rug rug air air fus fus gu
```

Strike the keys evenly and sharply.

Control Drill

Keep your book at your right.

```
is is us us if if did did jar jar rug rug lid lids
rid rid ark ark kid kid jug jug sir sir rig rig is
dig digs flag flags girl girls laud lauds lurk lug
glad glad raid raid laid laid full full dial dials
```

Think the position of the letter as you strike the key.

Skill Building

```
a raid is; a glad girl; air is full; if a jar lid;
furl a flag; a lass sails; a dark rug is; did aid;
laid a dark rug; all is fair; a full jar; is dark;
a drug did; a jug is; a guard is; a lad is afraid;
```

Space once after the semicolon.

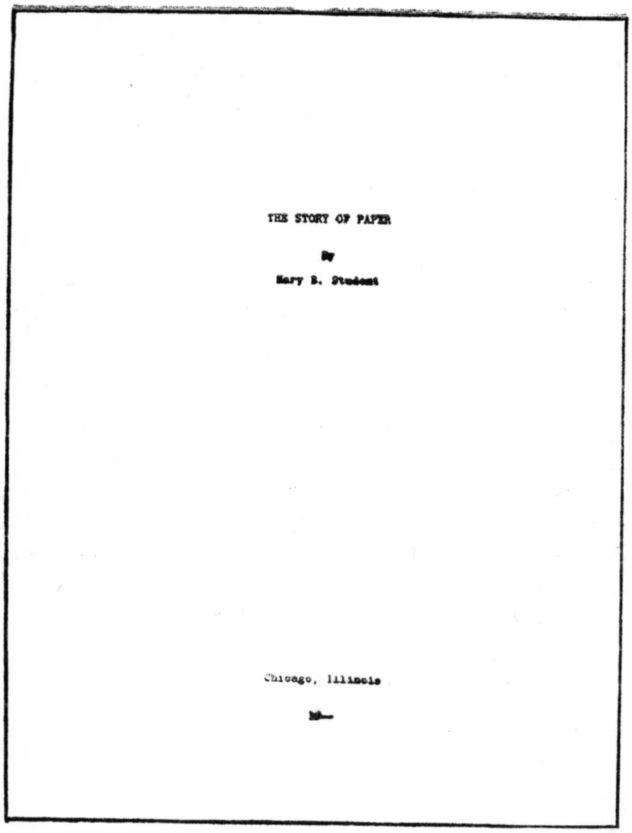

THE STORY OF PAPER

By

Mary B. Student

Chicago, Illinois

19—

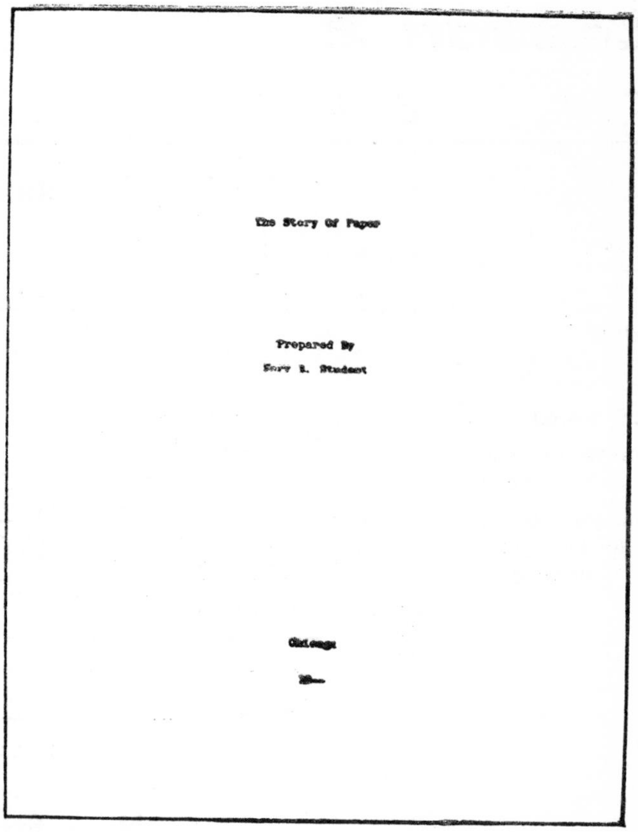

The Story Of Paper

Prepared By

Mary B. Student

Chicago

19—

ILLUSTRATION 109
Title Page Styles

There are a number of other styles in which the title may be typed on the title page and on the first page of the manuscript. Here are some of the more frequently used styles.

ALL CAPITALS

1. Letters spread	T H E S T O R Y O F P A P E R
2. Letters spread and underscored	T H E S T O R Y O F P A P E R
3. Letters spread, words underscored	T H E S T O R Y O F P A P E R
4. Words underscored	THE STORY OF PAPER

Capitals And Small Letters

1. Letters spread	T h e S t o r y O f P a p e r
2. Letters spread and underscored	T h e S t o r y O f P a p e r
3. Letters spread, words underscored	T h e S t o r y O f P a p e r
4. Words underscored	The Story Of Paper

Lesson 3
t h e . Left Shift

Line of 50 spaces. **Set left margin stop.**
Type each line twice with single spacing.
Space twice after each 2-line group.

Review

```
if is jar jug rug rid sir lad did dug lag lug lids
said slid lurk lark jail jars glad glass drill aid
fills a glass; a lass drills; a radius; dig a fir;
```

LEFT HAND

F-finger reaches up and to the right to strike t.

D-finger reaches up to strike e.

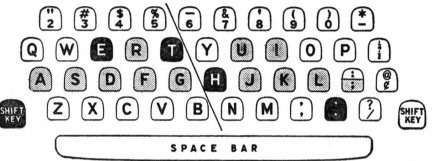

ILLUSTRATION 25

RIGHT HAND

J-finger reaches to the left to strike h.

L-finger reaches down to strike period (.).

New Stroke Drill

To capitalize a letter controlled by any finger of the *right* hand, depress the **LEFT** shift key with the *a*-finger. Hold down the shift key until you have completed the stroke; then release the shift key.

t h

e .

```
ftf ftf ftf ttt jhj jhj jhj hhh hat tah thi iht th
ded ded ded eee 1.1 1.1 1.1 ... del led sel les e.
jut Jut hie Hie kid Kid lid Lid irk Irk ugl Ugl is
he He us Us it Its his His jar Jar jr. Jr. lie Lie
```

Space once after the period which follows an abbreviation.

Control Drill

Are your capital letters on the line?

```
the this thus these head Head just Just hut Hut it
her hers his his their theirs lift Lift kite Kites
idle Idle hilts Hilts heights Heights light Lights
It is high tide.  Use a light shade.  Jud is here.
```

Space twice after the period at the end of a sentence.

Skill Building

Are you shifting with the a-finger?

```
hit heat sash ashes fuel tide threat little kettle
Judge Hart is here.  He is assured.  Kate is idle.
Use these lights.  Heat this jar.  Ida used these.
Les said he had a seal.  I liked this large suite.
```

Strike periods lightly.

Since the dawn of history man has carried on a constant search for a satisfactory method for preserving his thoughts and ideas.

How The Ancients Kept Records

Prehistoric man scratched notes and pictures on the walls of his cave. Later, Babylonians inscribed messages

ILLUSTRATION 108
Centered Subheading

Problem 3. You will now type the first page of a report to the stockholders of a corporation. Use a sheet of 8½ x 11 paper. Leave a top margin of 2 inches. Type the main heading in any style you select. Triple-space below the heading. Double-space the body of the copy. The centered subheadings should be typed with the first letter in each word capitalized. Underscore each subheading. In the last paragraph, type only enough of the copy to complete the last line on the page.

ANNUAL REPORT

It is a pleasure to submit to you and to the other stockholders the consolidated financial statements of your Company.

Earnings

Earnings for the year after all charges and tax provisions were $922,794, or 37¢ a share. The reduction in earnings in comparison with those of last year was caused by a combination of a heavy decline in our sales and an increase in unit costs.

Dividends Declared

A dividend of 30¢ a share was declared by the Board of Directors for both first quarter and second quarter distribution. When it became apparent that lower earnings were continuing in the third and fourth quarters, the dividend was reduced to 10¢ a share.

Claims For Tax Refunds

Your Company has pending before the Bureau of Internal Revenue several claims for substantial refunds of taxes paid.

New Enterprises

During the year your Company examined a number of enterprises with a view towards acquisition. Most of those investigated did not warrant an investment. The Management still has several under active consideration. Furthermore, we plan to continue an energetic search for diversification.

Management And Organization

It is with great sorrow that we report the death of our former President, Benjamin F. Park. For more than thirty years Mr. Park had been associated with the Company.

Title Page. When you have completed the typing of the body of the manuscript and have checked your work carefully, you are ready to prepare a title page. You will want to include on this page the following information: the title of the article or report, the name of the author, the place where the article was written, and the date.

Each line of the title page is usually centered horizontally. Here are two suggested arrangements for a title page for the article you have typed

Lesson 4

v m w o Right Shift

*Line of 50 spaces. Set left margin stop.
Type each line twice with single spacing.
Space twice after each 2-line group.*

Review

```
use these ideas; either height is right; this has;
Let us sit there.  I had real faith.  He did that.
Jud has large hats.  Karl liked the gift.  Use it.
```

LEFT HAND

F-finger reaches down to strike v.

S-finger reaches up to strike w.

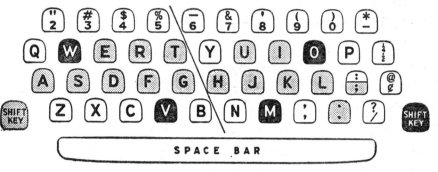

ILLUSTRATION 26

RIGHT HAND

J-finger reaches down to strike m.

L-finger reaches up to strike o.

New Stroke Drill

To capitalize a letter controlled by any finger of the *left* hand, depress the RIGHT shift key with the ;-finger. Hold down the shift key until you have completed the stroke; then release the shift key.

```
v  m   fvf fvf vfv vfv vvv jmj jmj mjm mjm mmm vim vmv vm
w  o   sws sws wsw wsw www lol lol olo olo ooo low wol wo
       via Via vile Vile must Must hive Hive time Time me
       wit Wit whit Whit oath Oath slow Slow lost Lost of
```

Control Drill

Are you shifting with the ;-finger?

```
avail Avails five Five river River visit Visits of
wish Wish evil Evil roam Roam goal Goal slow Slows
Five uses are listed.  Dim the light.  Tell Velma.
Work with the two old volumes.  Get more of these.
```

Are your capital letters on the line?

Skill Building

Are you sitting properly?

```
Ask Sam.  Drive this.  Vote for Ora.  Do it right.
Mark Wolf told us true tales.  Give them the work.
He wrote reviews for the various uses of the time.
I must get there just at five.  This mail is late.
```

Two spaces after the period at the end of a sentence.

tions--sulphite,[13] soda,[14] or sulphate.[15] The

13 An acid calcium bisulphite solution
14 An alkali caustic soda solution
15 A modification of soda with sodium sulphite

chemicals dissolve the glues and leave a mushy mass of pure wood fibers called pulp.

This pulp requires one more treatment, called beating, before it can be sent to the paper machine. After the beating and refining, the pulp--at this point nearly 99 per cent water--is run onto an endless wire mesh screen which may be perforated by as many as 6,000 tiny holes in each square inch. Because of the constant vibration of the screen, the cellulose fibers are interlaced. In the process much of the water is drawn off, leaving a very wet sheet of paper.

The sheet now passes through many pairs of heavy rollers which dry it out, press it together, and apply the desired finish.

The story of paper is also the story of communication. Adequate supplies of pulp and paper have helped to make America the best-informed nation in the world. Technical skill, scientific achievement, and productive forests promise to keep our country well supplied with paper for many generations to come.

Side Headings. Sometimes the author will decide to use side headings at the beginning of certain paragraphs in order to make the subdivisions of the manuscript stand out from the text matter. The typist will save time by using the "run-in" style. This type of side heading is indented 5 spaces and is followed by a period. The first letter of each word is capitalized. The side heading is underscored to make it more prominent. When a manuscript is set in type by the printer, such underscored lines are usually set in italics.

Study Illustration 106. Observe how the side heading at the beginning of the second paragraph has been arranged.

THE STORY OF PAPER

Since the dawn of history man has carried on a constant search for a satisfactory method for preserving his thoughts and ideas.

How The Ancients Kept Records. Prehistoric man scratched notes and pictures on the walls of his cave. Later, Babylonians inscribed messages on clay tablets

ILLUSTRATION 106
Run-in Side Heading

Another type of side heading begins even with the left margin and is typed on a line by itself. Like the run-in style of side heading, the *flush side heading* is underscored. Each word may begin with a capital. The period at the end of the line is omitted. Study Illustration 107.

THE STORY OF PAPER

Since the dawn of history man has carried on a constant search for a satisfactory method for preserving his thoughts and ideas.

How The Ancients Kept Records
Prehistoric man scratched notes and pictures on the walls of his cave. Later, Babylonians inscribed messages

ILLUSTRATION 107
Flush Side Heading

Centered Subheadings. The body of any manuscript may also be subdivided by using centered subheadings at various points. You may type such subheadings in any one of several styles. Usually each word in the heading is capitalized, but some typists use capitals only for the more important words. There are some authors who instruct the typist to underscore centered subheadings; other writers prefer to omit the underscores. The important point to remember is that any style which is adopted should be used consistently throughout the manuscript.

Illustration 108 shows how the side heading that appears in Illustrations 106 and 107 may be arranged as a centered subheading.

Lesson 5
x n   y ,

Line of 50 spaces. Set left margin stop.
Type each line twice with single spacing.
Space twice after each 2-line group.

Review

low river; useful time; five more; highest volume;
This is a wide mold. Most of them walked to work.
Mrs. Val worked with gifts. Walter lost the load.

LEFT HAND

S-finger reaches down to strike x.

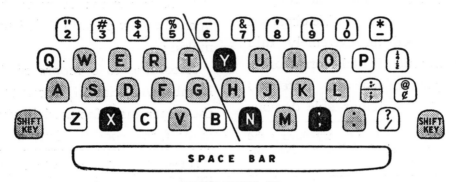

ILLUSTRATION 27

RIGHT HAND

J-finger reaches down and to the left to strike n.
J-finger reaches up and to the left to strike y.
K-finger reaches down to strike comma (,).

New Stroke Drill

x n sxs sxs xsx xsx xxx jnj jnj njn njn nnn six and xn

y , jyj jyj yjy yjy yyy k,k k,k ,k, ,k, ,,, yes so, y,

on ox fox six mix now new navy next oxen yank yarn

exit, north, yawl, oxide, wine, axle, foxy, laxity

Space once after the comma typed at the end of a word.

Control Drill

Are you sitting correctly at your machine?

names are; north of any town; this exit; many new;
Nora Yost is near an exit. He would know the way.
Ovens, novels, yarn, and flax are listed in these.
The onyx is a very fine stone. Examine the yawls.

Space once after each semicolon and comma, but twice after the period that ends a sentence.

Skill Building

Are both your feet flat on the floor?

Sixty navy men went through the exits to new work.
Within the last year he has gone around the world.
A later vogue shows a trend toward extreme styles.
Nora, Vida, and Jane are anxious to go on a train.

Make it a habit not to look up at the end of a line.

gress, during Washington's administration, appealed to the housewives to save every available rag and scrap of cloth for use in paper manufacture.

In other parts of the world men had been working for almost a century in an effort to solve the problem. In France, early in the Eighteenth Century, Rene de Reaumur spent several hours one day watching an industrious wasp build a nest. He observed that the insect used an extremely thin fibrous material which it had worn from a dry post and then mixed with secretions from its body.[8] This remarkable demon-

[8] George F. Kent, "French Industry during the Eighteenth Century," *Historical Review*, November, 1951, p. 132

stration set the French scientist to wondering whether it would be possible for man to duplicate the process and to make a paperlike substance by mixing together wood and water.

More than a century later a German named Kellar proved the soundness of de Reaumur's logic. By holding sticks of wood against a grindstone while adding water, he devised a mechanical method for duplicating the work of the nest-building wasp.[9]

[9] John D. Patterson, *Early European Paper-Makers*, Reese Publishing House, St. Louis, 1950, pp. 321-335

Two years later, in England, wood chips were cooked in a caustic soda solution to make pulp for paper.

Progress in the art of making paper continued at a rapid pace during the second half of the Nineteenth Century. In 1865 an American chemist, Benjamin Tilghman, discovered a sulphite process for cooking wood. The historian, Wainwright, observes that America offers the primary resources-- forests and water--which are so important to the paper industry.[10] The discovery in

[10] Frank S. Wainwright, *American Pioneers*, Howard Publishing Company, Cleveland, 1951, p. 372

this country of a completely new method for the treatment of wood by chemicals opened a new page in the history of paper-making.

According to a report of the American Lumber Association, about 97 per cent of the paper manufactured in this country is made from wood.[11] Only a relatively few

[11] Daniel R. West and others, *Report of America's Forest Resources*, American Lumber Association, New York, 1952, p. 439

paper products are made from the fibers of flax, straw, or rags. Today much waste paper is reprocessed and used again.

Many species of trees can be used for paper-making. Spruce, hemlock, pine, fir, cypress, larch, cedar, ash, aspen, poplar, beech, birch, tupelo, chestnut, alder, cherry, and maple are all used to make pulp and paper. One authority states that the first four species named--spruce, hemlock, pine, and fir--account for about 90 per cent of the nation's pulpwood.[12]

[12] Homer S. Robinson, "From Pulp to Paper," *Science Today*, January, 1952, p. 27

All wood consists of cellulose fibers that are held together by lignin, which is a resinous gumlike binder. To separate the fibers from the lignin, the paper-maker first slices the logs into chips. The chips are then cooked in any one of three chemical solu-

Lesson 6
Measured Typing

Line of 50 spaces. Set left margin stop. Type each sentence twice with single spacing. Space twice after the second writing.

Warm-up Practice

All the words in these three sentences are balanced-hand words.

It is their duty to go to the town for the title.

Jane may fix the signals when she turns the dial.

Rudy may sign the forms for the work he is to do.

Measured Typing

Set the line-space regulator for double spacing. Type Paragraph 1 with double spacing; then type it again. Type Paragraphs 2 and 3 in the same way—each paragraph twice.

To measure typing speed, we count five strokes (letters or spaces) as one word. Each line in these paragraphs has ten 5-stroke words; hence each paragraph has 30 words. When you type a paragraph in three minutes, you are typing at the rate of ten words a minute.

There is a ruler below each paragraph. The figures show the number of 5-stroke words in each line. This ruler makes it possible for you to determine instantly how many words you have typed. When you stop before finishing a full line, refer to the ruler to see how many words you typed in that line; then add that number to the word count given at the end of the preceding line.

Words

Are all your letters the same shade?

1 Those words that we use to talk of things that we 10

hold near and dear are the short words we learned 20

to know and use in our homes at a very early age. 30

Do not raise your eyes from the copy until after you have finished the paragraph.

```
   1    2    3    4    5    6    7    8    9
```

Type with uniform touch.

2 Long words are mostly for the minds of men; it is 10

the short words that get into their hearts. Long 20

words do not mean the same to those who use them. 30

Keep the carriage moving constantly.

```
   1    2    3    4    5    6    7    8    9
```

Strike the keys sharply and firmly.

3 One man who hears a long word gets one thought or 10

idea out of it, yet that thought or idea is often 20

not the same thought or idea that others may get. 30

Can you type each paragraph in three minutes?

```
   1    2    3    4    5    6    7    8    9
```

Problem 2. You will now type the article, THE STORY OF PAPER. Use a 6½-inch line and a 5-space paragraph indention. Follow carefully the instructions on page 279. Plan your work so that the footnotes and the reference numbers for each page appear on the same sheet.

Note: The material between the lines is to be typed as footnotes.

THE STORY OF PAPER

Since the dawn of history man has carried on a constant search for a satisfactory method for preserving his thoughts and ideas.

Prehistoric man scratched notes and pictures on the walls of his cave. Later, Babylonians inscribed messages on clay tablets which could be carried from place to place. The Egyptians wrote on thin strips of native wood called papyrus.[1]

---

[1] The paper reed still abounds on the marshy river banks of Palestine, Sicily, and Abyssinia. The plant is, however, now almost extinct in Egypt.

A young Chinese scholar, Ts'ai Lun, added an important milestone in man's progress in the art of paper-making. Davidson gives us the following account of the work of this early experimenter:

"Because he was dissatisfied with the silk and bamboo writing materials that were used in his native land, Ts'ai Lun decided to experiment with the inner bark of the mulberry tree. He pounded this material into pulp and added water. After the mixture had been thoroughly dried, it formed flat sheets of matted fiber on which messages could be written."[2]

---

[2] Herbert S. Davidson, *A Brief History of Paper-Making*, Watts Publishing Company, Chicago, 1952, p. 165

It was not until 1799 that a major improvement was made in the ancient method of Ts'ai Lun. In that year Louis Robert of France patented the first modern paper-making machine.[3] Later, in England, a

---

[3] Ibid., p. 198

---

firm of London stationers, the Fourdrinier Brothers, made certain improvements in Robert's invention.[4] The name of these

---

[4] William F. Garson, "The Romance of Printing," *Graphic Arts Monthly,* February, 1952, pp. 67 ff.

---

early experimenters is preserved today in paper-making machines which are referred to as "Fourdriniers."

All during this period the chief materials used in the making of paper were linen and cotton rags. Some experimenters also attempted to manufacture paper from raw hemp, jute, and asbestos.[5] In 1800 a book

---

[5] Thomas F. Cole (ed.) *Paper-Making Through The Ages,* H. N. Young & Sons, New York, rev. ed., 1952, vol. 3, pp. 216-220

---

was printed on paper that had been made from straw. These crude paper-making methods were unable to keep pace with the demand. According to Lewis,[6] paper sup-

---

[6] William F. Lewis, *The American Revolution,* Parker Press, Boston, 1951, p. 213

---

plies during the American Revolution were so limited that the officers in General Washington's Continental Army were compelled to write their commands on fragments of scrap paper. Some of these extremely important military communications have the general appearance of grocery lists. Lewis [7] also tells us that Con-

---

[7] Ibid., p. 237

Lesson 7

q c   p b

Line of 50 spaces. Set left margin stop. Type each line twice with single spacing. Space twice after each 2-line group.

Review

last year; autumn days; exit signs; yearly voyage;
high rivers, low lands, wide vales, very new home,
Lewis examined the note. Your values are extreme.

LEFT HAND

A-finger reaches up to strike q.

D-finger reaches down to strike c.

F-finger reaches down and to the right to strike b.

RIGHT HAND

;-finger reaches up to strike p.

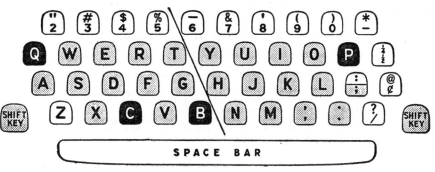

ILLUSTRATION 28

New Stroke Drill

q c aqa aqa qaq qaq qqq dcd dcd cdc cdc ccc can qua qu

p b ;p; ;p; p;p p;p ppp fbf fbf bfb bfb bbb bay cap pb

quick cost quite paid cope quack quart chapel pays
put Put bay Bay post Post chain Chain quest Quests

Control Drill

Are you using the correct shift key for the capitals?

brave couple; come quite early; buy the best cups;
quite badly; in a quart; due yearly; club profits;
Busy people can come. He paid a large cash bonus.
Plan your work. Work your plan. Pack quart jars.

Space correctly after each punctuation mark.

Skill Building

Are your capital letters properly typed?

Bright colors fade quickly. Bob is their brother.
It has quantity and quality. Paul bought the box.
Your request to pay by cash is now quite in order.
The exit was quite far back from the palace gates.

Use the paper release to remove the paper from the machine.

1 THE STORY OF PAPER

3 **2** Since the dawn of history man has carried on a constant search for a satisfactory method for preserving his thoughts and ideas.

Prehistoric man scratched notes and pictures on the walls of his cave. Later, Babylonians inscribed messages on clay tablets which could be carried from place to place. The Egyptians wrote on thin strips of native wood called papyrus.[1] **4**

A young Chinese scholar, Ts'ai Lun, added an important milestone in man's progress in the art of paper-making. Davidson gives us the following account of the work of this early experimenter:

5 "Because he was dissatisfied with the silk and bamboo writing materials that were used in his native land, Ts'ai Lun decided to experiment with the inner bark of the mulberry tree. He pounded this material into pulp and added water. After the mixture had been thoroughly dried, it formed flat sheets of matted fiber on which messages could be written."[2]

It was not until 1799 that a major improvement was made in the ancient method of Ts'ai Lun. In that year Louis Robert of France patented the first modern paper-making machine.[3] Later, in England, a firm of London stationers, the Fourdrinier Brothers, made certain improvements in Robert's **6** invention.[4] The name of these early experimenters is preserved today

---

7 [1] The paper reed still abounds on the marshy river banks of Palestine, Sicily, and Abyssinia. The plant is, however, now almost extinct in Egypt.

8 [2] Herbert S. Davidson, *A Brief History of Paper-Making*, Watts Publishing Company, Chicago, 1952, p. 165

9 [3] *Ibid.*, p. 190

10 [4] William F. Garson, "The Romance of Printing," *Graphic Arts Monthly*, February, 1952, pp. 67 ff.

1. Center the heading and type it in capital letters. Omit the period after the heading.

2. Triple-space between the title and the first line of the copy.

3. Indent five spaces for the first line of each paragraph.

4. Use superior figures to refer to footnotes. Footnotes may be either numbered consecutively from the beginning to the end of the manuscript or numbered consecutively for each page.

5. Use single spacing for quotations of three or more lines. Indent five spaces on each side.

6. Type an underscore across the page to separate the text matter from the footnotes. Single-space after the last line of the text matter; then type the underscore.

7. Single-space the lines in each footnote. Double-space after each footnote.

8. If the footnote refers to a book, arrange the data in the following order: name of author, title of book (underscored), name of publisher, place of publication, date of publication, page or pages.

9. If the footnote refers to the same work as the preceding footnote, use the abbreviation *Ibid.* (meaning *in the same place*). Give the page number only. Use *Ibid.* only when there are no intervening references.

10. If the footnote refers to an article in a magazine, arrange the data in the following order: name of author, title of article (in quotation marks), name of magazine (underscored), month and year date of the issue, page. The abbreviation *ff.* means *following*.

Lesson 8
Measured Typing

Line of 50 spaces. Set left margin stop.
Type each sentence twice with single spacing.
Space twice after the second writing.

Warm-up Practice

All the words in these three sentences are balanced-hand words.

Jane may sign the title for the land by the lake.

Six of them may wish to visit the ancient chapel.

Eight of the girls may handle the social problem.

Measured Typing

Set the line-space regulator for double spacing. Type Paragraph 1 with double spacing; then type it again. Type Paragraphs 2, 3, and 4 in the same way—each paragraph twice.

Words

1 We are so made that we get a thrill when we bring 10

a piece of work to a good end. That thrill comes 20

because we know we have done work that has value. 30

    1   2   3   4   5   6   7   8   9

2 Growth in any form of life always brings changes. 10

If a plant does not grow, it soon dies. Any mind 20

that does not grow will lose its power to change. 30

    1   2   3   4   5   6   7   8   9

3 We ought to look at and think about each new idea 10

that comes to us. When we show that we have some 20

desire to think, we show that our minds are open. 30

    1   2   3   4   5   6   7   8   9

4 We all like the person who does what he can to be 10

of help to others. Such a person has the will to 20

do for others what he would have them do for him. 30

    1   2   3   4   5   6   7   8   9

Margins
(Refer to illustrations on right)

Top margin of first page . . . 2 inches

Top margin of second and following pages . . . 1 ½ inches

Side and bottom margins . . . 1 inch

If the manuscript is to be bound, add, an extra ½ inch to the top or to the lefthand margin.

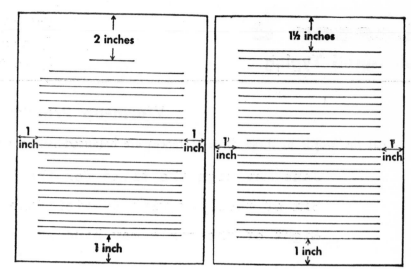

Spacing
(Refer to illustration on right)

For text matter: Double spacing

For quotations of three or more lines: Single spacing

For footnotes: Single spacing

Page numbering
(Refer to illustrations below)

Introductory pages: Small Roman numerals (i, ii, iii, iv, v, etc.) centered ½ inch from bottom edge.

First text page: Omit number

Second and following text pages: Arabic numerals (1, 2, 3, 4, etc.) centered ½ inch from the top edge.

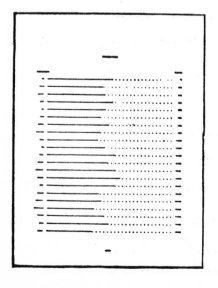

Lesson 9

z : / ?

Line of 50 spaces. Set left margin stop.
Type each line twice with single spacing.
Space twice after each 2-line group.

Review

Play ball. Paul came quickly. Cal quits at five.

Buy eleven bonds. Quote prices on pulp for paper.

Pay this bill. Question Pete about that capacity.

LEFT HAND

A-finger reaches down to strike **z**.

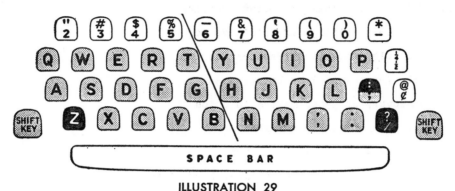

ILLUSTRATION 29

RIGHT HAND

The colon (:) is the shift of the semicolon (;).

The little finger moves down to strike the diagonal (/).

The question mark (?) is the shift of the diagonal.

New Stroke Drill

z aza aza zaz zaz zzz zinc zinc Zoe Zeke ozone ozone

: ;:; ;:; Dear Sir: Dear Madam: Dear Mrs. Zeigler:

/ ;/; ;/; /;/ /;/ /// James and/or Alfred will come.

? ;?; ;?; ?;? ?;? ??? How is he? What size is this?

Space twice after the colon and the question mark.

Control Drill

Is this an extra zone? Did Zucker and Mathews go?

We had six dozen eggs, five extra hams, and a box.

Gentlemen: Have you received the message we sent?

Have the students enjoyed the exhibits of zinnias?

Space once after the comma.

Skill Building

Throw the carriage quickly.

The zodiac has twelve signs. Knit with red yarns.

Were you amazed by the haze that covered the hill?

Here are their names: Mazure, Hazleton, and Zink.

Will you ship six sizes of these? How far was it?

Are you typing the capitals correctly?

THE STORY OF PAPER

I. Historical background

   A. Writing materials of ancient peoples

      1. Cave writings of primitive men

      2. Clay tablets of Babylonians

      3. Papyrus used by Egyptians

   B. Discovery of paper-making in China

      1. Use of silk and bamboo

      2. Experiments of Ts'ai Lun

         a. Made pulp from inner bark of mulberry tree

         b. Dried to form flat sheets of fiber

         c. Information about method spread slowly

   C. Work of European and American experimenters

      1. Louis Robert of France

         a. Made first major improvement over Chinese method

         b. Patented first modern paper-making machine

      2. The Fourdrinier Brothers of England

         a. Made changes in Robert's machine

         b. Name used for machine of present day

      3. Developments during 18th and 19th centuries

         a. Experiments of de Reaumur and Kellar

            (1) Based on observation of nest-building by wasp

               (a) Use of fibrous material

               (b) Body secretions

            (2) Mechanical method for reproducing wasp's work

ILLUSTRATION 105

Outline

Lesson 10

Measured Typing

Set the line-space regulator for double spacing. Type Paragraph 1 twice with double spacing; then type Paragraphs 2, 3, 4, 5, and 6 in the same way—each paragraph twice.

Words

1 You have to start from where you now stand; there   10   Use this copy to build your typing power.

is no other place from which to start. The thing   20

for us to do is to make a start, not stand still.   30

   1   2   3   4   5   6   7   8   9

2 You do not have to know what lies ahead. How can   10   Type evenly.

you know all that the future will bring? Make up   20

your mind to do the work you should do right now.   30

   1   2   3   4   5   6   7   8   9

3 You start right where you are; you take one step;   10   Throw the carriage quickly.

then the next one becomes clear. No matter where   20

you go, you must start by taking that first step.   30

   1   2   3   4   5   6   7   8   9

4 There is no sense in taking over worries from the   10   Increase your stroking rate when you type a paragraph the second time.

future. Be sure that doing what needs to be done   20

now will quickly show what needs to be done next.   30

   1   2   3   4   5   6   7   8   9

5 Worry is much like a rocking chair. It will give   10

you something to do, but you do not get anywhere.   20

Most things we worry about never do come to pass.   30

   1   2   3   4   5   6   7   8   9

6 If we can do something about the problem which is   10

the cause of our worries, then we should go right   20

ahead and do it; but if not, then why be worried?   30

   1   2   3   4   5   6   7   8   9

Lesson 10　　　**Measured Typing**　　　19

Division Ten—Outlines And Manuscripts

The first step in the writing of a manuscript is the preparation of an outline. A well-organized outline provides the author with a complete working plan.

In typing an outline, be sure to follow a uniform plan for listing the various items and for indenting the lines. Indentions are ordinarily five spaces. If an item requires more than one line, the second and subsequent lines are usually indented three spaces. Study the following illustration of an outline skeleton and note the correct arrangement of the various items.

HEADING CENTERED

```
I.  Roman numeral for main division
    A.  Capital letter for first subdivision
        1.  Arabic numeral for next subheading
            a.  Small letter for this subheading
                (1)  Arabic numeral in parentheses
                    (a)  Small letter in parentheses
```

ILLUSTRATION 104
Outline Skeleton

Note that periods have been typed after the numerals and letters, but that no periods are typed when parentheses are used. The outline is somewhat more "open" in appearance when the periods are followed by *two* spaces, as shown in the outline skeleton. It is also correct to omit periods entirely. When you do omit periods, always leave two spaces after the figure or letter.

Capitalize the first word of each line. **Do** not type periods at the end of the lines.

Let us say that a magazine writer decides to prepare an article about paper-making. After completing his research work, he arranges his facts in outline form. Illustration 105, page 277, is the first page of his outline.

Problem 1. Study the illustration carefully and compare the arrangement of the items with the outline skeleton shown in Illustration 104; then type this first page of the outline. Follow the arrangement shown in the illustration.

Manuscripts

After the author has completed his outline, he is ready to write the manuscript. Most writers first make a preliminary draft of the article. This first draft is then revised and rewritten. Punctuation and spelling are carefully checked. When all revisions and changes have been made, the manuscript is ready for final typing.

Let us assume that the author who prepared the outline for the article on paper-making has completed all the work of rewriting and revising. The manuscript is now ready for typing in final form. On page 278 are some general rules that the typist should follow in typing the final draft.

The illustrations and the accompanying instructions provide directions you will need to understand before you type Problem 2. Study them carefully.

On page 279 you will find an illustration which shows in reduced size the first page of the final draft of the manuscript. This illustration and the instructions printed below it give additional information to help you in typing Problem 2.

Lesson 11

a s d f Review

Line of 50 spaces. Set left margin stop.
Type each line twice with single spacing.
Space twice after each 2-line group.

Preliminary Practice

a   an an air air man man pal pal also also pair pair

s   so so is is us us sir sir sob sob isle isle risks

d   do do did did dog dog dug dug dock dock meld meld

f   of of for for fix fix fog fog five five firm firm

A   Amy is glad that she came and heard what he said.

S   Susie used this stamp and pasted it in the block.

D   Dickey walked the road that leads down the field.

F   Ford left those five gifts for his famous father.

Speed-up Sentences

Balanced-hand words.

It is the duty of the girls to pay for the burns.

Make the eight big emblems for the ancient autos.

Maud is proficient; she may mend the torn burlap.

Paragraph Typing

First, set the left margin stop for a line of 60 spaces.   Set the line-space regulator for double spacing.
Type each paragraph twice with double spacing.

Words

1 Few of us ever stop to think about how large a part of life   12

is made up of small things.   The way we do the small things   24

shows clearly how we shall act when we face the big things.   36

	1	2	3	4	5	6	7	8	9	10	11

2 No one can all at once change the way he acts and works and   12

thinks.   What a person thinks and the way he acts today and   24

in the future are just the outcome of his acts in the past.   36

	1	2	3	4	5	6	7	8	9	10	11

Paragraph Typing C

These paragraphs contain many figures, symbols, and capital letters.

1   Type this sentence: "On the 29th day of July the firm of Ford & Nicholson sold 84# of #3 grade seed for $70, less the regular discount of 15% for payment before the close of business (four o'clock) on August 26." The sentence has in it the figures from 0 to 9, but it does not have either the sign for at (@) or the sign for cents (¢). One word has an apostrophe--the word o'clock. The asterisk (*) is missing, but there are quotation marks at the beginning and the end.

2   In all ordinary cases use figures in typing the street numbers of houses and buildings; as, 148 Hunt Street. Some streets have numbers as their names. In order to avoid the difficulty that might arise in such cases, spell the street name; as, 1867 First Avenue, 1285 Forty-eighth Street. If, however, such a word as North, South, East, or West is part of the street name, it is all right to use figures for that name; as, 5308 North 131st Street, 1492 South 185th Avenue.

3   Kansas has 82,276 square miles and 105 counties. Iowa has 56,280 square miles and 99 counties. Idaho has an area of 83,557 square miles and 44 counties. Alaska has 586,400 square miles. New York, the "Empire State," has an area of 49,576 square miles and 62 counties. Mississippi covers an area of 47,716 square miles and has 82 counties. Minnesota has 84,068 square miles in 87 counties; California, 158,693 square miles; Massachusetts, 8,257; and Washington, 68,192.

Lesson 12

j k l ; Review

Line of 50 spaces. Set left margin stop.
Type each line twice with single spacing.
Space twice after each 2-line group.

Preliminary Practice

j   jam jam jig jig jog jog jays jays jamb jamb julep

k   key key bake bake sick sick work work forks forks

l   laps laps lamb lamb lent lent lane lane land land

;   right side; skies overhead; busy boys; depths of;

J   Just then each judge jotted down the jolly jests.

K   Kay has kept those kinds of keys in her work kit.

L   Lots less than eleven miles from us are for sale.

;   John K. Leidy; Larry J. Kent; King Lear; Joe Low;

Speed-up Sentences

Balanced-hand words.

The firms may then mend the big sign by the lake.

It is right for the firms to fight for the title.

He may land the rockfish with the aid of the men.

Paragraph Typing

First, set the left margin stop for a line of 60 spaces.   Set the line-space regulator for double spacing. Type each paragraph twice with double spacing.

Words

1 If you have used care and thought in your work in the past,   12

then you need not worry about the future.   You will be well   24

prepared because you have formed the habit of careful work.   36

    1   2   3   4   5   6   7   8   9   10   11

2 The fact that what you have done and thought in the past is   12

a part of you has its good side.   If you had to think about   24

each small act, you would never have time for anything new.   36

    1   2   3   4   5   6   7   8   9   10   11

Paragraph Typing B

Each of these paragraphs contains all the letters of the alphabet.

1 The matter of organizing yourself and your work can be developed. If you are lax in your methods of studying, you cannot hope to get far. The ability to concentrate on work is rare enough to be the subject of remarks. Nobody can go running off in all directions at once and still hope to get things done. There is nothing to the idea that you have no time to concentrate. Most people quit too soon and far too easily. They have not developed the inner urge to keep on.

11	
23	
35	
47	
59	
71	
83	
95	

2 Everybody has to learn to follow before he can hope to lead. He has to learn just how to do things accurately, to follow instructions precisely, and to do excellent work and not take forever and a day to do it. We live in a world of dazzling speed. There are many things to do, and they have to be done quickly. We have to take the maxim that time is money at its face value. If we show by our actions that we understand the value of time, we are on the way to success.

11	106
23	118
35	130
47	142
59	154
71	166
83	178
95	190

3 It is hard to rid ourselves of habits we have acquired through the years. Eventually, however, the time will come when we have to adjust ourselves to new ways. Certainly we must never close our minds and, in pure laziness, refuse to think about new and better methods. It is, of course, true that everything new is not necessarily better. At the same time we ought always to examine the new to discover whether it is actually better than what we have done in times past.

11	201
23	213
35	225
47	237
59	249
71	261
83	273
95	285

Lesson 13
Measured Typing

Line of 60 spaces. Set left margin stop.
Type each sentence twice with single spacing.
Space twice after the second writing.

Warm-up Practice

Each of these three lines contains all the letters you reviewed in Lessons 11 and 12—a s d f j k l.

Frank just had a chance to sail around that amazing island.
Harry said his house is just seven blocks from that avenue.
Jack did his full duty; his faith is an example for us all.

Measured Typing

Set the line-space regulator for double spacing. Type each paragraph twice with double spacing.

Words

1 It may be that you have not thought very much about what is   12
back of the work you do each day. It is well for us all to   24
know what study really is and how we can best use our time.   36

    1   2   3   4   5   6   7   8   9   10   11

2 The first kind of study to think about is just plain drill.   12
The purpose of all drill in any field is to aid you to form   24
those habits your teacher knows you need to get real skill.   36

    1   2   3   4   5   6   7   8   9   10   11

3 Right at the very start of any kind of drill make sure that   12
you have a strong desire to do this work. No one gets much   24
out of any drill unless he has a keen desire to do it well.   36

    1   2   3   4   5   6   7   8   9   10   11

4 The next step is to make sure that you know just what skill   12
you are working for. You will save a great deal of time by   24
having in your mind a vivid picture of what you want to do.   36

    1   2   3   4   5   6   7   8   9   10   11

5 Now you are set; you are very eager to learn; you know just   12
what you are going to do. You can thus begin your drill in   24
the right spirit to gain the good habit you want to master.   36

    1   2   3   4   5   6   7   8   9   10   11

Division Ten

Paragraph Typing A

Many of the words in these paragraphs are balanced-hand words.

Words

1   If a piece of cloth is torn, you may mend it or pay to   11
have it mended; if your auto breaks down, you may fix it or   23
pay to have it fixed. When a friendship is torn by strife,   35
however, or broken through the antics of one or both of the   47
friends, such friends cannot turn over to somebody else the   59
work of mending the rift. If they do not mend the break by   71
themselves, or if they do not laugh off the discord so that   83
they can make up and shake hands, nobody else can aid them.   95

2   If you want to make the world a finer world than it is   11   106
now, do not spend time trying to find things to blame about   23   118
the conduct of your neighbor. It is easy for most of us to   35   130
blame others while we try to shield our own faults from the   47   142
world and from ourselves. The man who overlooks the faults   59   154
of his neighbor and turns to the big job of mending his own   71   166
ways is apt to be kept busy for a long while; if he is both   83   178
frank and fair, he may find his neighbor better than he is.   95   190

3   Think of the brief span of time in which the world has   11   201
moved from short land trips by bicycle to lengthy air trips   23   213
by plane; it is then that you comprehend what men mean when   35   225
they say that the world is getting smaller. The person who   47   237
lives in another land is now a neighbor; we may go to visit   59   249
him whenever we wish to do so, and we may make our visit in   71   261
comfort. England, for example, is now so close to our land   83   273
by air that you may visit it tomorrow if you wish to do so.   95   285

273

Lesson 14

r u g i Review

Line of 50 spaces. Set left margin stop. Type each line twice with single spacing. Space twice after each 2-line group.

Preliminary Practice

r   or or rip rip ire ire rid rid work work real real

u   us us use use due due buy buy rush rush turn turn

g   go go log log fog fog dog dog goad goad sing sing

i   it it ivy ivy sit sit him him life life side side

R   Ruth led our short program for the winter review.

U   Use the trust fund to pay your tuition next year.

G   Gary will give the gander grain from his gardens.

I   It is a fine idea to aid the girl in buying kits.

Speed-up Sentences

Balanced-hand words.

Did six of the men handle the panelwork for Jane?

The field may make the usual profit for the firm.

When the signal is visible, rush the box to town.

Paragraph Typing

Set the left margin stop for a line of 60 spaces. Set the line-space regulator for double spacing. Type each paragraph twice with double spacing.

Words

1 Suppose that each day you would have to stop to think about   12

how to comb your hair or dress yourself or do all the other   24

routine things that you do each and every day of your life.   36

    1   2   3   4   5   6   7   8   9   10   11

2 You do not think about such acts, for they have become part   12

of you. Your mind is thus left free to think about how you   24

are going to meet the new facts that you are bound to face.   36

    1   2   3   4   5   6   7   8   9   10   11

Here are a few practical suggestions that apply to the interview you 14
will have when you apply for a position. Plan to arrive in plenty of 28
time; being late for the interview makes a bad impression. A young 41
man ought to take off his hat when he goes into an office and should 55
not play with his hat or roll it up. If he does so, people will get the 69
impression that he is of a nervous temperament. When you go into 82
the office, you may find a receptionist. Go up to her and tell her quietly 97
and clearly that you have an appointment for an interview. You may 110
be told to wait until the interviewer is ready to see you, as there may 124
be other applicants waiting for interviews. When you are taken into 138
the office of the interviewer, speak your name clearly. The interviewer 152
may or may not offer to shake hands with you, but he will probably 165
ask you to sit down. Do not put your purse, gloves, or other personal 179
belongings on the desk of the interviewer. Keep cool and collected; 193
answer all questions you are asked just as frankly and directly as you 207
can. Do not discuss personal or family matters unless you are asked 221
to do so. Let the interviewer do the talking; your part is to listen. 235

Avoid at the beginning of the interview making inquiries about 247
vacations and the hours of work. If you are employed, you will be 260
told before you leave the office the hours during which the employees 274
in that office work. Make it a point not to criticize anybody in anything 289
you say. Speak well of your school if the interviewer inquires about 303
it. Say nothing that would reflect unfavorably on a former employer. 317

In case you are applying for a position that involves taking and 330
transcribing dictation, the interviewer may give you dictation and then 344
ask someone to show you to a typewriter on which you are to transcribe. 358
An excellent impression is made if you use a notebook that you have 371
brought with you to the interview. Transcribe the dictation as quickly 385
as possible; before you take the sheet out of the machine, make sure 399
to read what you have typed. You may be under something of a strain, 413
and this precaution will enable you to catch any errors. 424

When you have finished transcribing, take your transcript to the 437
interviewer or to the person who has been designated to look over your 451
work. If you have made the right kind of impression and if your work 465
is satisfactory, you may be asked to report at the office on a certain 479
date. The interviewer, however, may not be ready to decide then and 493
there. He may have other applicants to interview. If he tells you that 507
he will get in touch with you later, ask whether it is all right for you 521
to come again tomorrow or to call him on the telephone. Sometimes 534
a little courteous persistence at this point will get the position for you. 549

Lesson 15

t h e . Review

Line of 50 spaces. Set left margin stop.
Type each line twice with single spacing.
Space twice after each 2-line group.

Preliminary Practice

t   to to toe toe lit lit sit sit kite kite tile tile

h   he he hat hat hit hit her her dish dish wish wish

e   me me key key die die tie tie meal meal envy envy

.   gr. gr. ea. ea. jr. jr. lb. lb. st. st. yrs. yrs.

T   This time the thought is to toss it into the air.

H   He taught him to be humble and to honor his home.

E   Each small table is filled with eight large jars.

.   These titles were used. Send the new daily list.

Speed-up Sentences

Balanced-hand
words.

They wish us to pay for the map of the six towns.

Both men may go to their aid and pay the penalty.

The problem for me is to make the sign authentic.

Paragraph Typing

Line of 60 spaces. Set the line-space regulator for double spacing. Type each paragraph twice with double spacing.

Words

1 There are three main factors to take into account in sizing   12
up your value as an office worker. Those factors are quite   24
simple; it will be well for you to know just what they are.   36

    1   2   3   4   5   6   7   8   9   10   11

2 You are judged on the basis of your attitude toward others,   12
your attitude toward your work, and your skill in doing the   24
work that is marked out for you or that you do on your own.   36

    1   2   3   4   5   6   7   8   9   10   11

There are many details of typewriter operation which form a part of | 13
the working equipment of the good typist. Attention to those details | 27
is necessary to turn out a good finished product. Become familiar with | 41
all the devices on your machine that play a part in its operation. It is | 56
so easy to overlook some device that will help you to improve the | 69
appearance of your work and the rapidity with which you turn it out. | 83
When you are writing without a carbon, it is well to use a backing | 96
sheet. Clearer impressions from the type are secured, and wear and tear | 110
on the platen are reduced. It is, of course, desirable to turn out work | 124
which does not call for erasing; but since the human equation enters | 138
into typewriting as it does into all other phases of activity, errors will | 153
sometimes occur and erasing becomes necessary. When you do erasing, | 167
take enough time to make a good erasure. Sometimes you may use an | 180
eraser shield to help you to make a good clean erasure. A noticeable | 194
erasure in a business letter or in any other kind of office typewriting | 208
makes a bad impression on the person who gets it. | 218

Remember that a letter which you type and which is signed and mailed | 232
is just as much a representative of your employer as is a salesman. A | 246
salesman whose shoes are run down at the heel, whose collar is frayed, | 260
or whose shirt is not clean is bound to make a bad first impression on | 274
the people to whom he is trying to sell a product or a service. In the | 288
same way a letter that contains a noticeable erasure, that has extremely | 302
uneven right margins, or that is poorly placed on the sheet makes a | 315
bad impression. Take real pride in turning out work that is so | 328
attractively arranged that the reader will get a favorable impression | 342
and will be encouraged to read what you have typed. | 352

You have surely come to realize that real skill in typing from plain | 366
copy lies at the base of your work. The more rapidly and accurately | 380
you write from such copy as this, the better you will be when you type | 394
from notes or when you set up tabulated material and work with other | 408
aspects of typewriting. When you have completed a page, it is always | 422
interesting for you to find out at what speed and with what accuracy | 436
you typed. It is important for you to do something about errors you | 450
make. Early in this course you were taught how to go about doing | 463
remedial practice that will help you to avoid making the same errors | 477
in the future. When you are typing from plain copy, you need to keep | 491
your attention on what you are writing. Close concentration on the | 504
copy is a vital factor in fast typing. The right time to take in the full | 519
meaning of what you typed is when you come to check your work with | 532
the copy to find out what errors, if any, you made. | 542

Lesson 16
Measured Typing

Line of 60 spaces. Set left margin stop.
Type each sentence twice with single spacing.
Space twice after the second writing.

Warm-up Practice

Each of these three lines contains all the letters you reviewed in Lessons 14 and 15—r u g i t h e.

Our duty is to believe in the good life and try to live it.
The urge to plan and work and win comes from inside of you.
You must have a deep inner motive to get you started right.

Measured Typing

Set the line-space regulator for double spacing.   Type each paragraph twice with double spacing.

Words

1 A famous author had spent years in writing a book.   One day — 12
a maid who was cleaning his study gathered up the sheets he — 24
had written so carefully and threw them into the fireplace. — 36

	1	2	3	4	5	6	7	8	9	10	11

2 You can understand the despair of that author when he found — 12
out that the result of his hard labor had gone up in smoke. — 24
For weeks he just moped around and could not write a thing. — 36

	1	2	3	4	5	6	7	8	9	10	11

3 When he was taking a walk one day, he stopped at a building — 12
that was going up.   There was one bricklayer who caught his — 24
eye; he stopped and for a long time watched the bricklayer. — 36

	1	2	3	4	5	6	7	8	9	10	11

4 He must have been a bricklayer who liked his work and found — 12
joy in it.   As he laid the bricks one by one, he would step — 24
aside now and then and take a look at the work he had done. — 36

	1	2	3	4	5	6	7	8	9	10	11

5 The author was so inspired by the earnestness of purpose he — 12
had seen displayed that he went home and set to work on the — 24
task of writing again all the material the maid had burned. — 36

	1	2	3	4	5	6	7	8	9	10	11

What you are rather than what you know determines the measure 12
of your joy and success in life. Ability can be put to good uses, or it 26
can be put to bad uses. If a person is to use his ability for the good of 41
himself and others, that ability must be backed up by high character, 55
honest thinking, and a firm resolution to do the right at all costs. It 69
is easy enough to give some of the marks of a person of character; it 83
is not easy to order each act of our lives in the light of the principles 98
that underlie right conduct. Often the right seems to shade off into 112
the wrong; it is hard to make sure just where the right ends and the 126
wrong begins. In all such cases we should bring cold reason to bear 140
on our acts. To act on the emotion of the passing hour may be fatal 154
to the best that is in us. Every person at times is confronted with 168
issues in which the right course and the wrong course are easily 181
determined. If he is a person of character, he chooses the right course 195
almost without thinking. It is when the right seems to shade off into 209
wrong that real strength of character shows itself. 219

From time to time in your school work you are given a test. The 232
object is to find out, for your own benefit, how well you have mastered 246
the subject you are studying. It is not so easy to give a test that will 261
show the progress you have made in forming character. Still, the 274
attempt now and then to measure yourself by high standards of right 287
thinking and right conduct will help you to avoid mistakes made in 300
the past and to build better in the future. 309

The first test of character is strict honesty in thought, word, and 322
deed. There is an old maxim which says that honesty is the best policy, 336
but the person who acts just on that principle is not truly honest. If 350
he pauses to debate an issue in which the right and the wrong are clearly 365
evident, he is a person who cannot be trusted. We need to develop 378
the habit of rigid honesty, not because honesty will help us to get on in 393
our careers, but because it is an end in itself. It is always sad to come 408
in contact with a person who acts on the idea that it is all right to do 422
something wrong if he can get away with it. 431

A wrong action is wrong, whether or not it is found out. Unless 444
we retreat from the wrong each time we meet it, we shall advance in 457
the path of wrong; and the further on we go, the longer it will take us 471
to come back. One who is honest will not lie or cheat, no matter what 485
others may say or do. He never betrays confidence that is placed in 499
him; he never shirks responsibility that is put on him. He is a trusted 513
person because he has shown that he is worthy of trust. When a person 527
is trusted by other people, he has passed the basic test of character. 541

Lesson 17

V m W O Review

Preliminary Practice

v   via via vow vow oven oven vogue vogue vigor vigor

m   vim vim move move mauve mauve vamp vamp ramp ramp

w   wit wit bowl bowl work work wine wine power power

o   coy coy worn worn cone cone pond pond clown clown

V   Vance More made many models of very fine violins.

M   Many marvel at the majestic monuments to bravery.

W   We shall wait until we know why he went that way.

O   Order a good book from those over on the low row.

Speed-up Sentences

Balanced-hand words.

The problem for May is to make their theory work.

Did Rickey and he turn down the giant ivory tusk?

The profit may go to Formand for the work he did.

Paragraph Typing

Line of 60 spaces. Set the line-space regulator for double spacing. Type each paragraph twice with double spacing.

Words

1 When you stop to think, you realize that most of us have to 12

live with and work with and have our being with others; not 24

one of us in these days can live and work by himself alone. 36

| 1 | 2 | 3 | 4 | 5 | 6 | 7 | 8 | 9 | 10 | 11 |

2 We can say three things about people whose work brings them 12

real rewards. First, they are workers who have learned how 24

to get along with their fellows in a happy and helpful way. 36

| 1 | 2 | 3 | 4 | 5 | 6 | 7 | 8 | 9 | 10 | 11 |

No. 27

Two young men were new employees in a division of a large business. 13
One day both were working on certain statistical statements which the 27
office supervisor wanted to give to the president before the latter 40
left on an inspection tour. It was necessary for one of the two to 53
work after office hours, for which the company pays at the regular 66
overtime rate. Both young men were equally loyal and equally 78
competent. The supervisor asked the first young man whether he could 92
stay at the office that evening. The young man explained that, while 106
he had a social engagement, he could arrange to cancel it and would be 120
quite willing to do so. The supervisor naturally did not want the young 134
man to make this sacrifice. He turned to the other man with a similar 148
request. That young man replied right away that he would like to stay. 162

Here we have a case of two men of equal ability and even of equal 175
loyalty, each willing to serve the company at the sacrifice of his own 189
convenience. The one made a decidedly favorable impression, and the 203
other at best made no impression whatever. The young man who 215
stayed on the job exercised business diplomacy because he expressed a 229
genuine interest in the problem of the supervisor. The other man, as 243
you can easily see, lost a valuable opportunity. 253

No one should be surprised to know that the employee who cultivates 266
and develops this kind of diplomacy is the one who gets ahead. Of 279
course, the first requirement for success in business is a stock of 292
knowledge. That stock must be increased from day to day by careful 305
observation and by systematic overtime study. Such knowledge has a 318
weight of about a third in the battle for success. In the second place, 332
a man must get his knowledge into action. A small idea that produces 346
something is a great deal better than a big idea that produces nothing. 360
During the business day a man should draw on pretty nearly everything 374
he has ever learned or experienced. The more he draws upon his 387
entire stock, the better he will do the work of each day. This using 401
of knowledge at the right time is likewise a third of the equipment 414
in the contest. Finally, a man must cultivate and develop business 427
diplomacy. He must be agreeable, pleasant, and wholesome; he must 440
develop the ability to present his strong points. In the matter of 453
getting ahead, we may allot another and final third to this ability. Of 467
course, there are many other qualities that enter into the situation; 481
but if you bear these three basic qualities of success in mind, you will 495
move onward and upward wherever you work. The man who knows 507
how to do the work that needs to be done is of no worth in business until 522
he goes into action in the right way and at the right time. 534

Lesson 18

x n y , Review

Preliminary Practice

x   ox ox tux tux mix mix fix fix axis axis coax coax

n   end end bend bend note note bonds bonds worn worn

y   sly sly may may pay pay say say lay lay keys keys

,   buy, buy, oxen, oxen, north, north, young, young,

X   Xi Chapter will fix fines for laxity in the exam.

N   Navy men have been nominated for many top honors.

Y   You and your young son may enjoy many quiet days.

,   This key will open the front, back, or side door.

Speed-up Sentences

Balanced-hand words.

Nan is to go to the island for the box of burlap.

The keys they own entitle them to visit the city.

The visitor laughs when she pays the big penalty.

Paragraph Typing

Line of 60 spaces. Set the line-space regulator for double spacing. Type each paragraph twice with double spacing.

Words

1 They seek to blend their work with the work of others; they   12

go out of their way to say good things about those who work   24

with them; they know the goal toward which all are working.   36

     1   2   3   4   5   6   7   8   9   10   11

2 It is also true that workers who achieve are those who work   12

with vim and vigor because they love their work and believe   24

in its value; they put their hearts into every job they do.   36

     1   2   3   4   5   6   7   8   9   10   11

Lesson 19
Measured Typing

Line of 60 spaces. Set left margin stop. Type each sentence twice with single spacing. Space twice after the second writing.

Warm-up Practice

Each line contains all the letters reviewed in Lessons 17 and 18—v m w o x n y—and the comma.

To express my idea clearly, I must not use any vague words.

I expect both of you to work with vim, vigor, and vivacity.

If every store does exhibit, we shall need much more space.

Measured Typing

Set the line-space regulator for double spacing.   Type each paragraph twice with double spacing.

Words

1 One of the most important outcomes of your education is the   12
ability to make yourself do the thing you have to do at the   24
time it ought to be done, whether you like doing it or not.   36

| 1 | 2 | 3 | 4 | 5 | 6 | 7 | 8 | 9 | 10 | 11 |

2 People are really valuable to a business only when they are   12
willing and able to work in harmony with other people.   One   24
who cannot or will not cooperate with others does not last.   36

| 1 | 2 | 3 | 4 | 5 | 6 | 7 | 8 | 9 | 10 | 11 |

3 The best art any of us can develop is the art of getting on   12
with other people easily, happily, congenially, and without   24
friction.   Nothing can hold down those who master that art.   36

| 1 | 2 | 3 | 4 | 5 | 6 | 7 | 8 | 9 | 10 | 11 |

4 People are important; all else is secondary.   When you work   12
every day in the spirit of true cooperation, your days will   24
be filled with the joy of working harmoniously with others.   36

| 1 | 2 | 3 | 4 | 5 | 6 | 7 | 8 | 9 | 10 | 11 |

5 To be a leader in anything, you must first learn to work in   12
the ranks.   The grandstand player soon fades from our view.   24
In business as on the football field, teamwork always wins.   36

| 1 | 2 | 3 | 4 | 5 | 6 | 7 | 8 | 9 | 10 | 11 |

Lesson 20

q c p b Review

Line of 50 spaces. Set left margin stop.
Type each line twice with single spacing.
Space twice after each 2-line group.

Preliminary Practice

q   aqua aqua quiz quiz quotes quotes request request

c   cut cut cry cry city city curls curls decks decks

p   pen pen pay pay put put pet pet ape ape hope hope

b   by by buy buy boy boy sob sob robe robe buck buck

Q   Quite a few requested copies of this unique quiz.

C   Check each column of these corrected copies soon.

P   Place the papers in the proper reading positions.

B   Buy the brands of butter that are in brown boxes.

Speed-up Sentences

Balanced-hand words.

Jay may then make the usual profit by the bushel.

The girls wish to visit England and to go by air.

Alan is kept so busy with rush work for the city.

Paragraph Typing

Line of 60 spaces. Set the line-space regulator for double spacing. Type each paragraph twice with double spacing.

		Words
1	Please keep in mind the fact that people who rise above the	12
	crowd are those who use their heads. They do not work in a	24
	listless way; they have their minds on what they are doing.	36

    1   2   3   4   5   6   7   8   9   10   11

		Words
2	Anybody who turns out large amounts of work follows a plan.	12
	He takes just one piece of work at a time; he learns all he	24
	can about that piece of work and just how it is to be done.	36

    1   2   3   4   5   6   7   8   9   10   11

Lesson 21

Z : / ? Review

Line of 50 spaces. Set left margin stop.
Type each line twice with single spacing.
Space twice after each 2-line group.

Preliminary Practice

z   doze doze lazy lazy hazy hazy quiz quiz size **size**

:   Send the following: paper, pencils, and baskets.

/   Mr. Hunt and/or Mr. Dill will represent the firm.

?   Is this a bronze box? How was the new quiz show?

z   Zelda found the topaz azaleas on her visit there.

:   Dear Sir: Please ship this order now by freight.

/   The squad will be trained by M/Sgt James Wingate.

?   How many words are on the quiz list? Why **so few?**

Speed-up Sentences

Balanced-hand
words.

The big oak sign by the field is visible to them.

Did he fit the lapels and make them right for us?

The eight anthems embody the lament of the world.

Paragraph Typing

Line of 60 spaces. Set the line-space regulator for double spacing. Type each paragraph twice with double spacing.

Words

1 The next step is to start work on the job and to keep at it   12

until you bring it to an end. You then put that job out of   24

your mind and turn at once to the next job that lies ahead.   36

     1   2   3   4   5   6   7   8   9   10   11

2 There is no other way to get things done. You need to know   12

what to do and how to do it; you then begin and keep at the   24

job to the end. You put it aside and take up the next job.   36

     1   2   3   4   5   6   7   8   9   10   11

Lesson 22
Measured Typing

Warm-up Practice

Each of these three lines contains all the letters you reviewed in Lessons 20 and 21—q c p b z— and the colon (:) and the question mark (?).

```
Gentlemen:  When can the new freezing equipment be shipped?
Dear Mr. Zorn:  Have you replied to the inquiry about zinc?
Dear Curt:  What do you take to be the purpose of the quiz?
```

Measured Typing

Set the line-space regulator for double spacing. Type each paragraph twice with double spacing.

Words

1 The first impression you get from a business letter is made   12
by its appearance as a whole. If you get a good impression   24
at first sight, you will probably start reading the letter.   36

> 1   2   3   4   5   6   7   8   9   10   11

2 Some time ago I received a letter from a company that sells   12
stocks and bonds. From reading even the first two or three   24
lines, I sensed how carefully the letter had been dictated.   36

> 1   2   3   4   5   6   7   8   9   10   11

3 What killed the letter was its poor appearance. Several of   12
the lines were as much as eight spaces shorter than others.   24
Worst of all, I saw some noticeable erasures in the letter.   36

> 1   2   3   4   5   6   7   8   9   10   11

4 If this company, I said to myself, is so careless as to let   12
letters of this kind go out of its office, it will probably   24
be just as careless when it is investing a sum of my money.   36

> 1   2   3   4   5   6   7   8   9   10   11

5 It may be that I did the company an injustice, as it was an   12
old and reliable business. The harm done was due wholly to   24
the gross carelessness of the one who had typed the letter.   36

> 1   2   3   4   5   6   7   8   9   10   11

Lesson 23

Measured Typing

Indenting for Paragraphs

To set the stop for a paragraph indention, proceed thus:

(1) Clear all tabs by moving the carriage to the extreme left, pressing down the Tab Clear Key, and returning the carriage.

(2) Release the Tab Clear Key.

(3) Strike the space bar five times.

(4) Press the Tab Set Key at this position.

You then have a paragraph indention of five spaces.

Indent for the first line of each paragraph by pressing the Tab Key with the little finger; or by pressing the Tab Bar (if your machine has a Tab Bar) with the first finger of either hand. The carriage will move automatically to the correct position for the 5-space indention. Hold down the Tab Key or the Tab Bar until the carriage comes to a complete stop.

Measured Typing

Beginning with this lesson, indent the first line of each paragraph 5 spaces. Use a 60-space line throughout. Type each paragraph twice with *double* spacing.

Words

1

It is true now, as indeed it has been true in all past — 11
time, that as a man thinks in his heart, so is he. To know — 23
the right is not the same as to do the right. A person may — 35
read the best of all books, but just to read that book will — 47
not help him unless he also feels the truths set out in it. — 59

	1	2	3	4	5	6	7	8	9	10	11

2

If a man feels the right in his heart, he will do what — 11
is right; but if he has not learned that right is right and — 23
wrong is wrong to the end, then all that he has in his mind — 35
will not keep him on the right track. Right acts and right — 47
thoughts always flow out of the heart, not out of the mind. — 59

	1	2	3	4	5	6	7	8	9	10	11

3

If you stop to think of an act in terms of the shorter — 11
word by which it is known, you will be sure to see that act — 23
in its true light. Let us say that you tell me that what a — 35
person said to you is a lie. I know exactly what you mean. — 47
If you say he is a prevaricator, then I am not at all sure. — 59

	1	2	3	4	5	6	7	8	9	10	11

Lesson 24

Measured Typing

Warm-up Practice

Type each sentence twice with single spacing.   Double-space after the second writing of each sentence. All the words in the four sentences are balanced-hand words.

Did the girl do the work for the chairman of the auto firm?

The problem is to halt the work when the men dig the rocks.

She paid the man for the pan of jam and laid it by the box.

The neighbor lent the bicycle and the hayfork to the girls.

Measured Typing

Set the line-space regulator for double spacing.   Type each paragraph twice with double spacing.

Words

1   Or let us say that a man steals money from the bank in   11
which he works. If you use the short word that we all know   23
and call him a thief, I know what you mean; but if you tell   35
me that his act is a defalcation, I may easily get the idea   47
that in some way the thief is not to be blamed for his act.   59

| 1 | 2 | 3 | 4 | 5 | 6 | 7 | 8 | 9 | 10 | 11 |

2   You see, his crime does not sound so bad as it does if   11
you speak of it as theft. We should know that words may be   23
used to hide the truth as well as to bring it to light. It   35
is for that reason that we shall do well to use those short   47
words of our native tongue that mean the same thing to all.   59

| 1 | 2 | 3 | 4 | 5 | 6 | 7 | 8 | 9 | 10 | 11 |

3   Words are the tools that we use each day of our lives.   11
At home and in school or college we must use words to speak   23
and to write. We use words in the work we do for a living.   35
It is through words that we make known our joys and griefs,   47
our hopes and fears. Words play a large part in our lives.   59

| 1 | 2 | 3 | 4 | 5 | 6 | 7 | 8 | 9 | 10 | 11 |

Lesson 25

Measured Typing

Warm-up Practice

Type each sentence twice with single spacing. Double-space after the second writing of each sentence. All the words in the four sentences are balanced-hand words.

```
The city also held the title to six of the ancient chapels.

Did Sidney pay for the ornament to go with the eight signs?

The maid may visit the town and lend the usual aid to them.

The man kept both the chair and the rug and paid the girls.
```

Measured Typing

Set the line-space regulator for double spacing. Type each paragraph twice with double spacing.

Words

1
```
     Words play on our minds all the time; they fly through        11
the air; they are flung at us from every side.  Often words        23
have changed the course of nations and of the world.  Words        35
have been used to stir up the beast in men, but others have        47
brought men real joy and peace in days of grief and strife.        59
```
1 2 3 4 5 6 7 8 9 10 11

2
```
     If you know a man who is out in front in his field and        11
ask him just why he has made good, he will tell you that it        23
is because he likes his work; he may even tell you that his        35
love for his work is what makes him keep on.  His heart and        47
soul are in his work, and he gives it all that in him lies.        59
```
1 2 3 4 5 6 7 8 9 10 11

3
```
     How can you get to like the work to which you set your        11
mind and hands?  The best way is to study the parts of that        23
work and make yourself master of those parts.  You can then        35
put those parts together and see for yourself what you have        47
done.  There is no joy like that of seeing an aim realized.        59
```
1 2 3 4 5 6 7 8 9 10 11

Lesson 26

Measured Typing

Warm-up Practice

Type each sentence twice with single spacing.   Double-space after the second writing of each sentence. All the words in the four sentences are balanced-hand words.

If the turkey burns, then he may also burn the pan of kale.

The title to the land and the right to the coal go to them.

It is right for the men to turn down the risk if they wish.

The girls laugh with vigor when they fish down by the quay.

Measured Typing

Each of these paragraphs contains all the letters of the alphabet.   Set the line-space regulator for double spacing.   Type each paragraph twice with double spacing.

Words

1   Everyone can report some feat of skill that stands out   11
in his mind.   One exciting sight I recall is the work of an   23
Australian boomerang thrower.   He was such a queer sight in   35
his native garb.   It was a joy to note his zest in throwing   47
the boomerang.   After each throw it came right back to him.   59

    1   2   3   4   5   6   7   8   9   10   11

2   I got to thinking about what I had seen.   In many ways   11
life is quite like that boomerang.   What we do each day and   23
what we express in words come back to give us joy or grief.   35
There are people in the world who blaze with desire to hurt   47
others, but what evil they do to others comes back to them.   59

    1   2   3   4   5   6   7   8   9   10   11

3   Not a single one of us is just a zero.   It may be that   11
the influence you exercise on those around you is quiet and   23
perhaps even limited.   It remains true that you meet people   35
and people meet you.   If what you give out is good, you may   47
rely on it that sooner or later good will come back to you.   59

    1   2   3   4   5   6   7   8   9   10   11

Lesson 27

Measured Typing

Warm-up Practice

Type each sentence twice with single spacing. Double-space after the second writing of each sentence. All the words in the four sentences are balanced-hand words.

```
The civic body is due to amend the pay forms for the towns.
Both of the men rush to bury the giant oak box by the lake.
When they visit us, they may also go to the city of Peoria.
Sidney Land kept the ornament; he also paid for the panels.
```

Measured Typing

Each one of these paragraphs contains all the letters of the alphabet. Set the line-space regulator for double spacing. Type each paragraph twice with double spacing.

Words

1   There are just two driving forces that will enable you   11
to get work done. First, you must want to do. Second, you   23
must organize yourself and your time. There are people who   35
kill time; they do not fill time. If you really want to do   47
something worthwhile, you will get the extra time required.   59

    1   2   3   4   5   6   7   8   9   10   11

2   The urge has to come from the inside. A strong motive   11
is the first requisite. Do you know just how to start on a   23
task and how to keep at it? Those who have to be coaxed do   35
not get anywhere. You will be amazed to learn how much you   47
can do when you make the right start and keep at your work.   59

    1   2   3   4   5   6   7   8   9   10   11

3   The difference between success and failure is often so   11
extremely small. Never allow yourself to become the victim   23
of routine. It is the one who does just a little more than   35
is required who makes his mark because he brings himself to   47
the notice of his superior who can authorize his promotion.   59

    1   2   3   4   5   6   7   8   9   10   11

Division Two—Figure and Symbol Keys

Lesson 28
4   7

Line of 60 spaces. *Set left margin stop.*
Type each line twice with single spacing.
Space twice after each 2-line group.

Preliminary Practice

The judge renders just decisions. Use the four new titles.
If they are to do it, then they must do it with great care.
He can aid the city official by his support of the problem.

LEFT HAND

F-finger reaches
up to strike 4.

Some typewriters
have a special
l-key controlled
by the *A*-finger.

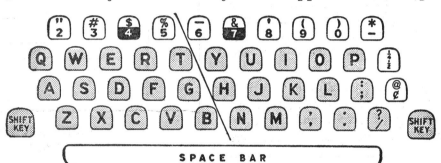

RIGHT HAND

J-finger reaches
up to strike 7.

ILLUSTRATION 30

New Stroke Drill

f4f f4f 4f4 4f4 444 j7j j7j 7j7 7j7 777 474 474 747 747 147
47 aisles; 74 signs; 41 docks; 14 fights; 71 keys; 17 hams;
474 James Court; 147 Kemp Road; 714 Lenton Drive; 417 Main;
There are 141 doctors, 171 dentists, and 47 nurses present.

Use small L for the figure 1.

Control Drill

The sum of 4 and 7 is 11, but what is the sum of 47 and 74?
The list dated June 4 includes 171 orders and 47 contracts.
To finish the entire job in 47 weeks, we shall need 74 men.
They were asked to ship 71 pounds each of grades 14 and 17.

Speed-up Sentences

The busy men make the usual bid for the 74 bushels of corn.
The problem of the panel is to pay for the 47 ancient maps.
The man may make an audit for the 47 girls of the sorority.
The auditors are to be paid to sign forms 14, 174, and 741.

Lesson 29

Measured Typing

Line of 60 spaces. Set left margin stop.

Warm-up Practice

Type each sentence twice with single spacing. Space twice after the second writing. All the words in the three sentences are balanced-hand words.

The title to the land is held by the chairman of the panel.
The duty of the girl is to rush to the aid of the neighbor.
Both men may then make a formal visit to the eight chapels.

Measured Typing

Type each paragraph twice with *double* spacing.

Words

1
One of these days you will reach the goal of your work | 11
in this course and will start to work in an office. Before | 23
you get started, you should know that there are really just | 35
two ways of mastering any aspect of business. The first is | 47
the way of chance; the second, the way of definite purpose. | 59

    1   2   3   4   5   6   7   8   9   10   11

2
In the first way you may learn something just by being | 11 70
around. In the second way you put your mind on the problem | 23 82
of learning what there is to know about the enterprise that | 35 94
claims your thought and attention. No thoughtful person is | 47 106
willing simply to go through the motions of his daily work. | 59 118

    1   2   3   4   5   6   7   8   9   10   11

3
Both ways have merit, but the second way is by far the | 11 129
more effective. When you really set yourself to the job of | 23 141
learning something, you can find out more about it in a day | 35 153
than you can find out by chance in a week or a month. Make | 47 165
it a point, therefore, to study and to keep your eyes open. | 59 177

    1   2   3   4   5   6   7   8   9   10   11

4
There is something else to bear in mind. Every one of | 11 188
us needs to learn how to work accurately and how to do good | 23 200
work without taking forever to do it. In the world we live | 35 212
in, there are always things that have to be done; they must | 47 224
be done quickly as well as correctly, for time means money. | 59 236

    1   2   3   4   5   6   7   8   9   10   11

Lesson 30
3 8

Line of 60 spaces. Set left margin stop.
Type each line twice with single spacing.
Space twice after each 2-line group.

Preliminary Practice

He assured me blithely that he had made the trip six times.

They saw the green sedan go into the parking lot near here.

We should have consulted you first, but you were very busy.

LEFT HAND
D-finger reaches
up to strike 3.

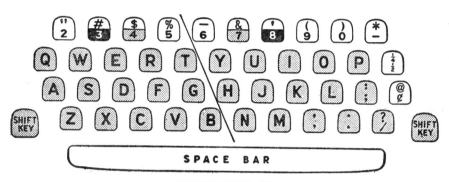

RIGHT HAND
K-finger reaches
up to strike 8.

ILLUSTRATION 31

New Stroke Drill

d3d d3d 3d3 3d3 333 k8k k8k 8k8 8k8 888 383 383 838 838 183

38 quarts; 83 cuts; 138 elevators; 381 rulers; 13 trenches;

Deliver 18 boxes each to 38 Rome Street and 83 Yancy Place.

Those 38 machines were shipped on February 8 in Lot No. 83.

Control Drill

Reports show that 14,738 people attended the May 8 concert.

Winning 38 games out of 47 put the team in the top bracket.

There will be 3,847 entries on 1,473 pages in his new book.

You will find the data in paragraphs 13 and 18 on page 148.

Speed-up Sentences

The man held the title for the 83 emblems for the bicycles.

The firm is also to make the audit for the 38 pajama firms.

It is then their duty to pay for the 3,847 bushels of corn.

The tutor and the 483 sorority girls go down to the island.

Lesson 31

Measured Typing

Warm-up Practice

Type each sentence twice with single spacing. Space twice after the second writing. All the words in the three sentences are balanced-hand words.

```
The pay for the bushel of corn is due by the eighth of May.
If she is busy with the problem, I may do half of the work.
The name of the tutor is Rieman; he is kept downright busy.
```

Measured Typing

Type each paragraph twice with *double* spacing.

Words

1
```
    Have you ever had a chance to stand in the wings, back    11
of the scenes, at the time when a play was being given in a   23
theater?  If you have had such a chance, you saw the actors   35
waiting for the moment to come when it was their turn to go   47
on stage to speak the words they had learned at rehearsals.  59
      1     2     3     4     5     6     7     8     9    10    11
```

2
```
    The actors are waiting for their cues, which will give   11   70
them the chance to go out and say something.  It is just as   23   82
important for those players to remember their cues as it is   35   94
for them to recall their lines.  If they do not go on stage  47  106
at just the right time, the play is likely to be a failure.  59  118
      1     2     3     4     5     6     7     8     9    10    11
```

3
```
    We are all like the players in a great piece, with the   11  129
world as the stage on which we play our parts to add joy or   23  141
sadness to the spectacle; but if we are to achieve the goal  35  153
we have set before us, there is one thing we must remember,  47  165
and that is the daily need for our being ready for the cue.  59  177
      1     2     3     4     5     6     7     8     9    10    11
```

4
```
    Of course, the players in the theater have a number of   11  188
advantages over the actors on the world stage.  Their lines  23  200
are prepared for them; they know just the parts they are to  35  212
play day after day.  They go over those parts and the whole  47  224
action many times, so that they will never miss their cues.  59  236
      1     2     3     4     5     6     7     8     9    10    11
```

Lesson 32
5   9

Line of 60 spaces. Set left margin stop.
Type each line twice with single spacing.
Space twice after each 2-line group.

Preliminary Practice

It is so much easier to avoid an error than to correct one.

Always use your best efforts for the most effective result.

The age in which we live calls for a broader point of view.

LEFT HAND

F-finger reaches up and to the right to strike 5.

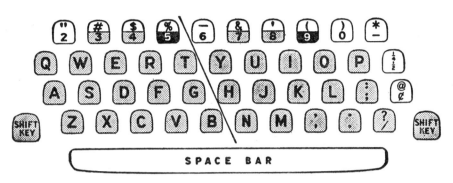

RIGHT HAND

L-finger reaches up to strike 9.

ILLUSTRATION 32

New Stroke Drill

f5f f5f 5f5 5f5 555 191 191 919 919 999 595 595 959 959 519

59 signals; 95 fields; 159 islands; 951 rocks; 591 anthems;

What is the total of 59 and 95? The divisor to use is 159.

Will you ship the 59 crates? Are there 95 members present?

Control Drill

Remember these dates: June 5, August 19, and September 15.

Will the new addresses in Toledo be 5 and 9 Linden Terrace?

The gauge shows that he has driven 5,397 miles on the trip.

Can you sell 159 cars if they are shipped to you next week?

Speed-up Sentences

Lend the 59 forms, the 47 maps, and the 38 keys to the men.

The problem is to mend the 59 signs and the 95 big emblems.

What is the right total of 13, 15, 37, 48, 57, 95, and 159?

She may divide 15 by 5, 39 by 13, 413 by 59, and 595 by 85.

Lesson 33

Measured Typing

Warm-up Practice

Type each sentence twice with single spacing. Space twice after the second writing. All the words in the three sentences are balanced-hand words.

```
Both girls clap their hands and laugh when they make a bid.
The six ensigns may also wish to visit their sick neighbor.
He is to augment and codify the audit to make it authentic.
```

Measured Typing

Type each paragraph twice with *double* spacing.

Words

1
```
     The real actors on the stage of life must look out for      11
themselves.  When they see that their chance has come, they      23
must be ready to take it.  They must be always on the alert      35
for the cue that is to give them their chance to enter.  If      47
they fail to grasp that chance, somebody else will take it.      59
```
```
     1     2     3     4     5     6     7     8     9     10     11
```

2
```
     In other words, it is the ability to recognize the cue      11   70
that is one of the marks of every person who has set a goal      23   82
for himself.  He not only knows his cue, but he is ready to      35   94
act on it at once.  When an opportunity comes your way, you      47   106
must seize upon it right away and take the action required.      59   118
```
```
     1     2     3     4     5     6     7     8     9     10     11
```

3
```
     Opportunity does not often take the trouble to send an      11   129
advance agent; therefore we have to be on the alert all the      23   141
time to grasp every opportunity which comes our way.  There      35   153
is not the slightest doubt that many a fine opportunity has      47   165
been lost because no attention was paid to the opportunity.      59   177
```
```
     1     2     3     4     5     6     7     8     9     10     11
```

4
```
     Opportunity does come knocking at our door.  If we are      11   188
asleep or busy about other things, we may not even take the      23   200
time or trouble to answer the summons.  Perhaps we open the      35   212
door and fail to realize that opportunity has called on us.      47   224
Thus we have lost a chance that may not come our way again.      59   236
```
```
     1     2     3     4     5     6     7     8     9     10     11
```

Lesson 34
2 0

Preliminary Practice

A good battery will give me starting power in zero weather.

How can I best fit into the upset conditions of these days?

Lewis drove the truck over the winding road of these hills.

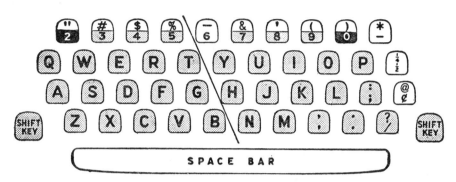

LEFT HAND
S-finger reaches
up to strike 2.

RIGHT HAND
;-finger reaches
up to strike 0.

ILLUSTRATION 33

New Stroke Drill

s2s s2s 2s2 2s2 222 ;0; ;0; 0;0 0;0 000 202 202 020 020 220
200 quarts; 121 zones; 10 Dock Street; 100 cubes; 210 vats;
Ship the following: 20 boxes, 21 cartons, and 121 barrels.
These are the correct totals: 472, 730, 201, 920, and 721.

Control Drill

This fine dictionary has 1,205 pages with 827 colored maps.
Refer the girl to paragraphs 2 and 10, Section 29, page 70.
We shall need 30 cans of varnish to finish the 27 cabinets.
She has reached the stroking rate of 20 net words a minute.

Speed-up Sentences

Their problem is to make a total of 20 visits to the laity.
When may the pals make their usual visit to the 27 chapels?
Two of the 20 ensigns may make handy maps of the big field.
I may divide 80 by 20, 210 by 30, 320 by 40, and 840 by 20.

Lesson 35

Measured Typing   *Line of 60 spaces.   Set left margin stop.*

Warm-up Practice

Type each sentence twice with single spacing.   Space twice after the second writing.   All the words in the three sentences are balanced-hand words.

```
To go to their city by auto, make a right turn by the lake.
I also wish to visit Lake Maud when I go by air to England.
The girl is shaken by the dismal sight of the burnt burlap.
```

Measured Typing

Type each paragraph twice with *double* spacing.

Words

1   A man who is a real leader in business in his city had   11
as his guests several men who were prospects for putting an   23
industry in his city. Right after lunch he took his guests   35
to the garage where he had left his new car to be oiled and   47
greased. He also told the manager to have the oil changed.   59

    1   2   3   4   5   6   7   8   9   10   11

2   The host had his guests get into the car and told them   11   70
that he wanted to take them on a tour about the city. When   23   82
they had driven some ten miles and had had a number of fine   35   94
places pointed out to them, things began to happen with the   47   106
car. It started to shake, and finally the motor went dead.   59   118

    1   2   3   4   5   6   7   8   9   10   11

3   As the car had been driven less than a thousand miles,   11   129
the host could not understand what had occurred. He called   23   141
the garage to send a man right away. After a wait that was   35   153
much too long for the fuming host, the mechanic finally got   47   165
there. He looked at the motor block and up went his hands.   59   177

    1   2   3   4   5   6   7   8   9   10   11

4   A gadget of some kind had come through the block. One   11   188
of the guests who was an engineer said to his host that the   23   200
man at the garage who had been instructed to change the oil   35   212
had either failed to put oil back into the engine or he had   47   224
neglected to put the plug back when he had changed the oil.   59   236

    1   2   3   4   5   6   7   8   9   10   11

Lesson 36
6 -

Line of 60 spaces. *Set left margin stop.*
Type each line twice with single spacing.
Space twice after each 2-line group.

Preliminary Practice

All we have to do is to set the dials if we want even heat.

The store carries a full line of consoles to fit all needs.

Come early and save money from these special bargain sales.

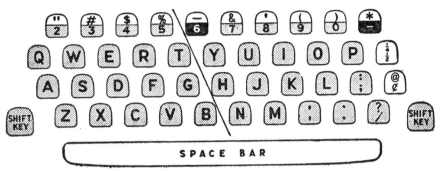

ILLUSTRATION 34

RIGHT HAND

J-finger reaches up and to the left to strike 6.

;-finger reaches up and to the right to strike the hyphen (—).

New Stroke Drill

Do not space before or after a hyphen *within* a word.

j6j j6j 6j6 6j6 666 ;-; ;-; -;- -;- --- first-class anthems
that 3-point landing; 60-page pamphlets; 628-630 Akers Road
How quickly can you total 46, 38, 63, 126, 96, 34, and 276?
I signed the 60-day note. These high-grade boxes are hers.

Control Drill

The school enrolled 626 students in the 26 English courses.
The 16-story office building is located at 65-67 West Road.
The new and up-to-date hotel has 16 floors and 1,823 rooms.
We can use 60 stamps, 126 large envelopes, and 64 journals.

Speed-up Sentences

They wish me to go with them to the city for the 674 forms.
I am to take 6 hams, 60 turkeys, and 86 ducks to the field.
The eight busy sorority girls may go with us to the ritual.
May 16 is when Jan is to be the chairman of the civic body.

No. 21

Loyalty is the watchword of every good secretary. She is loyal and true to the interests of her employer. Loyalty never means being subservient and just agreeing with the employer. True loyalty often consists of bringing to the attention of the employer facts and situations which may be distasteful to him. In being loyal in that way, the secretary has the larger interests of the employer in mind. She is able to think of the future in terms of the present, as well as of the present in terms of the future. It would be disloyal for her not to present all the facts that ought to enter into a conclusion.

The work of the secretary is of a highly confidential nature. Many matters that pass through her hands are not intended for the eyes or ears of other people, not even for the eyes and ears of other employees in the same office. She is always on the alert not to betray, by a slip of the tongue or by idle talk, matters that have been entrusted to her care. She is dependable and trustworthy because she is loyal in every fibre of her being. If you cannot keep things to yourself and if you do not have the ability to stay loyal through thick and thin, you may be sure you are not cut out to be a secretary.

Initiative is still another quality which has a large place among the characteristics of the successful secretary. A person who has real initiative not only starts things, but he gets those things done. He does not wait for somebody to find work for him to do, and he does not have to have that work outlined for him step by step. On the contrary, he is continually on the alert to start things himself, to initiate improvements, and to find new and better ways of doing the daily work of the office or getting it done. There is hardly an hour in the day when the secretary does not need to bring initiative to bear on small things as well as on things that loom large in importance. She makes sure that a sufficient supply of working materials is always at hand. She thinks ahead and senses that her employer will need certain papers in arriving at a decision on a business problem; she uses her initiative and gets those papers together so that they will be ready when they are needed. From time to time she brings to the attention of her employer news items or other material which she knows will be of interest to him. For that reason she scans the trade papers which come to the desk of her employer. Often she is able to boil down an article and then present it, in abstract form, to her employer. In all these ways she makes herself useful and, indeed, indispensable in activities that lie beyond the plane of the mechanical and the routine. She is a creative worker who enjoys the confidence and respect of all.

Words
13
26
40
55
68
82
97
111
121
134
148
162
176
190
204
218
232
241
255
268
283
297
311
324
338
352
366
380
394
408
422
435
448
461
474
488
502
515
528
542

Lesson 37

Measured Typing   *Line of 60 spaces.   Set left margin stop.*

Warm-up Practice

Type each sentence twice with single spacing.   Space twice after the second writing.   All the words in the three sentences are balanced-hand words.

He is to pay the firm to make the usual audit of the forms.
Both the girls kept busy with social work for the sorority.
Leo is proficient; he is the right man to work the problem.

Measured Typing

Type each paragraph twice with *double* spacing.

Words

1   Have you ever given thought to asking yourself what is   11
the most important quality you can develop while you are in   23
school or college? It is just the ability to make yourself   35
do the things you should do at the time you should do them.   47
Doing only what you feel like doing can become a bad habit.   59

     1   2   3   4   5   6   7   8   9   10   11

2   Some people get in the habit of allowing tasks to hang   11   70
over them. Let us say that you have a lesson to prepare or   23   82
some practice work to do. You decide you do not have to do   35   94
the work right now, and you let it ride. You tell yourself   47   106
that you will feel much more like doing it some other time.   59   118

     1   2   3   4   5   6   7   8   9   10   11

3   In almost every case it is just a matter of getting at   11   129
the work that lies before you. When you avoid the habit of   23   141
putting off a job you know you should do and get at it, you   35   153
will surprise yourself by the amount of work you can do and   47   165
how readily you do the things you felt would be hard to do.   59   177

     1   2   3   4   5   6   7   8   9   10   11

4   You will be certain to feel better and to do better if   11   188
you will not permit your work to pile up and if you make it   23   200
a point to keep your current work cleared up; then you will   35   212
be able to turn your mind and hands freely to new work. Be   47   224
sure to plan everything you do and then work out your plan.   59   236

     1   2   3   4   5   6   7   8   9   10   11

ARTICLE IV--OFFICERS

Section 1. The officers of this Association shall be a President, a Vice-President, a Secretary, and a Treasurer to be elected from the active members by a majority vote of the member lines represented at the annual meeting.

Section 2. The term of office shall be one year, but any officer shall be eligible to succeed himself or to be elected to a different office for a succeeding term.

Section 3. All officers of this Association shall, at the time of their election, be officers or employees of different member lines.

ARTICLE V--DUTIES OF OFFICERS

The officers shall perform the customary duties of their respective offices.

ARTICLE VI--BOARD OF DIRECTORS

The Board of Directors shall consist of the four officers and three additional directors elected annually. Sections 1 and 2 of Article IV shall apply to the election of the three additional directors. Section 3 of Article IV shall not apply.

ARTICLE VII--MEETINGS

Section 1. This Association shall hold an annual meeting in January at a place in Indiana, Michigan, or Ohio selected by the Board of Directors.

Section 2. Special meetings may be called by the Board of Directors.

Section 3. The Secretary shall notify each member line of the time and place of any meeting at least forty-eight (48) hours before the meeting.

Section 4. The Board of Directors shall meet monthly and at such other times as the President may direct.

ARTICLE VIII--QUORUM

Section 1. A majority of member lines shall constitute a quorum for any meeting of the Association.

Section 2. Four members of the Board of Directors shall constitute a quorum of the Board of Directors.

ARTICLE IX--AMENDMENTS

The By-Laws may be amended at any annual meeting by an affirmative vote of two-thirds of the member lines present.

Line of 60 spaces. Set left margin stop.
Type each line twice with single spacing.
Space twice after each 2-line group.

Preliminary Practice

Do I have the ability to get these people to work together?
Automatic signals were used to speed up all late shipments.

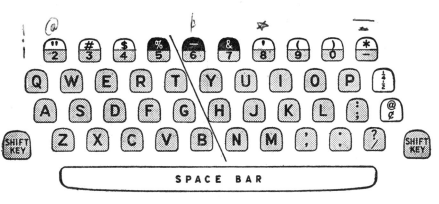

LEFT HAND

The per cent sign (%) is the shift of 5.

ILLUSTRATION 35

RIGHT HAND

The ampersand (&) is the shift of 7.

On a manual typewriter the underscore (_) is the shift of 6.
On an electric typewriter it is the shift of the hyphen.

New Stroke Drill

To underscore a word on a manual typewriter: (1) type the word; (2) backspace to the first letter; (3) lock the shift key; (4) strike the underscore for each letter. To underscore a word on an electric typewriter, follow steps 1 through 3; (4) hold down the underscore key. To use the repeat action of the hyphen and underscore, depress the key and hold it down for the number of repetitions you want. To type one hyphen or one underscore at a time, release the key quickly.

```
          f5f f5f f%f f%f %f% %f% %%% 15% discount; 30% gross profit.
          j7j j7j j&j j&j &j& &j& &&& B & O; Carter & White; C L & M;
Electric  ;-; ;-; ;_; ;_; _;_ _;_ ___ Six larger signs can be posted.
Manual    j6j j6j j_j j_j _j_ _j_ ___ Six larger signs can be posted.
          Hart & Company; 5%, 9%, and 15% basic increases; 8% and 6%;
```

Control Drill

Do you know the difference between principal and principle?
Melton & Hahn will give 20% discount on all Wearlong tires.

Speed-up Sentences

The firm of Landor & Mandl may pay the duty of 9% by proxy.
The sign & is for and in such a firm name as Krup & Tidmor.

By-Laws. The By-Laws make up the set of rules by which an organization is governed. They are divided into parts called *Articles*. Subdivisions of the Articles are called *Sections*.

Illustration 101 shows the style generally used for typing By-Laws. The number and the title of each Article are centered. Each Section is indented.

Problem 48. You are to cut stencils for reproducing the following set of By-Laws. Before you do so, however, type the By-Laws on plain paper.

Use Illustration 101 as your model for style. Leave a top margin of one inch.

BY-LAWS

of the

TRI-STATE ASSOCIATION OF
MOTOR FREIGHT LINES

Adopted June 30, 19--

ARTICLE I--NAME

The name of this organization shall be the Tri-State Association of Motor Freight Lines.

ARTICLE II--PURPOSES

The purposes of this Association shall be to advance the interests of the motor freight industry in the states of Indiana, Michigan, and Ohio; to provide its members with the organizational means of solving cooperatively such problems as are of common interest; and to promote good will and understanding among its members.

ARTICLE III--MEMBERSHIP

Section 1. Any motor line that hauls freight on any of the highways of Indiana, Michigan, and Ohio, or of any one of these states, shall be eligible for membership provided that it has been in operation for a period of at least one year and provided

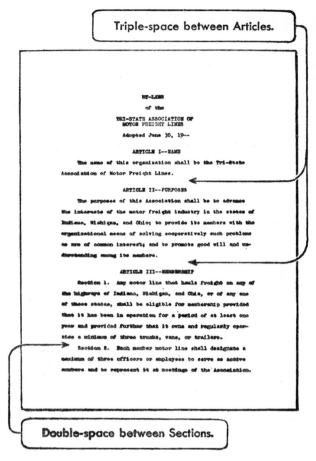

ILLUSTRATION 101
By-Laws

further that it owns and regularly operates a minimum of three trucks, vans, or trailers.

Section 2. Each member motor line shall designate a maximum of three officers or employees to serve as active members and to represent it at meetings of the Association.

Section 3. Membership classes and dues shall be determined by the Board of Directors.

Section 4. A member motor line shall be dropped from membership in this Association only upon the affirmative vote of four-fifths of the member lines.

Section 5. Each member line shall have one vote only.

Lesson 39

Measured Typing *Line of 60 spaces. Set left margin stop.*

Warm-up Practice

Type each sentence twice with single spacing. Space twice after the second writing. All the words in the three sentences are balanced-hand words.

```
She did dismantle the ancient auto and the antique bicycle.
Is the ivory ornament for the panel the handiwork of Helen?
The firm may make a bid to the city to dismantle the docks.
```

Measured Typing

Type each paragraph twice with *double* spacing.

Words

1
```
     When you judge every new idea that comes to you on its      11
merit rather than by your first reaction, you show that you      23
have reached maturity in your thinking.  There is something      35
to the old maxim about not being the first to adopt the new      47
or the last to discard the old, but it has its limitations.     59
```
          1   2   3   4   5   6   7   8   9   10   11

2
```
     What was good in the past should be kept.  At the same   11   70
time we should make certain that we do not think and act in   23   82
certain ways now just because we thought and acted in those   35   94
ways in the past.  If we simply will not change in any way,   47  106
we shall fall into a rut; then we just jog along every day.   59  118
```
          1   2   3   4   5   6   7   8   9   10   11

3
```
     Of course, no person who does any real thinking is for   11  129
change just for the sake of change.  Still, there is such a   23  141
thing as refusing to think through a matter and of taking a   35  153
stand in the spirit of stubbornness.  There are some people   47  165
who are sure they are always right and others always wrong.   59  177
```
          1   2   3   4   5   6   7   8   9   10   11

4
```
     To get a new idea into the mind may mean some pain and   11  188
suffering, yet resistance to all new ideas is the sure sign   23  200
of decay.  Keep your mind wide open; take time to study the   35  212
new ideas which come to you.  Try to avoid the closed mind,   47  224
for the closed mind always holds back progress in anything.   59  236
```
          1   2   3   4   5   6   7   8   9   10   11

Minutes. The minutes form the official record of a meeting. The secretary of the organization, board, club, or committee is responsible for the preparation and safe-keeping of the minutes in a "minutes book."

Minutes are set up in article form, with provision at the end for the secretary's signature.

Problem 47. Type a stencil for the following minutes. Use Illustration 100 as your model for style.

MINUTES OF THE
MONTHLY MEETING
of the

Executive Committee

TWIN CITIES DEPARTMENT STORE ASSOCIATION

March 23, 19--

The meeting was held in the Board Room of Kittredge Brothers, Inc. Mr. Herman Bostwick, President, called the meeting to order at 3:30 p.m.

The following members were present: Messrs. Bostwick, Francisco, Scott, Fox, Hansen, Jergenson, Kittredge, Lopez, McGrady, Morris, and Olson. Mr. Kline was absent.

Minutes of the last meeting were read by the Secretary and approved as read.

There being no other reports or old business, the President called for new business and recognized Mr. Hansen. Mr. Hansen suggested that the Committee act at this meeting on the summer schedule to be followed by Association members.

After a discussion participated in by Messrs. Bostwick, Francisco, Jergenson, and Fox, it was moved by Mr. Francisco and seconded by Mr. McGrady that all member stores close for nine consecutive Saturdays, starting with June 28 and ending with August 23, both dates inclusive.

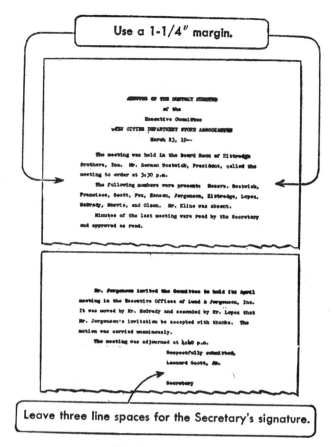

ILLUSTRATION 100
Minutes

The motion was carried by a show of hands, Mr. Jergenson dissenting.

The President instructed the Secretary to notify all members of the Committee's action and to prepare a news release for distribution to the press.

Mr. Jergenson invited the Committee to hold its April meeting in the Executive Offices of Lund & Jergenson, Inc. It was moved by Mr. McGrady and seconded by Mr. Lopez that Mr. Jergenson's invitation be accepted with thanks. The motion was carried unanimously.

The meeting was adjourned at 4:40 p.m.

> Respectfully submitted,
> Leonard Scott, Jr.
> Secretary

Lesson 40
$ ' *

Line of 60 spaces. Set left margin stop.
Type each line twice with single spacing.
Space twice after each 2-line group.

Preliminary Practice

It is easy to find a good job when you are prepared for it.
You can speed up your typing rate by using good techniques.
The result of the voting was quite conclusive in all areas.

LEFT HAND
The dollar sign
($) is the
shift of 4.

SPACE BAR

ILLUSTRATION 36

RIGHT HAND

On a manual typewriter the apostrophe (') is the shift of 8.

On an electric typewriter it is on the home row next to the semicolon. Use the ;-finger. Do not shift.

On a manual typewriter the asterisk (*) is the shift of the hyphen (−).

On an electric typewriter it is the shift of 8.

New Stroke Drill

f4f f4f f$f f$f f f $$$ $5; $600; $23.45; $67.89; $100;

Electric
{ ;'; ;'; ;'; ';' ';' ';' ''' women's and children's dresses;
{ k8k k8k k*k k*k *k* *k* *** Read Blacklin's current* study.

Manual
{ k8k k8k k'k k'k 'k' 'k' ''' women's and children's dresses;
{ ;-; ;-; ;*; ;*; *;* *;* *** Read Blacklin's current* study.

Men's suits range from $39 to $79. Dunn* isn't the author.

Control Drill

Unless an exclamation point is on the keyboard of your typewriter, type the exclamation point in the following manner: (1) strike the apostrophe; (2) backspace; (3) strike the period. Space twice after the exclamation point at the end of the sentence. The apostrophe is used for *feet.*

Oh, yes, I will! In an hour's time I'll call Tom's office.
The four o'clock bus* arrives at Daytona about six o'clock.
The lot, which is 100' x 150', is offered to us for $2,345.

Speed-up Sentences

Don't dare to go! Isn't Henry to be here by eight o'clock?
Mr. Mayfield's study* is on the authenticity of the emblem.
What is the total of $5.14, $7.48, $1.29, $9.60, and $7.58?

Resolutions. Resolutions are worded as though they consisted of one continuous sentence. When typed, they are set up in paragraph form.

Problem 46. This problem consists of typing a set of resolutions to be presented at a Board meeting. Type the material *on a stencil* for duplication. Study carefully the instructions for "Typing A Stencil" before you start to work.

RESOLUTIONS

Adopted by the Board of Directors

STOLL DRUG AND CHEMICAL CORPORATION

May 8, 19--

WHEREAS, the experiments of Dr. Kennedy D. Lawson with the antibiotic commonly known as HRWH have brought prestige to this Corporation and hope to victims of diseases heretofore thought incurable; and

WHEREAS, Dr. Lawson has been invited by the Directors of The L. T. Crandell Memorial Foundation to establish a laboratory under that Foundation in which further benefits to mankind from HRWH may be explored; and

WHEREAS, he has requested a six months' leave of absence from his duties with this Corporation as Assistant Chief of Research in order to accept this invitation,

BE IT RESOLVED that Dr. Lawson be granted, and he is hereby granted, the requested leave of absence; and

BE IT FURTHER RESOLVED that his salary be, and it is hereby ordered to be, continued in full during his leave.

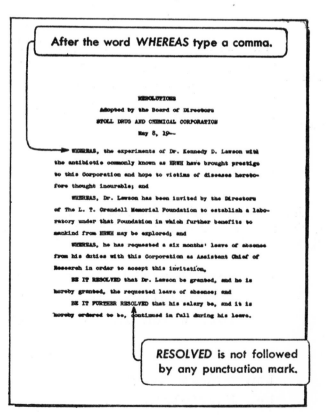

ILLUSTRATION 99
Resolutions

Lesson 41

Measured Typing   *Line of 60 spaces.   Set left margin stop.*

Warm-up Practice

Type each sentence twice with single spacing.   Space twice after the second writing.   All the words in the three sentences are balanced-hand words.

```
Both firms make big maps of the Orient; both make a profit.
With the aid of the auditor, I may make the eighth proviso.
The theory is right, and she is to work the problem for us.
```

Measured Typing

Type each paragraph twice with *double* spacing.

		Words

1   One of the most vivid memories of my boyhood is a fire — 11
that burned up the barn on our farm. I can still see those — 23
flames shooting into the sky and the dense clouds of smoke. — 35
I can also picture in my mind a number of our neighbors who — 47
had come running from their homes when they saw the flames. — 59

```
    1    2    3    4    5    6    7    8    9    10   11
```

2   The next day those neighbors and a few others appeared — 11   70
on the scene and cleared up things; then they began work on — 23   82
a new barn. They did not pay for any of the materials, but — 35   94
they would not take a cent for their labor. They were glad — 47   106
to help out, for they knew that others would help them out. — 59   118

```
    1    2    3    4    5    6    7    8    9    10   11
```

3   In our hurried times we should have more of the spirit — 11   129
those neighbors displayed. Many of us tend to lose contact — 23   141
with people. We go our own way and pay little attention to — 35   153
other people even when those people are in trouble. In the — 47   165
end we may become so selfish as to think only of ourselves. — 59   177

```
    1    2    3    4    5    6    7    8    9    10   11
```

4   There is no such thing in the world of today as living — 11   188
unto ourselves alone; we all have to live with and have our — 23   200
being with others. Just as a motor cannot run without oil, — 35   212
so no enterprise can be successfully carried on without the — 47   224
oil of neighborliness which enables us to work with others. — 59   236

```
    1    2    3    4    5    6    7    8    9    10   11
```

Insurance Reports. The report of injury shown in Illustration 98 is typical of many forms you will be asked to type in business.

Get the blank report form from your Workbook and study it. Insert it in your machine and make sure that it is absolutely straight.

Disengage the ratchet release. Use the cylinder knob to get each line in proper position for typing.

Here is the material you are to type on the report.

Problem 45. (Form 8-45)

1. Joslin Paint Corporation
2. 300 Dexter Street Cumberland Maryland
3. Penn Fidelity and Bonding Company
4. Paint manufacturer
5. (a) 300 Dexter Street, Cumberland, Maryland Warehouse B Yes
   (b) (Leave blank)
6. May 2, Tuesday 4:12 (p.m.)
7. May 2, (Cross out a.m.)
8. Yes
9. At once; foreman saw the accident.
10. Andrew W. Waldecker
11. Clinton G. Tremby 981-02-3826
12. 391 Logan Drive Cumberland Maryland
13. Type x after the following: *Married Male*
14. American U. S. A. Yes
15. 38 No
16. (a) Warehouseman (b) Yes
17. (a) 5 years (b) Time (c) 2.20
18. (a) 8 plus overtime (b) 17.60 minimum (c) 5 or 6 (d) 92.00
    (e) None furnished
19. Fork lift truck
20. Electrical
21. Axle
22. (a) None applies (b) (Leave blank)
23. No
24. Employee was operating a partially loaded fork lift truck. The front axle snapped without warning. He was thrown out on the warehouse floor, and the truck toppled over on him.
25. Mr. Andrew W. Waldecker, 26 Cottage Grove Avenue, Cumberland, Maryland
26. Broken left ankle
27. 8 weeks 28. No
29. (Leave blank)
30. (a) Dr. R. W. Hoyle, 970 Pine St., Cumberland, Md.
    (b) Duncan Memorial Hospital, Cumberland, Md.
31. No

Date May 3, 19--

Firm name Joslin Paint Corporation

Signed by Howard L. Karr

Official Title Office Mgr.

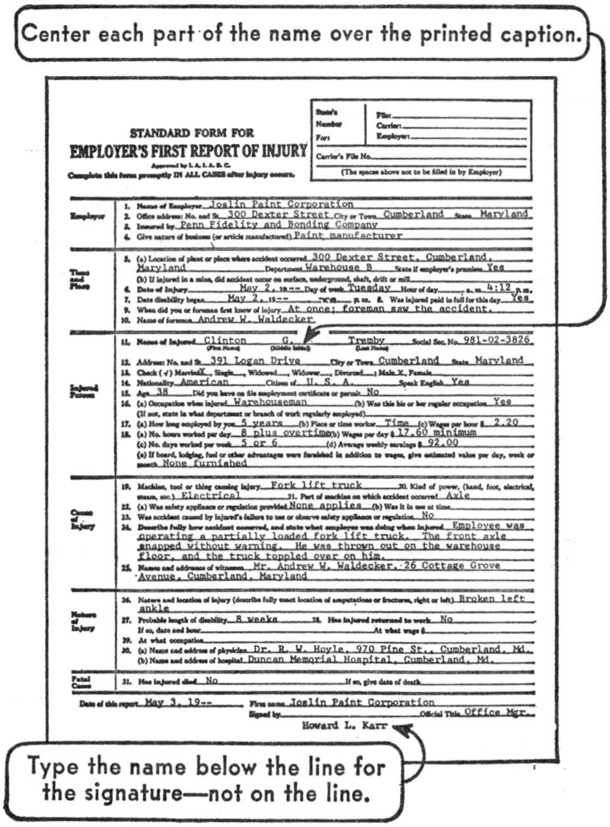

STANDARD FORM FOR
EMPLOYER'S FIRST REPORT OF INJURY
Approved by I. A. I. A. B. C.
Complete this form promptly IN ALL CASES after injury occurs.

State's Number For: File: Carrier: Employer:
Carrier's File No.
(The spaces above not to be filled in by Employer)

Employer
1. Name of Employer Joslin Paint Corporation
2. Office address: No. and St. 300 Dexter Street City or Town Cumberland State Maryland
3. Insured by Penn Fidelity and Bonding Company
4. Give nature of business (or article manufactured) Paint manufacturer

Time and Place
5. (a) Location of plant or place where accident occurred 300 Dexter Street, Cumberland, Maryland Department Warehouse B State if employer's premises Yes
(b) If injured in a mine, did accident occur on surface, underground, shaft, drift or mill
6. Date of Injury May 2, 19-- Day of week Tuesday Hour of day a. m. 4:12 p.m.
7. Date disability began May 2, 19-- a.m. p. m. 8. Was injured paid in full for this day Yes
9. When did you or foreman first know of injury At once; foreman saw the accident.
10. Name of foreman Andrew W. Waldecker

Injured Person
11. Name of Injured Clinton (First Name) G. (Middle Initial) Tremby (Last Name) Social Sec. No. 981-02-3826
12. Address: No. and St. 391 Logan Drive City or Town Cumberland State Maryland
13. Check (√) Married X, Single, Widowed, Widower, Divorced; Male X, Female
14. Nationality American Citizen of U. S. A. Speak English Yes
15. Age 38 Did you have on file employment certificate or permit No
16. (a) Occupation when injured Warehouseman (b) Was this his or her regular occupation Yes
(If not, state in what department or branch of work regularly employed)
17. (a) How long employed by you 5 years (b) Piece or time worker Time (c) Wages per hour $ 2.20
18. (a) No. hours worked per day 8 plus overtime (b) Wages per day $ 17.60 minimum
(c) No. days worked per week 5 or 6 (d) Average weekly earnings $ 92.00
(e) If board, lodging, fuel or other advantages were furnished in addition to wages, give estimated value per day, week or month None furnished

Cause of Injury
19. Machine, tool or thing causing injury Fork lift truck 20. Kind of power, (hand, foot, electrical, steam, etc.) Electrical 21. Part of machine on which accident occurred Axle
22. (a) Was safety appliance or regulation provided None applies (b) Was it in use at time
23. Was accident caused by injured's failure to use or observe safety appliance or regulation No
24. Describe fully how accident occurred, and state what employee was doing when injured Employee was operating a partially loaded fork lift truck. The front axle snapped without warning. He was thrown out on the warehouse floor, and the truck toppled over on him.
25. Names and addresses of witnesses Mr. Andrew W. Waldecker, 26 Cottage Grove Avenue, Cumberland, Maryland

Nature of Injury
26. Nature and location of injury (describe fully exact location of amputations or fractures, right or left) Broken left ankle
27. Probable length of disability 8 weeks 28. Has injured returned to work No
If so, date and hour At what wage $
29. At what occupation
30. (a) Name and address of physician Dr. R. W. Hoyle, 970 Pine St., Cumberland, Md.
(b) Name and address of hospital Duncan Memorial Hospital, Cumberland, Md.

Fatal Cases
31. Has injured died No If so, give date of death

Date of this report May 3, 19-- Firm name Joslin Paint Corporation
Signed by Official Title Office Mgr.
Howard L. Karr

ILLUSTRATION 98

Insurance Report

Lesson 42

" # ( )

Line of 60 spaces. Set left margin stop.
Type each line twice with single spacing.
Space twice after each 2-line group.

Preliminary Practice

Large dividends will be paid this year to all stockholders.
The price of the security may be subject to change any day.

LEFT HAND

On a manual typewriter the quotation marks (") are the shift of 2.

The number sign (#) is the shift of 3.

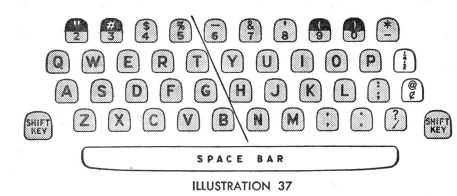

ILLUSTRATION 37

RIGHT HAND

On an electric typewriter the quotation marks (") are the shift of the apostrophe.

The left parenthesis [( ] is the shift of 9.

The right parenthesis [ )] is the shift of 0.

New Stroke Drill

Type the period inside the quotation marks. The sign # in front of a figure means *number;* after a figure, *pound* or *pounds.*

Electric ;'; ;'; ;"; ;"; ";" ";" """ He said, "Don't go over there."
Manual s2s s2s s"s s"s "s" "s" """ He said, "Don't go over there."
d3d d3d d#d d#d #d# #d# ### 345#; #4567; 32 dozen #10 ties;
191 191 l(l l(l (l((l((((;0; ;0; ;); ;););));)))) (9)
twenty-nine (29) #92; AMOCO (American Oil Company); 3,849#;

Control Drill

Type the ? mark *after* the quotation marks when the whole sentence is a question.

Buy 100 cases of Stock #486 (Mayfield Points) at $5 a case.
Who wired us thus: "Ship at once 400# of #1483 Fullerton"?
"The plan," said the chairman, "may pay a direct dividend."

Speed-up Sentences

Type the ? mark *before* the quotation marks when the quoted sentence is a question.

The sixth form (#47) has the title, "Problem in Panelwork."
"Doesn't that firm (Cox & Kay) have #850 enamel?" he asked.
Fulton Mackay (1889-1958) is the author of "Duke's Lament."

Name	Net Pay	$20	$10	$5	$1	50¢	25¢	10¢	5¢	1¢
Ambrose, Charles H.	89.64	4		1	4	1		1		4
Appleton, Mary W.	81.24	4			1			2		4
Baker, Morgan R.	73.27	3	1		3		1			2
Ballard, Leonard B.	58.68	2	1	1	3	1		1	1	3
Barnes, Viola C.	85.10	4		1				1		
Bates, Letitia S.	70.82	3	1			1	1		1	2
Blythe, Willard, Jr.	65.40	3		1			1	1	1	
Boswell, O. Edward	58.84	2	1	1	3	1	1		1	4
Bryant, Nettie A.	76.48	3	1	1	1		1	2		3
Butler, Foster J.	91.51	4	1		1	1				1
Calvert, Mitchell N.	52.46	2	1		2		1	2		1
Cannon, Jessica R.	71.25	3	1		1		1			
Caplan, Dolores	54.62	2	1		4	1		1		2
Carr, T. Donald	84.66	4			4	1		1	1	1
Cassidy, Roland McG.	65.76	3		1		1	1			1
Coleman, Horace H.	71.77	3	1		1	1	1			2
De Carlo, Joyce K.	64.40	3			4		1	1	1	
De Marco, Matthew V.	67.18	3		1	2			1	1	3
Dempsey, Rosina	57.28	2	1	1	2		1			3
Devlin, H. Melvin	95.23	4	1	1				2		3
Diffendall, Hilda D.	71.65	3	1		1	1		1	1	
Dillon, Leroy L.	89.75	4		1	4	1	1			
Dominick, Carl T.	94.98	4	1		4	1	1	2		3
Donnelly, Beatrice W.	72.16	3	1		2			1	1	1
Douglas, Terence F.	98.66	4	1	1	3	1		1	1	1
	1862.76	79	16	12	50	13	13	21	10	44

Lesson 43

Measured Typing *Line of 60 spaces. Set left margin stop.*

Warm-up Practice

Type each sentence twice with single spacing. Space twice after the second writing. All the words in the three sentences are balanced-hand words.

The tutor is also to blame, for he kept the key to the box.
The neighbor may go to England to visit the town of Sidlay.
He owns the land and may cut the quantity to eight bushels.

Measured Typing

Type each paragraph twice with *double* spacing.

Words

1   Impress on your mind the fact that learning to type is   11
not something routine. The more real thinking you bring to   23
bear on your daily work, the more helpful the training will   35
be to you. Your teacher has been over the ground and knows   47
what skill you should get each day and how you will get it.   59

    1   2   3   4   5   6   7   8   9   10   11

2   Perhaps you have seen pictures of a bookkeeper of long   11   70
ago. He is seated on a high chair in front of a desk where   23   82
his books are spread out. He is usually shown with a green   35   94
shade over his eyes. Seldom does he lift his eyes from his   47   106
books. Looking at the picture, you know he is a routinist.   59   118

    1   2   3   4   5   6   7   8   9   10   11

3   If you allow yourself to fall into a rut in your work,   11   129
you will be just like that old bookkeeper. Perhaps you can   23   141
have what seems an easy time of it when you follow the line   35   153
of least resistance. You can do just enough to get by, but   47   165
before so long you are just bound to be brought up sharply.   59   177

    1   2   3   4   5   6   7   8   9   10   11

4   On the other hand, you can determine not to get into a   11   188
rut. You can put yourself into an inquiring frame of mind,   23   200
always wanting to know how the work you are doing fits into   35   212
the work that other people around you are doing. Keep your   47   224
eyes and your mind open; then you will not fall into a rut.   59   236

    1   2   3   4   5   6   7   8   9   10   11

Name		M	T	W	Th	F	Sat	Total	Rate	Amount	Total Earn.	Deduct.	Net Pay
Cannon, Jessica R.	Reg.	8	8	8	8	8		40	2.15	86.00	86.00	14.75	71.25
	O.T.		2			2		4	2.55	10.20			
Caplan, Dolores	Reg.	8	8	8	0	8		32	1.70	54.40	64.60	9.98	54.62
	O.T.		2½				5½	8	3.27	26.16			
Carr, T. Donald	Reg.	8	8	8	8	8		40	2.18	87.20	113.36	28.70	84.66
Cassidy, Roland McG.	Reg.	0	8	8	8	8		32	2.50	80.00	80.00	14.24	65.76
Coleman, Horace H.	Reg.	4½	8	8	8	8		36½	2.38	86.87	86.87	15.10	71.77
De Carlo, Joyce K.	Reg.	8	8	8	8	8		40	2.00	80.00	80.00	15.60	64.40
	O.T.		2½					2½	3.60	9.00			
De Marco, Matthew V.	Reg.	8	8	0	8	6		30	2.40	72.00	81.00	13.82	67.18
Dempsey, Rosina	Reg.	5	8	8	8	8		37	1.80	66.60	66.60	9.32	57.28
	O.T.		2½				6	8½	4.02	34.17			
Devlin, H. Melvin	Reg.	0	8	8	8	8		32	2.68	85.76	119.93	24.70	95.23
Diffendall, Hilda D.	Reg.	7	8	8	8	8		39	2.15	83.85	83.85	12.20	71.65
	O.T.		2½				4	6½	3.30	21.45			
Dillon, Leroy L.	Reg.	8	8	8	8	8		40	2.20	88.00	109.45	19.70	89.75
	O.T.						6	6	3.57	21.42			
Dominick, Carl T.	Reg.	8	8	8	8	8		40	2.38	95.20	116.62	21.64	94.98
Donnelly, Beatrice W.	Reg.	8	8	8	8	8		40	2.20	88.00	88.00	15.84	72.16
	O.T.		2½				5½	8	3.60	28.80			
Douglas, Terence F.	Reg.	8	8	8	8	8		40	2.40	96.00	124.80	26.14	98.66

Payroll Distribution Sheet. After the net pay due each employee is entered on the payroll, most companies "break down" that amount into the number of bills and coins needed to fill the pay envelope. The sheet showing that break-down is called a payroll distribution sheet.

You will save time in your work with payroll distribution sheets by setting tabulator stops for the columns. Be sure to line up the totals with the figures in the columns.

The largest possible denominations are used for the distribution of the amount due an employee. Thus, $49 in bills is broken down into two 20's, one 5, and four 1's—not into four 10's and nine 1's or into some other possible combination of bills. In the same way, 72¢ in coins is broken down to include a 50-cent piece instead of two quarters.

Study Illustration 97 carefully. It shows the payroll distribution sheet for the payroll that you typed in Problem 43. You will type this sheet from the data given in Problem 44 on page 244. Use the illustration as a model for your work.

Type across the form. To help your eye in following the copy, use a ruler or the edge of a sheet of paper.

Leave a 2-space left margin.

PAYROLL DISTRIBUTION SHEET
PARK LANE LAUNDRY CO.
Page No. 1 of 12 Pages
Week Ending September 25, 19—

NAME	NET PAY	$20	$10	$5	$1	50¢	25¢	10¢	5¢	1¢
Ambrose, Charles H.	89.64	4		1	4	1		1		4
Appleton, Mary W.	81.24	4			1		2			4
Baker, Morgan R.	73.27	3	1		3	1				2
Ballard, Leonard B.	58.68	2	1	1	3	1		1	1	3
Barnes, Viola C.	85.10	4		1				1		
Bates, Letitia S.	70.82	3	1			1	1		1	2
Blythe, Willard, Jr.	65.40	3			1		1	1	1	
Boswell, O. Edward	58.84	2	1	1	3	1	1			4
Bryant, Nettie A.	76.48	3	1	1	1		1	2		3
Butler, Foster J.	91.51	4			1	1				1
Calvert, Mitchell N.	52.46	2	1		2		1	2		1
Cannon, Jessica R.	71.25	3	1		1					
Caplan, Dolores	54.62	2	1		4	2		1		2
Carr, T. Donald	84.66	4			4	1		1	1	1
Cassidy, Roland McG.	65.76	3		1		1	1			1
Coleman, Horace H.	71.77	3	1		1	1	1			2
De Carlo, Joyce K.	64.40	3			4		1	1	1	
De Marco, Matthew V.	67.18	3		1	2			1	1	3
Dempsey, Rosina	57.28	2	1	1	2		1			3
Devlin, H. Melvin	95.23	4	1		1			2		3
Diffendall, Hilda D.	71.65	3	1		1	1		1	1	
Dillon, Leroy L.	89.75	4		1	4	1	1			
Dominick, Carl T.	94.98	4	1		4	1	1			3
Donnelly, Beatrice W.	72.16	3	1		2			1	1	1
Douglas, Terence F.	98.66	4	1	1	3	1		1	1	1
TOTALS	1862.79	79	16	12	50	13	13	21	10	44

Set up the columns so that the totals will be centered.

ILLUSTRATION 97
Payroll Distribution Sheet

Lesson 44

$\frac{1}{2}$ $\frac{1}{4}$ ¢ @

Line of 60 spaces. Set left margin stop.
Type each line twice with single spacing.
Space twice after each 2-line group.

Preliminary Practice

This test is designed to measure your ability to type well.
Be sure that you record the number of each name on my card.
There is some doubt whether or not this law is enforceable.

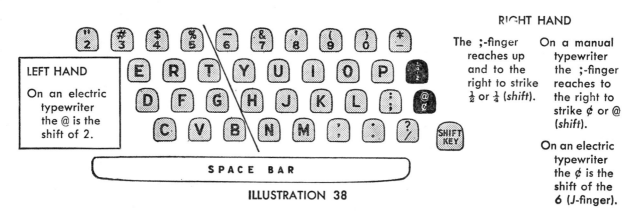

LEFT HAND

On an electric typewriter the @ is the shift of 2.

SPACE BAR

ILLUSTRATION 38

RIGHT HAND

The ;-finger reaches up and to the right to strike $\frac{1}{2}$ or $\frac{1}{4}$ (*shift*).

On a manual typewriter the ;-finger reaches to the right to strike ¢ or @ (*shift*).

On an electric typewriter the ¢ is the shift of the 6 (*J-finger*).

New Stroke Drill

Any fraction not on the keyboard is made by typing the diagonal between the figures that make the fraction. When one (or more) of the fractions in a series is a made fraction, type all the fractions in the series as made fractions.

;$\frac{1}{2}$; ;$\frac{1}{2}$; $\frac{1}{2}$;$\frac{1}{2}$ $\frac{1}{2}$;$\frac{1}{2}$ $\frac{1}{2}\frac{1}{2}\frac{1}{2}$;$\frac{1}{4}$; ;$\frac{1}{4}$; $\frac{1}{4}$;$\frac{1}{4}$ $\frac{1}{4}$;$\frac{1}{4}$ $\frac{1}{4}\frac{1}{4}\frac{1}{4}$ Add 4$\frac{1}{2}$, 9$\frac{1}{4}$, and 7$\frac{1}{2}$.

Electric j6j j6j j¢j ¢j¢ ¢¢¢ s2s s2s s@s @s@ @@@ 93 packages @ 38$\frac{1}{4}$¢;

Manual ;¢; ;¢; ¢;¢ ¢;¢ ¢¢¢ ;@; ;@; @;@ @;@ @@@ 93 packages @ 38$\frac{1}{4}$¢;

7 2/3; 6 4/5 acres; 3/4 plus 5/6; 9 3/4 tons; 7 3/8 pounds;
Five @ 38$\frac{1}{2}$¢; eleven @ 27$\frac{1}{4}$¢. Add 14 7/8, 4 1/4, and 28 1/2.

Control Drill

The area is 47$\frac{1}{2}$ feet long, 39$\frac{1}{4}$ feet wide, and 8$\frac{1}{2}$ feet deep.
They sold 5% @ $35, 7% @ $96, and 3 5/8% @ $184 net profit.
You type 1/2 or 1/4 in a sentence that has other fractions.

Speed-up Sentences

The quotation he made is 92$\frac{1}{2}$¢ a bushel, an increase of 3$\frac{1}{4}$¢.
Take 1/3 of 39; 1/5 of 75; 1/6 of 54; 1/7 of 84; 1/8 of 96.
We use @ in typing invoices to show the price of each unit.

Payrolls. The typing of payrolls calls for careful planning. Alignment on the payroll must be perfect. No name, figure, or amount should ever cut into any of the printed lines on the form.

Most payroll forms are printed to correspond with the spacing on the typewriter. Before you start to type, therefore, insert the form in your machine and check to see whether you will have to use the variable line spacer.

Space across the form to see whether the lines dividing dollars and cents can be made to match the spaces on your machine.

Set tabulator stops where needed. When only *one or two* spaces separate columns, no time is saved by setting tabulator stops.

Time worked by employees is divided into regular time and overtime, for which different rates of pay apply. The overtime rate is normally one and one-half times the regular rate.

The payroll that you will type is the one shown in the illustration. The names are given at the bottom of this page and at the top of the next page.

Get the payroll form from your Workbook. Type across the form. Use a ruler or the edge of a sheet of paper to help your eye follow each line.

Remember to take the fractions into account when you center the Hours Worked columns.

Begin your typing two spaces from the left edge of the sheet.

ILLUSTRATION 96
Payroll

Problem 43. (Form 8-43). *Page No.* 1 *of* 12 *Pages*   *Week Ending* September 25, 19--

Name		M	T	W	T	F	S	Total	Rate	Extension	Total	Deductions	Net Pay
	O.T.						6	6	3.30	19.80			
Ambrose, Charles H.	Reg.	8	8	8	8	8		40	2.20	88.00	107.80	18.16	89.64
	O.T.		2½					2½	3.15	7.88			
Appleton, Mary W.	Reg.	8	8	8	8	8		40	2.10	84.00	91.88	10.64	81.24
	O.T.		2½			4		6½	2.82	18.33			
Baker, Morgan R.	Reg.	8	8	8	8	8		40	1.88	75.20	93.53	20.26	73.27
Ballard, Leonard B.	Reg.	8	8	8	8	8		40	1.70	68.00	68.00	9.32	58.68
	O.T.		2			2		4	3.15	12.60			
Barnes, Viola C.	Reg.	8	8	8	8	8		40	2.10	84.00	96.60	11.50	85.10
Bates, Letitia S.	Reg.	8	8	8	8	8		40	2.15	86.00	86.00	15.18	70.82
Blythe, Willard, Jr.	Reg.	8	8	8	8	8		40	2.00	80.00	80.00	14.60	65.40
Boswell, O. Edward	Reg.	8	8	4	8	8		36	1.90	68.40	68.40	9.56	58.84
	O.T.		2					2	3.15	6.30			
Bryant, Nettie A.	Reg.	8	8	8	8	8		40	2.10	84.00	90.30	13.82	76.48
	O.T.					4		4	3.75	15.00			
Butler, Foster J.	Reg.	7½	8	8	8	8		39½	2.50	98.75	113.75	22.24	91.51
	O.T.						6	6	2.82	16.92			
Calvert, Mitchell N.	Reg.	0	0	8	8	8		24	1.88	45.12	62.04	9.58	52.46

242

Lesson 45

Measured Typing *Line of 60 spaces. Set left margin stop.*

Warm-up Practice

Type each sentence twice with single spacing. Space twice after the second writing. All the words in the three sentences are balanced-hand words.

```
If they kept the gown, it is their duty to pay the penalty.
The goal of the auditor is to cut down the work of the men.
The firm of Leigh & Odman is to pay for the eighty bushels.
```

Measured Typing

Type each paragraph twice with *double* spacing.

Words

1
```
     Your goal in typing is to weld a chain of habits which      11
will enable you to type correctly, rapidly, and without any      23
wasted effort.  The links in a real chain correspond to the      35
letters in a word.  When you started your course in typing,      47
you were thinking of every letter at the time you typed it.      59
```
```
     1    2    3    4    5    6    7    8    9    10   11
```

2
```
     As you gained skill and confidence, you found that you      11   70
could type words as words; you could put together the links      23   82
in correct order.  The strand of letters that formed a word      35   94
became the unit of your typing instead of letters, with the      47  106
result that you were able to type more rapidly than before.      59  118
```
```
     1    2    3    4    5    6    7    8    9    10   11
```

3
```
     Your eyes will soon begin reading all the copy you are      11  129
typing by phrases or word groups.  The words combine into a      23  141
short chain.  Every time your eyes see that chain of words,      35  153
you set up a chain of acts that enable you to reproduce the      47  165
word group.  You see why you must always keep eyes on copy.      59  177
```
```
     1    2    3    4    5    6    7    8    9    10   11
```

4
```
     Speed and accuracy in typing from copy lie at the base      11  188
of success, but they are not the entire story.  As you make      23  200
progress, you will get training in the various applications      35  212
of typing skill.  Right now your one aim is to master those      47  224
basic skills which are the foundation of success in typing.      59  236
```
```
     1    2    3    4    5    6    7    8    9    10   11
```

Bills of Lading. The bill of lading is a standard business form used in making freight shipments—whether by rail, truck, ship, or plane. Most transportation companies use a form like the one shown in Illustration 95.

Bills of lading are prepared in triplicate. The *original* is sent to the company or person that will receive the shipment (the consignee). The *duplicate* is the transportation company's copy. The *triplicate* is kept by the shipper (the consignor).

In your Workbook you will find an original of a bill of lading. Before you start typing, familiarize yourself with the form. You will notice that only portions of the form are intended for use by the shipper.

Use Illustration 95 as a style model for typing the following bill of lading.

Problem 42. (Form 8-42)

Station St. Louis   *State* Missouri

From Lander Manufacturing Company

Bill of lading date 3/28/--

Customer's No. 903

ILLUSTRATION 95
Bill Of Lading

Consigned to Cleary Office Supply Company

239 Western Avenue, Chester, Pennsylvania

Destination Chester   *State of* Pennsylvania   *County of* Delaware

Route B & O

Type *X* after *Yes* for *Pick-up service.*

Type *X* after *Yes* for *Delivery service requested.*

Shipper Lander Manufacturing Company

Permanent post office address of shipper 1408 South River Avenue, St. Louis, Missouri   63102

No. Pkgs.	Description	Weight
3	Office Desks (crated)	594 lbs.
10	Cartons Office Chairs	281 lbs.
2	Metal Storage Cabinets (crated)	167 lbs.
5	Cartons Manila File Folders	326 lbs.

Lesson 46

Symbol Review

Type each sentence twice with single spacing. Space twice after the second writing.

The invoice reads thus: "38 doz. May-Kin brushes @ $1.27."
Some firms use the form List No. 138; others use List #138.
The # before a figure means number; after a figure, pounds.

Letter and Figure Review

Type each paragraph twice with double spacing. This first paragraph contains all the capitals.

In another envelope you are getting the required cards
for the following: Ada B. Cole, David E. Fall, G. H. Ivor,
Janice K. Langdon, Morris Nathan Olney, Paul Quentin Ralph,
Samuel T. Underwood, Vera Winship, and Xavier Y. Zimmerman.

This paragraph contains all the letters and all the figures.

In our conversation of May 28 about Order No. 17069, I
explained why we are required to deliver the sixty boxes of
frozen fruit to 384 Vinal Street, Kingston, before July 15.

Measured Typing

Type each paragraph twice with *double* spacing.

Words

1   Do you have a purpose of your own and an honest desire   11
to make the work you are now doing better each day? Do you   23
have before you a goal which is higher than you can readily   35
reach right now? Are you giving some thought day by day to   47
what you would like to be doing one year or five years from   59
today? In other words, do you have a real purpose in life?   71

  1   2   3   4   5   6   7   8   9   10   11

2   The status of your life depends largely on how you can   11   82
answer questions of this kind. Some people can answer such   23   94
questions in the affirmative. A good many others, however,   35   106
could not answer even one of them without stopping to think   47   118
and to take stock of themselves to find out whether they do   59   130
have a goal on which they keep their minds fixed every day.   71   142

  1   2   3   4   5   6   7   8   9   10   11

Promissory Notes. As in the case of checks, the typing of promissory notes involves writing on printed lines.

> Set the margin stop for the two lines that start at the far left.

ILLUSTRATION 92
Promissory Note

Here is the material that you are to type on the two promissory notes you will find in your Workbook.

Problem 38. (Form 8-38)

1260.00   May 17,   One Hundred Twenty Days   We   Ruxton Electric Company   One Thousand Two Hundred Sixty and no/100 $3\frac{1}{2}\%$ *No.* 6
Due September 14, 19--

Problem 39. (Form 8-39)

239.75   July 5,   Three Months We   Steele Brothers Company Two Hundred Thirty-nine and 75/100
4%   *No.* 25   *Due* October 5, 19--

Receipts. Receipts are often printed on small forms. For top efficiency, follow the procedure you learned for typing labels.

Your Workbook contains a form like the receipt shown in Illustration 93. Get it now and type the following material on it.

Problem 40. (Form 8-40)

26.25   March 23,   Matthew L. Krew   Twenty-six and 25/100   9664
75.50

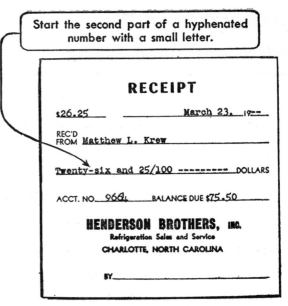

> Start the second part of a hyphenated number with a small letter.

ILLUSTRATION 93
Receipt

The petty cash slip shown in Illustration 94 is actually a receipt. In this case, however, the slip is prepared by the person who *pays out* the money.

Here is the material that you are to type on the petty cash slip you will find in your Workbook.

Problem 41. (Form 8-41)

January 29,   Four and 26 Express charges on shipment from Kent Brothers, Inc., Akron, Ohio   4.26

> Center the cents over the printed figure.

ILLUSTRATION 94
Petty Cash Slip

Lesson 47

Review—Measured Typing   *Line of 60 spaces.   Set left margin stop.*

Symbol Review

Type each sentence twice with single spacing.   Space twice after the second writing.

Good usage prefers the words <u>cents</u> and <u>per cent</u> to ¢ and %.
Chapter 8, "TV Contests," is in the May "Television Guide."
Boyd & Lang (formerly Boyd & Preston) is a well-known firm.

Letter and Figure Review

Type each paragraph twice with double spacing.   The first paragraph contains all the capitals.

The following directors were present: Adams, Burdick,
Clay, Davids, Eaton, Frost, Gray, Harrison, Inman, Jenkins,
Kane, Land, Mathews, Nugent, Oldham, Packer, Quinlan, Rock,
Stow, Todd, Ulman, Victor, Weston, Xanthos, Yeager, Zeller.

This paragraph contains all the letters and all the figures.

During the winter campaign which you started for us on
November 13, we kept six quiz programs on the air, received
a total of 6,475 inquiries, and wrote up just 2,890 orders.

Measured Typing

Type each paragraph twice with *double* spacing.   **Words**

1   Too many people seem to be content to spend their time   11
in just carrying out the purposes of others. They work for   23
nothing but the pay; they think more about the pay than the   35
purpose. Give them the pay, and somebody else can have the   47
purpose, for all they care. In this way millions of people   59
live unhappy lives just because they do not have a purpose.   71

| 1 | 2 | 3 | 4 | 5 | 6 | 7 | 8 | 9 | 10 | 11 |

2   You can and should have a purpose of your own. At the   11   82
same time you can serve the purpose of another and serve it   23   94
even better. You can still have the pay and yet be working   35 106
out your own purpose. Remember that all good purposes tend   47 118
in the same direction and go hand in hand. Decide now that   59 130
you will have a purpose; then your life will be the richer.   71 142

| 1 | 2 | 3 | 4 | 5 | 6 | 7 | 8 | 9 | 10 | 11 |

Checks. The two checks shown in Illustration 91 are typical of voucher checks used in business offices today. The voucher stub, or "statement," as it is often called, shows the payee exactly what the check is intended to pay.

Use the ratchet release to make sure that your typing is on the printed lines of the check. Notice how carefully the typing on lines is done on the two checks in Illustration 91. Observe, too, the use of hyphens on both checks.

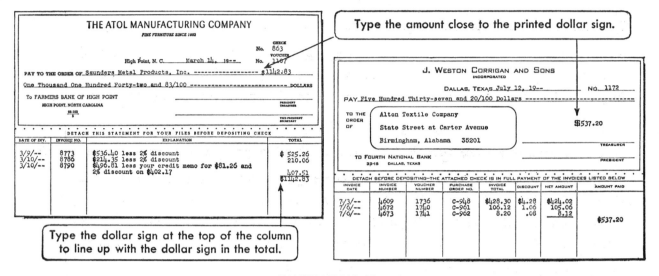

ILLUSTRATION 91

Voucher Checks

Problem 36. (Form 8-36)

March 14, *Check No.* 863 *Voucher No.* 1107 *Pay to the order of* Saunders Metal Products, Inc. 1142.83 One Thousand One Hundred Forty-two and 83/100

Date of Inv.	Invoice No.	Explanation	Total
3/9/--(this year)	8773	$536.40 less 2% discount	$ 525.26
3/10/--(this year)	8786	$214.35 less 2% discount	210.06
3/10/--(this year)	8790	$496.81 less your credit memo for $81.26 and 2% discount on $402.17	407.51
			$1142.83

Problem 37. (Form 8-37) July 12, 19-- No. 1172

Pay Five Hundred Thirty-seven and 20/100 Dollars 537.20

to the order of Alton Textile Company
State Street at Carter Avenue
Birmingham, Alabama 35201

Invoice Date	Invoice Number	Voucher Number	Purchase Order No.	Invoice Total	Discount	Net Amount	Amount Paid
7/3/--(this year)	4609	1736	C-948	$428.30	$4.28	$424.02	
7/6/--(this year)	4672	1740	C-961	106.12	1.06	105.06	
7/6/--(this year)	4673	1741	C-962	8.20	.08	8.12	
							$537.20

Lesson 48

Review—Measured Typing   *Line of 60 spaces.   Set left margin stop.*

Type each of the sentences in Symbol Review and each of the Speed-up Sentences twice with single spacing.   Space twice after the second writing.

Symbol Review

The asterisk (*) is used to refer the reader to a footnote.
The apostrophe (') comes before the s in men's and women's.

Speed-up Sentences

All the words in these sentences are balanced-hand words.

The problem is to make a profit and pay for the eighth fur.
The firm paid the auditor for the work he did for the city.
Kalen kept their formal bid for the big quantity of burlap.
He is a busybody and is to blame for the fury of the fight.
The oriel of the ancient chapel is visible to the neighbor.

Letter and Figure Review

Type this paragraph twice with double spacing.   It contains all the letters and all the figures.

At the convention held in Quebec from August 19 to 23,
the group made an adjustment in our Vera Cruz business that
will enable you to take care of 476,580 tons for exporting.

Measured Typing

Type each paragraph twice with *double* spacing.   **Words**

1   Before there can be a harvest, there must be a time of   11
planting. No farmer is ever so foolish as to expect a crop   23
of wheat or rye to grow unless he first plants the seed and   35
tills the ground. Producing anything of value always calls   47
for thinking, planning, and preparing. In this world there   59
is no such thing anywhere as getting something for nothing.   71

      1   2   3   4   5   6   7   8   9   10   11

2   Sometimes I find a student who seems to expect to reap   11   82
almost as soon as he has sown. He does not stop to realize   23   94
that it takes time to get an education and to build a skill   35   106
of any kind. He does not seem to get it into his head that   47   118
he must work and study and practice, for it is only through   59   130
thoughtful practice that anybody will become a good typist.   71   142

      1   2   3   4   5   6   7   8   9   10   11

Statements of Account. Most companies that sell "on account" mail their customers periodic statements—usually once a month. The statement helps the customer to check his own record of purchases and payments.

Study the typical statement of account shown in Illustration 90. The "Balance Forwarded" is the amount that was owed on the date on which the previous statement was prepared. Each charge or credit since that date is listed separately on the statement.

Your first step in typing statements is to set margin and tabulator stops. Note how the columns are arranged in Illustration 90. Use the longest figure in each column for centering the typing in that column.

Here is the material that you are to type on the two statement forms in your Workbook. Separate the two forms before you start. Use Illustration 90 as a style model. That illustration shows the statement you will type in Problem 34.

ILLUSTRATION 90
Statement Of Account

Problem 34. (Form 8-34)

Mason Drug Stores, Inc.
700-720 Foster Avenue
Pittsburgh, Pennsylvania   15209

November 1, 19--

Date	Invoice No.	Charges	Credits	Balance
Balance Forwarded				306.19
10/2	14311	115.20		421.39
10/5	14866	47.61		469.00
10/7			306.19	162.81
10/8	14892	322.15		484.96
10/14	15005	102.38		587.34
10/22	15396	29.40		616.74

Problem 35. (Form 8-35)

Gratz Processing Company
290 North Commerce Street
Little Rock, Arkansas   72203

November 1, 19--

Date	Invoice No.	Charges	Credits	Balance
Balance Forwarded				1752.63
10/8			238.12	1514.51
10/10			617.40	897.11
10/12			310.88	586.23
10/13	14998	62.95		649.18
10/15	15012	1409.27		2058.45
10/19			586.23	1472.22
10/22	15391	8.17		1480.39

Lesson 49

Review—Measured Typing *Line of 60 spaces. Set left margin stop.*

Type each of the sentences in Symbol Review and each of the Speed-up Sentences twice with single spacing. Space twice after the second writing.

Symbol Review

How much is the sum of 5½, 9¼, 27½, 38½, 49¼, 51½, and 71¼?
Type 1/2, 1/4 in a series with fractions such as 1/5, 3/12.

Speed-up Sentences

All the words in these five sentences are balanced-hand words.

The air corps is to halt the dirigible by the field for us.
If the corn and rye burn, the penalty is borne by the firm.
When work irks Mr. Ridman, he may go to the island to fish.
I wish them to do the work for Laurie with the usual vigor.
He paid eight of their own men to handle the big panelwork.

Letter and Figure Review

Type this paragraph twice with double spacing. It contains all the letters and all the figures.

You will like the pictures on pages 157 and 284 of the
catalog sent you on May 3; they show just a very few of the
690 exquisite designs to be bought at amazingly low prices.

Measured Typing

Type each paragraph twice with *double* spacing.   Words

1   The three rules to apply in building a business career   11
are old and simple. First, you need to get knowledge. You   23
must learn why things are as they are. Second, you need to   35
get skill in putting knowledge into practice. You need, in   47
other words, to learn the how as well as the why. Finally,   59
it is your attitude that will determine success or failure.   71

| 1 | 2 | 3 | 4 | 5 | 6 | 7 | 8 | 9 | 10 | 11 |

2   Through your practice you obtained control of the keys   11   82
on the keyboard. You are learning how to apply the control   23   94
to the typing of sentences and paragraphs. As you go along   35   106
in your work, you will learn how to apply the skill you are   47   118
now getting to the typing of letters and other applications   59   130
of your skill in typing which you will be called on to use.   71   142

| 1 | 2 | 3 | 4 | 5 | 6 | 7 | 8 | 9 | 10 | 11 |

Credit Memorandums.

Credit Memorandums. The most frequent use of a credit memorandum is to show the amount of credit for merchandise returned to the seller.

The reasons for such returns vary. Sometimes merchandise is ordered by mistake. Goods may be damaged in shipment or found to be defective. An order may be incorrectly filled.

Unless a letter accompanies a credit memo, a mere listing of items will not always make clear to the customer why his account has been credited. See the note of explanation typed at the bottom of the credit memo in Illustration 89.

A business form may not provide a ruled column for unit prices. On such a form, type the @ symbol and tabulate the prices in the usual way.

Use Illustration 89 as a style model for typing the following credit memos.

Type the @ symbols in a straight, vertical line. Use the same tabulator stop set for the date.

CREDIT MEMO

ROMAINE VITREOUS PRODUCTS, INC.

264 WEST DELAWARE STREET — NEWARK, N. J. 07106

TO Rodney Construction Company   DATE September 14, 19--
1108-16 North Bay Street
Providence, Rhode Island   02902

WE HAVE CREDITED YOUR ACCOUNT AS FOLLOWS:

Quantity	Explanation		Amount
17	No. 6899 Porcelain Brackets	@ 1.12	19.04
2 doz.	No. 9104 Porcelain Clamps	@ 2.10	4.20
			23.24
	Less 30% discount		6.97
	This credit to apply against Invoice No. 5339 for items lost in transit		
	TOTAL CREDIT		16.27

Type the sum of an addition directly below the underscore.

ILLUSTRATION 89
Credit Memorandum

Problem 32.   (Form 8-32)

To Rodney Construction Company   *Date* September 14, 19--
1108-16 North Bay Street
Providence, Rhode Island   02902

Quantity	Explanation		Amount
17	No. 6899 Porcelain Brackets	@ 1.12	19.04
2 doz.	No. 9104 Porcelain Clamps	@ 2.10	4.20
			23.24
	This credit to apply against Invoice No. 5339 for items lost in transit	Less 30% discount	6.97
		TOTAL CREDIT	16.27

Problem 33.   (Form 8-33)

To Lycoming Electric Company   *Date* August 3, 19--
Main and Oak Streets
Allentown, Pennsylvania   18107

Quantity	Explanation		Amount
6	Type RM-70 Insulators	@ 7.20	43.20
2	No. 6871 Tubes	@ .90	1.80
			45.00
		Less 30% discount	13.50
		TOTAL CREDIT	31.50

Lesson 50

Measured Typing *Line of 60 spaces. Set left margin stop.*

Measured Typing

Type each paragraph twice with *double* spacing.

Words

1   Always make it a point to plan your work and then work   **11**
your plan. It is the lack of system and order which brings   **23**
about the feeling that we are swamped. The disorderly mind   **35**
always results in disorderly and haphazard working methods.   **47**
When you really organize your thinking, you will find it so   **59**
simple to organize your doing; you will get your work done.   **71**

```
    1     2     3     4     5     6     7     8     9    10    11
```

2   Do not try to do everything at once, but do what needs   **11** **82**
to be done right now. When you follow that method of work,   **23** **94**
you will have the satisfaction of bringing that part of the   **35** **106**
job to a conclusion; then you can start the next task which   **47** **118**
lies before you. You get results when you concentrate your   **59** **130**
mind on one task at a time and work at it until you finish.   **71** **142**

```
    1     2     3     4     5     6     7     8     9    10    11
```

3   The ease or difficulty of any piece of work depends on   **11** **153**
how you think about it. If you permit yourself to think it   **23** **165**
is hard, then it will be hard; but if you persuade yourself   **35** **177**
that it is easy, it will be easy. A person who just throws   **47** **189**
up his hands and says that a job which he is asked to do is   **59** **201**
too hard will never in his life do anything that has value.   **71** **213**

```
    1     2     3     4     5     6     7     8     9    10    11
```

4   Resolve to become thoroughly proficient in any job you   **11** **224**
set out to do. Remember that study and knowledge will give   **23** **236**
you power over your work and that lack of study will always   **35** **248**
lead to failure. Find the right way to do anything, for it   **47** **260**
is always easier to work in the right way than in the wrong   **59** **272**
way. Doing a task in the wrong way wastes time and effort.   **71** **284**

```
    1     2     3     4     5     6     7     8     9    10    11
```

Problem 30. (Form 8-30)

Date March 9, 19--
Invoice No. T-5583

Sold Cleveland Brothers, Inc.
To Bixby Street at Third Avenue
Tulsa, Oklahoma 74101

Shipped Furniture Warehouse
To Cleveland Brothers, Inc.
456 West Osage Street
Tulsa, Oklahoma 74103

Your Order No. 302   *Shipped by* Bard's Motor Express   *Terms* 1% 10 days; net 30

Quantity	Catalog No.	Description	Unit Price	Total
10	C-002	Colonial Fiber Rug--6' x 9'--green	7.50	75.00
12	C-004	Colonial Fiber Rug--6' x 9'--burgundy	7.50	90.00
20	X-94	Bancroft Rug--9' x 12'--brown	12.80	256.00
				421.00
		Less 10%		42.10
				378.90
		Transportation prepaid		11.86
				390.76

Problem 31. (Form 8-31)

Date March 9, 19--
Invoice No. T-5584

Sold Kester and Boggs, Inc.
To 1400 Waller Building
1 East Pontiac Street
Detroit, Michigan 48208

Shipped The Kester Store
To 785 South Windsor Avenue
Flint, Michigan 48501

Your Order No. V-70   *Shipped by* Southern Railway   *Terms* 1% 10 days; net 30

Quantity	Catalog No.	Description	Unit Price	Total
48	S-5100	Sun-Glo Scatter Rug--24" x 48"--oval	4.80	230.40
60	S-5104	Sun-Glo Scatter Rug--36" x 60"--oval	9.30	558.00
108	Y-431	Scotty Plaid Rug--27" x 50"--rose	4.20	453.60
108	Y-433	Scotty Plaid Rug--27" x 50"--green	4.20	453.60
120	Z-1104	Colonial Rainbow Rug--36" x 60"	5.10	612.00
				2307.60
		Less 10%		230.76
				2076.84

Lesson 51

Measured Typing   *Line of 60 spaces. Set left margin stop.*

Measured Typing

Type each paragraph twice with *double* spacing.

Words

1   There are certain attitudes which everybody should try   11
hard to develop. It cannot be too often said that it is by   23
the way we look at things that we determine what we get out   35
of our work and our lives. A person may have the best that   47
is to be had in the way of training; but unless he also has   59
the right attitude, he is certain to work under a handicap.   71

    1   2   3   4   5   6   7   8   9   10   11

2   The first right attitude to develop is to realize that   11   82
you are not carrying the world on your own shoulders. This   23   94
world could and would get on without you. There is no such   35   106
thing as one who cannot be replaced. It is for that reason   47   118
that you will do well never to take yourself too seriously.   59   130
If you do, you may find that people will tend to avoid you.   71   142

    1   2   3   4   5   6   7   8   9   10   11

3   Tell yourself every day that you really like and enjoy   11   153
the work you are doing. When you do so, you will find that   23   165
your work will become a pleasure. If you should ever catch   35   177
yourself thinking about your work as drudgery, make up your   47   189
mind right then and there to change your attitude. You can   59   201
get joy out of any work to which you really apply yourself.   71   213

    1   2   3   4   5   6   7   8   9   10   11

4   Practice and learn the art of relaxing. When you find   11   224
that you are under pressure, ease up. Never give in to the   23   236
feeling of stress and strain. Take things in stride and do   35   248
the best you can right now. Time is a vital factor both in   47   260
the education you are now getting and in every other aspect   59   272
of life. Work along steadily with no pressure; be relaxed.   71   284

    1   2   3   4   5   6   7   8   9   10   11

Problem 29. (Form 8-29)

Date April 7, 19--

P. O. No. N-3672

To Morgan Electronics, Inc.
1406-1412 South 13th Street
Brooklyn, New York   11242

Ship **Parts Division**
To   Kent and Collins Television Company
489 North Granite Street
Bangor, Maine   04401

Ship by **Railway Express**   *F.O.B.* Brooklyn, N. Y.   *Terms* 1/15; net 30

Item No.	Quantity	Part No.	Description	Unit Price
1	12	RDW-312	Capacitor--100 mmf., 500 v., silver mica	.14
2	30	RDW-314	Capacitor--150 mmf., 300 v., ceramic	.19
3	4	RDK-009	Capacitor--10 mf., 150 v., electrolytic	1.73
4	120	RTT-575	Resistor--3.3 meg., $\frac{1}{2}$ w., carbon	.08
5	48	RTT-1006	Resistor--22,000 ohms, $\frac{1}{2}$ w., carbon	.08
6	36	RTT-1089	Resistor--100,000 meg., $\frac{1}{2}$ w., carbon	.12
7	1	XBL-23	Coil--horizontal oscillator coil for Model 74-B Premier Veltone	1.54
8	3	XBL-38	Coil--converter plate coil	2.48
9	2	XBL-70	Coil--focus coil	5.18
10	18	ZJM-2137	Reactor--filter reactor	1.76

By **V. Leroy Kent, Purchasing Agent**

Invoices. Most businesses use an invoice form similar to the one in Illustration 88.

Because the invoice is usually typed more frequently than any other form used in the office, the form is designed for maximum typing speed. Note how the invoice in Illustration 88 is planned so that you can make effective use of tabulator stops and margin settings.

Your work with invoices in business will usually include the necessary mathematical calculations. Those calculations have been made for you, so that you can concentrate on your typing.

Use the style of Illustration 88 in setting up and typing the invoices in Problems 30 and 31, page 236.

Set your line space regulator for single spacing. Speed up your work by setting tabulator stops before you start to type.

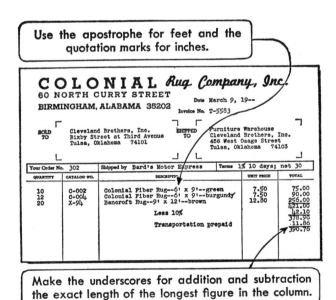

ILLUSTRATION 88

Invoice

Lesson 52

Measured Typing

Measured Typing

Type each paragraph twice with *double* spacing.

Words

1   Train your mind not to put off until tomorrow what you   11
can do today. Putting off work always makes it harder than   23
it would otherwise be. Do not permit yourself to drag over   35
to today the burdens of yesterday. The past is done; there   47
is nothing you can do about it. Keep your daily work up to   59
date; then you will close your day with a sense of elation.   71

| 1 | 2 | 3 | 4 | 5 | 6 | 7 | 8 | 9 | 10 | 11 |

2   It is well for you to know that there is no such thing   11   82
as accidental success in business. It does happen at times   23   94
that luck puts someone into an important position, but luck   35   106
will not keep him there. The work you are now doing has as   47   118
its purpose the job of training you in certain skills which   59   130
are called for in business. Your object is to master those   71   142
skills and become competent in doing office work. What you   83   154
are doing is laying the foundation on which you can build a   95   166
career that will be useful to others and profitable to you.   107   178

| 1 | 2 | 3 | 4 | 5 | 6 | 7 | 8 | 9 | 10 | 11 |

3   The person who wants to go ahead in business is always   11   189
asking himself what he is doing day by day, month by month,   23   201
and year by year to strengthen his personal assets, as well   35   213
as his business knowledge and producing ability. You ought   47   225
to analyze yourself at times to find out whether you really   59   237
have developed such assets as the eagerness and the ability   71   249
to work hard, to think about what you do, and to check your   83   261
own work. Do you get along with other people and cooperate   95   273
with them? Such personal assets are basic to your success.   107   285

| 1 | 2 | 3 | 4 | 5 | 6 | 7 | 8 | 9 | 10 | 11 |

Problem 28. (Form 8-28 original and carbon).

Number C-52   *Date* March 26, 19--   *Needed* At once   *Deliver to*
Correspondence Department--Attention: Miss Jackson

On Hand	Wanted	Description
37	100	Tabbed Manila Folders--Letter Size--1/3 cut tabs (TRUFILE Stock No. 308 or comparable)
48	200	Tabbed Manila Folders--Letter Size--1/5 cut tabs (TRUFILE Stock No. 309 or comparable)
0	2 sets	Card Index Guides--Size 5 x 3--A to Z divisions (25 cards to set)

Approved J. N. Murray

Purchase Orders. Illustration 87 shows a typical purchase order. Study it to see how tabulator stops have been used in arranging the typed material attractively on the form.

The purchase order is the first business form you have studied that includes a price column. Note that prices are typed so that all decimal points fall in a straight, vertical line.

Contrast the arrangement of the first and second columns of the purchase order with the arrangement of the third and fourth columns. Stock numbers, like the descriptions that follow them, are generally typed to line up at the left. When the numbers in a column represent *quantities* or make up a *number series* (1, 2, 3, etc.), they are typed to line up at the right.

The abbreviation *F.O.B.* (which you will generally type with small letters) is used in business to indicate whether the seller or the purchaser will pay shipping charges. On this purchase order the purchaser agrees to pay express charges from Brooklyn, New York, to Bangor, Maine.

The terms under which a purchase is made are usually stated briefly in a way similar to the one shown here. Terms of "1/15; net 30" mean that a discount of 1% will be given for payment in 15 days and that the full net amount will be due in 30 days.

Individual office practice determines whether the purchase order is single spaced or double spaced. When you type the purchase order in Problem 29, use Illustration 87 as a style model.

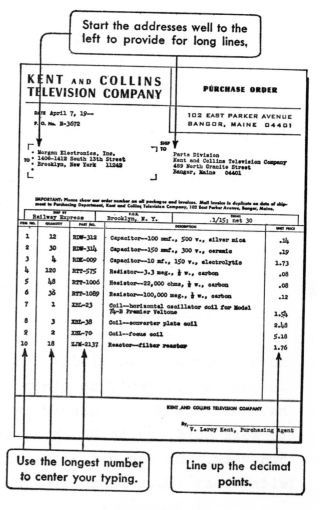

ILLUSTRATION 87.
Purchase Order

Division Three
Speed and Accuracy Development

Read the following paragraphs carefully. They contain instructions that will enable you to profit greatly from your work in this Division. Your instructor may have you type the paragraphs either now or later. If so, use a 60-space line with a 5-space paragraph indention.

Words

Your ability to write fast and accurately is certainly   11
the basic skill you want to develop. As you work along day   23
by day, you will learn the many business applications which   35
are a highly important part of your training. As you learn   47
those applications of typing, you will also do special work   59
with various kinds of drills and type straight copy to help   71
you keep up your speed and, indeed, increase it day by day.   83

In this Division you are going to have a chance to get   11   94
the kind of training in building speed and accuracy that is   23   106
needed for the work ahead. Each Lesson, you will find, has   35   118
five sections: (1) Warm-up Practice, (2) Sentence Writing,   47   130
(3) Technique Improvement, (4) Speed Building, and, lastly,   59   142
(5) Brief Timed Writing. Keep your attention on your work.   71   154

(1) Warm-up Practice. Here you have many common words   11   165
and phrases. You need to learn to type all kinds of matter   23   177
with an even touch; hence these drills vary both in content   35   189
and in degree of difficulty. Use the first five minutes of   47   201
every period for this Warm-up Practice. Type each line two   59   213
or three times. Your goal is to develop correct technique.   71   225

(2) Sentence Writing. To build your speed, you should   11   236
drive for the maximum typing rate for a brief period during   23   248
each day. If you are now typing accurately, let us say, at   35   260
30 words a minute, you should try to force up your stroking   47   272
rate to 40 or even 50 words a minute for a short spurt. As   59   284
you will see, the sentence which is the fourth line of each   71   296
group of sentences contains all the letters; the final line   83   308

Credit Inquiry Forms. To simplify the checking of credit references, many companies use printed inquiry forms such as the one shown in Illustration 85.

Notice that only the upper part is filled in by the company requesting credit information. The form is then mailed in a window envelope. (Refer back to page 143, if necessary, for instructions on folding for insertion in a window envelope.) The lower part, the *Credit Report,* is used for the reply.

Type the date two line spaces below the letterhead. Omit the salutation.

When you fill in the reply section, use the variable line spacer to type on the printed lines. Begin your typing two spaces after each question mark.

Here is the material you are to type on the two parts of the credit inquiry form in your Workbook.

McNARY
BROTHERS, INC.

2000 S. WINDSOR STREET – – BUFFALO, NEW YORK 14209

February 5, 19--

Taggery Metal Products, Inc.
5609 Island Avenue
Brooklyn, New York 11203

Your name has been given to us as a credit reference by

Fenster & Wilkinson
4326 East Penn Street
Camden, New Jersey 08102

from whom we have just received a first order.

The amount of credit requested is $185.00.

We'll appreciate your telling us your credit experience with this customer. Please fill in the Credit Report at the bottom of this sheet and return the entire sheet to us in the enclosed envelope.

The information you give us will be held in strict confidence.

McNARY BROTHERS, INC.
Credit Department

Credit Report

(1) How long has this customer had an account with you? 3½ years
(2) What are your terms? 3/10, n/60 (3) What is the largest amount this customer has ever owed you? $1,728.59 (4) How much is now owed? $366.20
(5) How much of that amount is now past due? $25.92 (6) Please mark with an "X" the phrase that best describes this customer's method of payment.

☐ Excellent ☒ Satisfactory ☐ Slow ☐ Unsatisfactory

Date February 6, 19-- Signed
Title Credit Manager

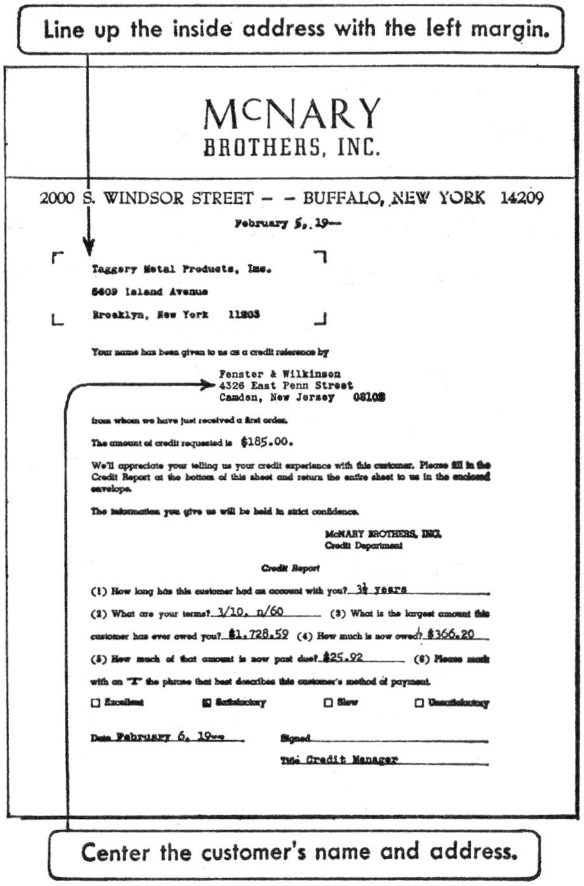

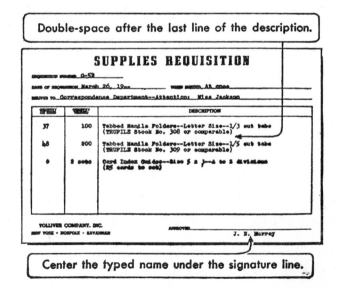

ILLUSTRATION 85

Credit Inquiry Form

Problem 27. (Form 8-27).

February 5, 19--

Taggery Metal Products, Inc. 5609 Island Avenue Brooklyn, New York 11203

Fenster & Wilkinson 4326 East Penn Street Camden, New Jersey 08102

$185.00.

Credit Report (1) 3½ years (2) 3/10, n/60 (3) $1,728.59 (4) $366.20 (5) $25.92 (6) Satisfactory

February 6, 19--

Credit Manager

Requisitions. A requisition, as the name of the form indicates, is a request—not an order—for supplies. It is customarily prepared in one office or branch of a company and sent to the company's purchasing department.

As a precaution to prevent waste, the form often includes a statement of the quantity of each item on hand. Note the first column of the supplies requisition shown in Illustration 86.

Your Workbook contains two requisition forms. You will use one of them for the original and the other for a carbon copy of the requisition you are to type in Problem 28, page 234.

SUPPLIES REQUISITION

Requisition number O-52
Date of requisition March 26, 19-- When needed At once
Deliver to Correspondence Department--Attention: Miss Jackson

		DESCRIPTION
37	100	Tabbed Manila Folders--Letter Size--1/3 cut tabs (TRUFILE Stock No. 308 or comparable)
48	200	Tabbed Manila Folders--Letter Size--1/5 cut tabs (TRUFILE Stock No. 309 or comparable)
0	2 sets	Card Index Guides--Size 5 x 3--A to Z divisions (25 cards to set)

TOLLIVER COMPANY, INC.
NEW YORK · NORFOLK · SAVANNAH

APPROVED
J. N. Murray

ILLUSTRATION 86

Requisition

reviews the figure strokes and the symbol strokes. Give at 95 320
least five minutes each day to practice on these sentences. 107 332

(3) Technique Improvement. Type these drills each day 11 343
for five to ten minutes. Their purpose is to aid you to do 23 355
correct stroking. Each drill is given over to some special 35 367
phase of typing that is briefly explained in the line above 47 379
the drill. You will gain much from typing these exercises. 59 391

(4) Speed Building. You will find that the paragraphs 11 402
for continuous writing are carefully graded. Start each of 23 414
these writings at your normal typing rate; then try hard to 35 426
increase your rate, but gradually. Should you complete the 47 438
copy before your teacher calls time, just go back and start 59 450
over again at the beginning; stop when the signal is given. 71 462

(5) Brief Timed Writing. Write this paragraph several 11 473
times. At each writing try to increase the number of words 23 485
you write during the timed period. Repeated writing of the 35 497
paragraphs is a splendid way to develop speed and accuracy. 47 509

Remedial Practice. When you have done all the work on 11 520
a lesson, read over your typing carefully and check all the 23 532
errors. Study each error and try to determine just why you 35 544
made it. That study will help you to avoid making the same 47 556
error in the future. Were you uncertain about the location 59 568
of the key or about the stroke? Did you look away from the 71 580
copy and lose your place? Was your mind on your work? Was 83 592
your posture correct during the typing? Have you developed 95 604
the right kind of stroke and a uniform, smooth typing rate? 107 616

To profit from your corrective practice, proceed thus: 11 627

(1) Type three times the letter you wrote incorrectly, 22 638

(2) Type correctly three times the word wrongly typed. 33 649

(3) Type several times the word that comes just before 44 660
the word in which you made the mistake; then type correctly 56 672
the word wrongly written; finally, type the following word. 68 684

If you transposed letters, type slowly three times the 11 695
word in which you made the error. This slow typing will be 23 707

Index Cards. The index card most frequently used in business is five inches wide by three inches deep. The typing runs the five-inch way.

Your first objective in arranging material on an index card is to make the top line—the line that determines the order in which the cards will be filed—stand out from the rest of the typing.

The practice in some offices is to capitalize that line. Other offices follow the style shown in Illustration 84. The double spacing and the indenting make the top line stand out from the others and make it easy to read.

You will speed up your work with index cards by inserting the cards at the center of the platen. Move the paper guide to the right and set the left margin stop three spaces from the edge of the card.

A holder such as the one you made to type labels may also be used for index cards.

Your Workbook contains five forms that are the size of index cards. If 5 x 3 cards are available, use them for your work and use the Workbook forms for practice. Use the card holders and the paper holders.

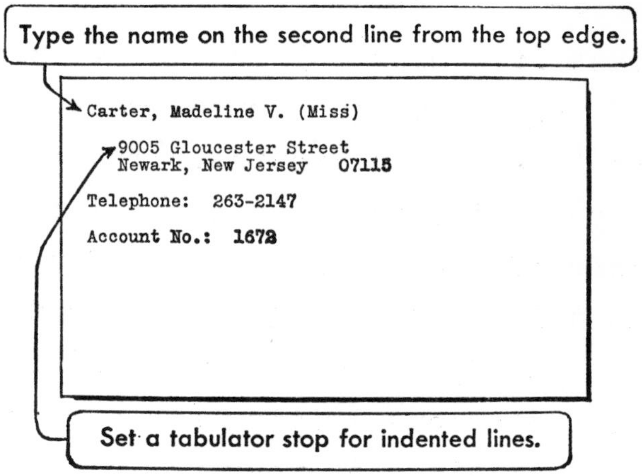

Problem 22. (5 x 3 card or Form 8-22)

Carter, Madeline V. (Miss)

9005 Gloucester Street
Newark, New Jersey   07115

Telephone: 263-2147

Account No.: 1672

Problem 23. (5 x 3 card or Form 8-23)

Cassells, Rosamond B. (Mrs. F. L.)

642½ Colony Street
Hillside, New Jersey   07200

Telephone: 539-6778

Account No.: 10578

Type the name on the second line from the top edge.

Carter, Madeline V. (Miss)

9005 Gloucester Street
Newark, New Jersey   07115

Telephone: 263-2147

Account No.: 1672

Set a tabulator stop for indented lines.

ILLUSTRATION 84
Index Card

Problem 24. (5 x 3 card or Form 8-24)

Cline, D. Margaret (Miss)

28 East Dover Avenue
Newark, New Jersey   07115

Telephone: 327-0480

Account No.: 3618

Problem 25. (5 x 3 card or Form 8-25)

Crafton, Marie T. (Mrs. James R.)

7805 West Stephens Road
Newark, New Jersey   07113

Telephone: 539-2111

Account No.: 32056

Problem 26. (5 x 3 card or Form 8-26)

Creel, Beatrice C. (Mrs. Claude T.)

5751 Donald Place
East Orange, New Jersey   07017

Telephone: 433-1685

Account No.: 65928

sure to impress on your mind the correct order in which the   35   719

letters should have come. Write three times the three-word   47   731

series made up of the word before, the word itself, and the   59   743

word after. Type evenly and gradually increase your speed.   71   755

    To correct errors you have made in spacing, type three   11   766

times the word before and the word after the omitted space.   23   778

Extra spaces between words are most often caused by failure   35   790

to raise the right thumb quickly enough from the space bar.   47   802

To help you to understand and carry through the effective method of corrective practice described, study these illustrations.

Wrong letter typed. Let us say that you typed *v* instead of *b* in the word *bought* (that is, you typed *vought* instead of *bought*) in the following sentence.

These machines in our factory were bought from your agency.

Here is the way you would do your corrective practice work.

    bbb bought bought bought were were were bought from were

    bought from were bought from *etc.*

Transposed letters. Assume that you transposed the letters *t* and *h* in the word *with* (that is, you typed *wiht* instead of *with*) in this sentence.

You did the job with the care that marks everything you do.

You would do your corrective practice work in this way.

    with with with job with the job with the job with the *etc.*

Kinds Of Errors

In addition to errors that are the result of typing wrong letters or of transposing letters, there are certain other kinds of errors made in typing. Read and study the following short paragraphs; they describe those errors. Your instructor may have you type the material now or later. If so, use a 60-space line with a 5-space paragraph indention. Space twice after the periods which follow the numbers. When you indent for the paragraphs that begin with 10, 11, and 12, backspace once so that the second figure in those numbers will line up with 1, 2, 3, 4, 5, 6, 7, 8, and 9.

Words

1. Incorrect division of a word at the end of a line.   11

2. Inaccurate indention of first line of a paragraph.   22

3. Wrong vertical spacing of any line in your typing.   33

4. A line that is out of position at the left margin.   44

5. An extra letter or a blank space left in any word.   55

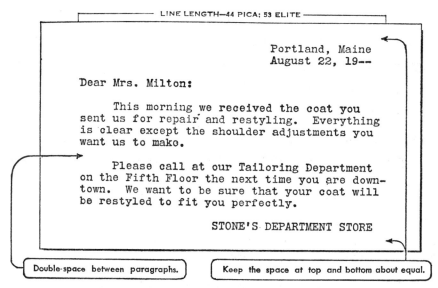

Portland, Maine
August 22, 19--

Dear Mrs. Milton:

This morning we received the coat you
sent us for repair and restyling. Everything
is clear except the shoulder adjustments you
want us to make.

Please call at our Tailoring Department
on the Fifth Floor the next time you are downtown. We want to be sure that your coat will
be restyled to fit you perfectly.

STONE'S DEPARTMENT STORE

Double-space between paragraphs.   Keep the space at top and bottom about equal.

ILLUSTRATION 82
Message Side Of Postal Card

In some offices the message is typed the narrow way on a postal card. Study Illustration 83.

Notice that the line length is short—only 24 pica or 29 elite—but that there are 33 lines available.

You are to type the following message for a postal card to be arranged in the style shown in Illustration 83. Before you start, make a careful study of the illustration. It shows the proper placement of the message side of your card.

Problem 21. (Postal card or Form 8-21)
Address Side Clarke & Townley, Inc.   400 Pioneer Street   Portland, Oregon   97203
Message Side   900 Dexter Building Chicago, Illinois   60609   October 15, 19-- Gentlemen: Thank you for your Order No. 483-B for 20 dozen Style 76 sweaters. Your sweaters will be shipped early next week. (¶) Another shipment of this fast-selling style is on the way to us from the mill. Your order will be among the first ones to be filled from the new stock. **KRALLER WOOLENS, INC.**

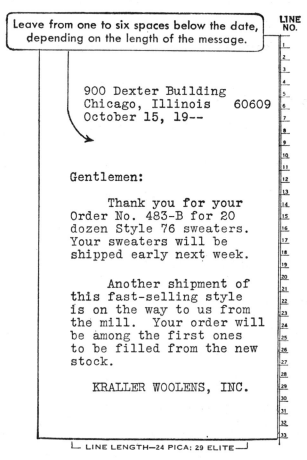

Leave from one to six spaces below the date, depending on the length of the message.

LINE NO.

900 Dexter Building
Chicago, Illinois   60609
October 15, 19--

Gentlemen:

Thank you for your
Order No. 483-B for 20
dozen Style 76 sweaters.
Your sweaters will be
shipped early next week.

Another shipment of
this fast-selling style
is on the way to us from
the mill. Your order will
be among the first ones
to be filled from the new
stock.

KRALLER WOOLENS, INC.

ILLUSTRATION 83
Message Typed Narrow Way

6. Not spacing between words (counts just one error).   66

7. A letter struck so lightly that it cannot be read.   77

8. An extra space or extra spaces following any word.   88

9. An error in typing a punctuation mark, leaving out   109
a punctuation mark, or incorrectly putting in a mark.   120

10. Violating the spacing rules for punctuation marks.   131

11. A capital or any other shift character that is off   142
the line because of improper use of the shift key.   152

12. Two letters that are typed in such a way that they   163
are "piled" or overlap.   168

Remedial Practice

The errors you make are not likely to be the same errors that someone else makes. To help you in planning special remedial practice for yourself, you will find it convenient to keep a chart to classify your errors.

Study Illustration 39 below. Opposite Lesson 53 the student has noted the errors that he made in typing the Speed Building paragraph in Lesson 53, page 67. Notice that *i* was typed instead of *e*. Other errors made in the typing of the Speed Building paragraph in Lesson 53 are these: *d* typed instead of *k*; *f* typed instead of *r*. The four wider columns at the right of the chart provide spaces for recording other errors.

The chart you are to use in recording your errors is the first page in your Workbook. In the first column under "Number" write the number of the Lesson; as, 53. Record the errors you made in the manner shown in the filled-in chart below. In the last column at the right, enter the total number of errors you made in typing the Speed Building paragraph.

When you have recorded the errors, you have taken the first step toward better typing. The second—and more important step—is for you to do practice work that will prevent you from making the same errors again. Individual remedial practice plays a vital part in building speed.

NUMBER	A	B	C	D	E	F	G	H	I	J	K	L	M	N	O	P	Q	R	S	T	U	V	W	X	Y	Z	,	.	?	;	—	FIGURES	SPACING	Mechanical	OTHERS	TOTAL
53				i							d							f																		3
54																				g		s											✓			3
55	Perfect																																			0
56			d	c̃																													✓			4
57												o								b			l											m omitted		4
58	s													i					r																	3
59	g,v																																	left margin		3
60																w																				1
61				r									,	b																						3
62																		f																indention		2
63															o																					1
64							g																													1
65	Perfect																																			0
66	s								l																											2
67	v													m																						2

ILLUSTRATION 39
Error Classification Chart

Postal Cards. A postal card—purchased at the post office and bearing printed postage—is 5½ inches wide by 3¼ inches deep.

Move the paper guide to the right and feed the postal cards into the center of the platen. Be sure to use the card holders and the paper holders.

Your Workbook contains two forms that are postal card size. If you can get cards of the correct size, do your work on those cards and use the forms for practice.

Here is a time-saving device for reversing the card. Twirl the cylinder knob after you finish the address side and while the card is still in your machine. With just a little practice, you can make the card drop against the paper rest in position to be fed back into the machine. Give the knob another twirl, and you are ready to start typing the message side.

After you have had experience in addressing cards, your eye will tell you the proper placement. Meantime, learn and follow the placement plan in Illustration 81.

Problem 20A. (Postal card or Form 8-20) *Address Side* Mrs. Howard W. Milton 787 Oak Lane   Portland, Maine   04110

You will next type the message side of the postal card you have just addressed. First, study the card in Illustration 82, page 231.

Notice that the inside address and the complimentary close are omitted. It is also customary to omit identifying initials.

Although there is no objection to varying the line length according to the length of the message, you will usually get the most attractive arrangement by following the plan shown in Illustration 82. In your work use a one-half inch margin for all messages and vary the amount of space at the top and bottom.

Use Illustration 82 as a style model for the message side of your first card.

Problem 20B. *Message Side* Portland, Maine   August 22, 19--   Dear Mrs. Milton: This morning we received the coat you sent us for repair and restyling. Everything is clear except the shoulder adjustments you want us to make. (¶) Please call at our Tailoring Department on the Fifth Floor the next time you are downtown. We want to be sure that your coat will be restyled to fit you perfectly. STONE'S DEPARTMENT STORE

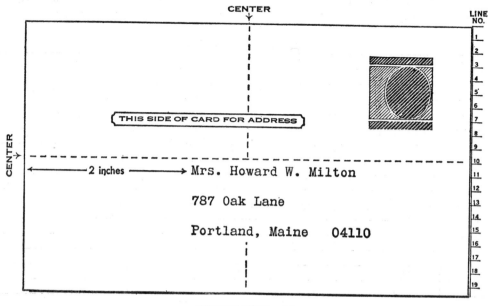

ILLUSTRATION 81
Address Side Of Postal Card

Perfecting Your Control

In this Division you will perfect your typing control and will prepare yourself for the training you will get in applying that control to a wide variety of practical typing problems and situations.

Each Lesson has five parts. The purpose of each part is explained on pages 62 and 63. Read those pages again, so that you will understand precisely how each part will help you to realize your ambition to become a superior typist.

Type Lessons 53 to 57 (inclusive) line for line, just as shown. Each line contains exactly 60 strokes and spaces, allowing one stroke at the end of the line for carriage return.

Write the first three parts of each Lesson—

Warm-up Practice, Sentence Writing, and Technique Improvement—with *single* spacing—each line two or three times. Space twice after each 2-line or 3-line group.

Type the remaining parts of each Lesson—Speed Building and Brief Timed Writing—each twice with *double* spacing. Indent the paragraphs *five* spaces. When you have finished your work on these two parts, check your typing carefully; then be sure to do remedial practice in the way described on pages 63 to 65.

Set the left margin stop for a line of 60 spaces. You are now ready to begin by typing the Warm-up Practice in Lesson 53.

Lesson 53

Warm-up Practice

High frequency words and phrases

act add age ago aid aim air all and any are arm art ask ate
able also auto away back ball bank base beat been best bill
about above admit after again agree ahead allow along among
as soon as, if you wish to, at present, we shall be glad to
at the same time, as well as, at that time, there have been

Sentence Writing

You may avoid many errors by keeping your eyes on the copy.
Always be sure that it is your fingers which do the typing.
You can save energy and reduce fatigue by sitting properly.
Freight to me sixty dozen quart jars and twelve black pans.
Unpaid checks are No. 89 for $76.54 and No. 630 for $21.85.

Many business forms are arranged in such a way that you can greatly simplify your typing by setting stops on your machine. You will often find, too, that the ruling is exactly right for single spacing or for double spacing, so that you won't have to use the variable line spacer. Make it a practice to study the pattern of each new form.

Get the two routing slips from your Workbook and separate them at the perforation.

Insert Form 8-16 into your machine. Use the variable line spacer to line up the date line; then set the line space regulator for single spacing.

Type the following material on the two routing slips.

Problem 16. (Form 8-16). August 3, 19--
To Mr. Crenshaw   *From* Mr. Lohrman
1 Mr. Daniels   *2* Miss Stanwood
3 Miss Cavanaugh   *4* Mrs. Lord
Return to N. W. Lohrman   *Remarks* Please study this plan carefully. Call me by Tuesday at the latest to tell me how you feel about its adoption. NWL

Problem 17. (Form 8-17). November 16, 19--   *To* Accounting Department   *From* R. McNeale   *1* Mr. Downs   *2* Mr. Fisher   *Return to* Accounting Department *Remarks* Ask Mr. Downs and Mr. Fisher to check the receiving date and the condition of this shipment. If we're at fault, write the customer and make a proper adjustment. RMcN

Long Distance Call Record. Many business forms require typing after printed words or headings. The long distance call record shown in Illustration 80 is a typical example.

Note that this form also requires the typing of an *x* in a small printed square.

Unless the center of the printed square corresponds exactly with the spacing on your machine, move the carriage to the space just beyond the center of the square and use the backspace

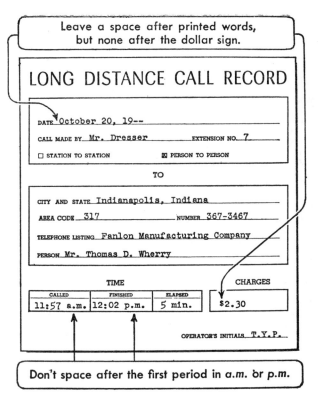

ILLUSTRATION 80
Long Distance Call Record

key. Hold the backspace key while you strike the *x*.

Your Workbook contains two forms like the one shown in Illustration 80. Here is the material you are to type on them. Use your own initials.

Problem 18. (Form 8-18). October 20, 19--   Mr. Dresser   *Extension No.* 7
X *Person to Person*

To Indianapolis, Indiana   317 367-3467 Fanlon Manufacturing Company Mr. Thomas D. Wherry   *Time* 11:57 a.m. to 12:02 p.m.--5 min.   *Charges* $2.30

Problem 19. (Form 8-19). July 8, 19-- Mr. Saunders   *Extension No.* 463   **X** *Person to Person*

To New Orleans, Louisiana   504 675-7741 LeCompte Brothers, Inc. Mr. Maurice F. LeCompte   *Time* 10:18 a.m. to 10:20 a.m.--2 min.   *Charges* $1.95

Technique Improvement

Drill on the index fingers of the left and right hands

try hurt fry numb rut jury mug burn ruby fun turn bunt tuft
hunt thumb buff truth myth burnt mum gruff hymn funny grunt
Burn 65 huts. Ruth turns. Hunt 56 rugs. Buy but 74 hubs.
Turn the burnt fur rug, but try to buy 576 jugs in a hurry.
Gruff Hugh hums as he hunts tuneful hymns that have rhythm.

Speed Building

	Words
America is truly the land of opportunity. In no other	11
country in the world do people have the chance to rise from	23
poverty to important places of leadership. To the founders	35
of our nation we owe a debt of thanks. They had the vision	47
to create a country where men have equality before the law.	59

| 1 | 2 | 3 | 4 | 5 | 6 | 7 | 8 | 9 | 10 | 11 |

Brief Timed Writing

	Words
No matter who you are or where you live, you have just	11
as much opportunity as any other person to win out in life.	23
Your success depends on your willingness to study and work.	35

| 1 | 2 | 3 | 4 | 5 | 6 | 7 | 8 | 9 | 10 | 11 |

Lesson 54

Warm-up Practice

High frequency words and phrases

bad bag bat bay bed bee beg bid big bit box boy but buy can
blow body bond both busy came care case cent city come copy
aware basis begin being below blank block brief build carry
a few weeks, at all times, there will not, in a few minutes
it may be, you can have, shall be glad to, will not be able

Problem 13. (Form 8-13). *Your Order No.* 12-765 *Our Invoice No. 834* *To* **M. and L. Sporting Goods Company** East 20th Street at Blair Omaha, Nebraska 68105

Problem 14. (Form 8-14). *Your Order No.* 607-T *Our Invoice No. 835* *To* Train's Stationery Company 14 North 112th Street Cleveland, Ohio 44109

File Folder Labels. Labels for file folders are manufactured in perforated strips. Labels in strips can be typed more easily than separate labels.

Study Illustration 78. Notice that each label in the strip is marked off into two parts. Insert the strip into your machine so that the shorter part of each label—the part above the fold—is at the top.

Type labels for file folders in ALL CAPITAL LETTERS without punctuation.

Problem 15. (Form 8-15)

Detach the strip of nine file folder labels in your Workbook. The names you are to type on the labels are listed in the next column.

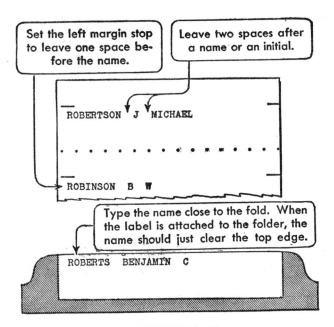

ILLUSTRATION 78
File Folder Labels

Before you start to type, put the card holders and the paper holders in position to hold the labels.

```
ROBBINS    CHARLES
ROBBINS    CHARLES  D
ROBBINS    CLIFFORD
ROBERTS    ALVIN  R
ROBERTS    BENJAMIN  C
ROBERTS    HENRY  L
ROBERTS    WARREN
ROBERTSON  J  MICHAEL
ROBINSON   B  W
```

Correspondence Routing Slips. Companies with several offices or departments often use routing slips to make sure that letters and other papers get to all the persons who should see them. The routing slip is stapled or clipped to the correspondence.

Study the routing slip shown in Illustration 79. Note that it has been designed so that all but two lines of typing start either at the left margin or at a point just beyond the center.

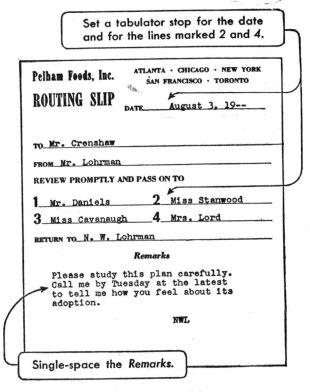

ILLUSTRATION 79
Correspondence Routing Slip

Sentence Writing

Be relaxed and avoid a feeling of strain when you practice.
Speed in typing is always built on a firm base of accuracy.
An expert typist does not pump arms and wrists up and down.
May just saved much time by taking an extra follow-up quiz.
Get our J & M "ready-to-eat" foods; buy now and save money.

Technique Improvement

Second-finger drills

die died eke eked ice iced cede ceded kick kicked dead keep
Dick deck Ed Eddie did decide kid Keck cede ceded dike dice
Deck 83 dikes. Cede 38 dikes. Kick 838 dice. Keep 3,838.
Did he kick the edges of the decayed keels as he descended?
Eddie decided to cede the dike to Dick; Eddie did the deed.

Speed Building

Words

When you are planning a vacation trip, you first get a   11
map of the region and find the location of the spot you are   23
to reach. You then decide the road you will take to get to   35
the end of your trip. You will do well to decide your life   47
journey in the same way. Decide at the start what your aim   59
is to be; then plan out the right way to achieve your goal.   71

| 1 | 2 | 3 | 4 | 5 | 6 | 7 | 8 | 9 | 10 | 11 |

Brief Timed Writing

It is not easy for you to decide what your aim in life   11
is to be or to determine for yourself the best way to reach   23
it. You will add purpose to your life when you plan ahead.   35

| 1 | 2 | 3 | 4 | 5 | 6 | 7 | 8 | 9 | 10 | 11 |

Shipping Labels. Labels are easy to type. You can speed up your work by making a label holder yourself. Here is how to make the holder.

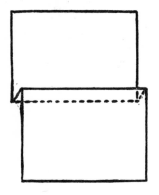 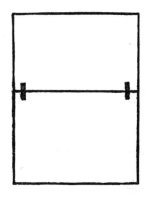

1. Fold carefully a pleat about ¼ inch deep across the center of a sheet of paper. Be sure the creases are straight.

2. Press down the fold until it is as flat as you can make it. Use strips of tape, if available, at the edges of the sheet.

Make the fold flat, with good sharp creases. Feed the sheet into your machine until the pocket made by the fold just clears the platen. Drop a label into the pocket and roll it back into typing position.

On the pleated sheet make a vertical pencil mark at the left edge of the first label to guide you when inserting additional labels of the same size.

Keep the holder in your typewriter. As one label is finished, roll it out of the front of your typewriter and feed another one into the pocket.

Even with your own special holder, you should also use the card holders.

Set the left margin stop and move the paper holders to grip the top of the label.

Your Workbook contains supplies of the shipping labels shown in Illustration 77. Separate those labels from the sheet and address them individually. Use a holder like the one described. Follow Illustration 77 for style.

Here is the copy to be typed on each label.

Problem 8. (Form 8-8). *Invoice No.* 1063 *Your Order No.* 4-1933 *To* Platt & Haskins, Inc. 5782 San Joaquin Avenue Fresno, California 93702

Problem 9. (Form 8-9). *Invoice No.* 1064 *Your Order No.* 395 *To* Kent McTavish Company 287 East Daggett Street Carson City, Nevada 89701

Problem 10. (Form 8-10). *Invoice No.* 1065 *Your Order No.* 798-43 *To* J. Bancroft and Sons Grandview at Ninth San Francisco, California 94121

Problem 11. (Form 8-11). *Invoice No.* 1066 *Your Order No.* N-8724 *To* Telgar Brothers Company 395 North Alhambra Street Phoenix, Arizona 85011

Problem 12. (Form 8-12). *Your Order No.* 1742 *Our Invoice No.* 833 *To* Bob's Hobby Shop 5690 West Lake Street Duluth, Minnesota 55808

Use the block style.

Type straight across the label. Notice that the order and invoice numbers fall on the same typed lines with parts of the address.

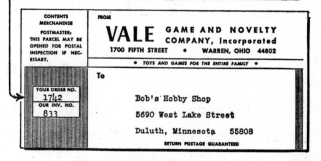

ILLUSTRATION 77
Shipping Labels

Lesson 55

Warm-up Practice

High frequency words and phrases

cap car cat cow cry cup cut dad day did die dog dry due ear
cost dark data date deal desk does done down each easy else
chair check chief claim class clear could count cover delay
we are having, how many, we shall send, as well, what to do
which will be, you should have, shall be glad, by this time

Sentence Writing

High speed in typing comes from the right kind of practice.
Keep your eyes on your copy and think while you are typing.
In typing, you need to use your head as well as your hands.
Jo may equal the fine record by solving six puzzles a week.
During February and March Mr. West's sales were $68,724.39.

Technique Improvement

Third-finger drills

loss sow wool low wood zoo solo woes slot sob wolf sole woo
soils allows slow sloops sold swallow oleo six soy owls old
Allow 29 zoos, 92 owls, 292 dolls, 929 soles, 2,929 sloops.
The zoos will allow the six old yellow owls to swallow soy.
Old Sol saw sixty sloops slowly wallow in the swollen seas.

Speed Building

	Words
The first step you need to take in order to reach your	11
goal in life is to make a list of all your talents. Put in	23
all the things you believe you can do well. It may be that	35
you like to meet people and talk with them. If so, selling	47
may be just the work in which you can best use your talent.	59

```
   1      2      3      4      5      6      7      8      9     10     11
```

Problem 7.   (Form 8-7)

Miss Doris Mears
1542 Beech Avenue
Oneida, New York   13421

Miss Mildred Ramsey
1810 Blackhawk Street
Bryan, Ohio   43506

Mr. Walker F. Nevin
Woodward Oil Company
Oberlin, Ohio   44074

Mr. Philip R. Fenn
Davidson Company, Inc.
300 Sixth Street
Oswego, New York   13126

Mr. Howard Callow
Purchasing Agent
J. Lord and Sons, Inc.
1608 East Nelson Street
Canton, Ohio   44701

Mr. Glenn J. Randall, Jr.
In care of Clark Hotel
Ripley, Ohio   45167

Mr. J. M. Brooker
Mannion and Brooker, Inc.
609 Fidelity Building
Rome, New York   13441

Mr. C. K. Dillon
The R. Cope Corporation
1600 Northern Boulevard
Cadiz, Ohio   43807

Mrs. S. S. Orr
Sycamore Valley
Ohio   43789

Mr. Alfred A. Sanders
Director of Personnel
Killigrew Brothers
Market Street at Ninth
Rome, New York   13443

Kenneth D. Voss, Esq.
Voss, Miller & Grant
211 Hunter Building
3000 East Erie Road
Dayton, Ohio   45403

Dr. Clifford Q. Drake
Mount Hope Hospital
Duke and Ostend Streets
Toledo, Ohio   43603

Mr. Donald Frazier, Jr.
869 Mohawk Street
Utica, New York   13511

Mr. W. John Henderson
Secretary-Treasurer
Henderson and Sons, Inc.
Dover, Ohio   44622

Colonel Kent W. Strom
2947 Pacific Avenue
Warren, Ohio   44485

Dr. Melvin H. Jennings
702 Medical Building
1304 Mountain Avenue
Vestal, New York   13850

Mr. David Reed Cather
Apartment 3-R
Mead Apartments
3080 Shore Road
Kent, Ohio   44241

Miss Lillian G. Campbell
Training Supervisor
Lane's Department Store
Cove and Third Streets
Zanesville, Ohio   43701

Professor N. Blayne Howe
1692 University Drive
Ada, Ohio   45810

Mrs. James T. Swythe
946 Ponca Boulevard
Lima, Ohio   45805

Mr. Bevin C. McVail
P. O. Box 205
Tulsa, Oklahoma   74011

Mrs. Foster R. Mason
Pine Grove Apartments
340-344 Calhoun Street
Akron, Ohio   44312

Mr. W. W. Rust
Great Western Airways
Municipal Airport
Newark, Ohio   43055

Mr. V. Alvin Boone
Michaelson Corporation
840 North River Road
Tulsa, Oklahoma   74106

Brief Timed Writing

When you have made a list of all your talents and have	11
chosen the one thing you are certain you can do better than	23
anything else, you have started on the proper road for you.	35

```
1    2    3    4    5    6    7    8    9    10   11
```

Lesson 56

Warm-up Practice

High frequency words and phrases

eat egg end eye far fat fed fee few fit fix fly for fun **fur**
even ever fact fail fair fast feel fell file fill find five
doubt dozen drive every extra fifth fifty final first force
be sure, send us, it may be that, a few weeks, at this time
I was, he will be, to give me, out of the question, must **be**

Sentence Writing

You can live within an income more easily than without one.
Good personal traits are just as important as good ability.
Business leaders know how to work easily with other people.
Five dozen black Roman jeeps were bought by a queer expert.
"My best offer is $9.50 a foot--that's final," said George.

Technique Improvement

Fourth-finger drills

ape equip papa abate equal paper crazy plaza aqua zip apace
apply par adapt apart parade papaw bazaar quay daze parapet
At the bazaar papa won a paper parasol, a queer quiz prize.
Apply 90 scraps of opaque paper to the part of the parapet.
The dazed paraders gazed when the haze on the plaza abated.

Many companies write a confirming letter for each telegram. Such a letter is mailed to the addressee and quotes the body of the telegram.

Your Workbook contains two telegram blanks. Use them to type the following telegrams.

Follow the style shown in Illustration 75 at the bottom of page 224.

Problem 5.   (Form 8-5)

Telegram

September 29, 19--
Baker Textile Company
5100 East Normandy Street
High Point, North Carolina
Report immediately on our Order Number 9942 for 80 dozen Style 64-N socks. Stock needed for sale next week.

                              Kinzer & Sons

300 North Morrow Street
685-7500
RKK: *(Add your initials)*

Problem 6.   (Form 8-6)

Overnight Telegram

October 2, 19--
Valley Fruit Company
5308 Park Road
San Jacinto, California
Our Sales Manager, Wayne Morgan, flies to Los Angeles Tuesday. He will have authority to make necessary arrangements. Please wire whether your representative can meet him at Hotel Crown, Los Angeles, Wednesday morning at ten.

                        Tunis Brothers, Inc.

2367 Tower Building
448-6997
CRT: *(Add your initials)*

Address Labels. Many offices use perforated sheets of labels to save time in envelope addressing. The entire sheet, which contains 24 labels, is typed at one time; then the labels are separated and pasted on envelopes.

Form 8-7 in your Workbook is a sheet of 24 labels. Problem 7, page 226, gives the addresses to be typed on that sheet. They are already arranged for you, so that you can type straight across the page. Single-space each address in the block style.

When you have typed the 24 addresses on Form 8-7 and before you take the sheet out of your typewriter, check your work.

Illustration 76 shows how the sheet should look after it is typed. Study the illustration carefully before you start.

Leave two single line spaces at the top of each row of labels. Any 3-line, 4-line, or 5-line address will then fall into proper position.

Miss Doris Mears 1542 Beech Avenue Oneida, New York 13421	Miss Mildred Ramsey 1810 Blackhawk Street Bryan, Ohio 43506	Mr. Walker F. Nevin Woodward Oil Company Oberlin, Ohio 44074
Mr. Philip R. Fenn Davidson Company, Inc. 300 Sixth Street Oswego, New York 13126	Mr. Howard Callow Purchasing Agent J. Lord and Sons, Inc. 1608 East Nelson Street Canton, Ohio 44701	Mr. Glenn J. Randall, Jr. In care of Clark Hotel Ripley, Ohio 45167
Mr. J. M. Brooker Mannion and Brooker, Inc. 609 Fidelity Building Rome, New York 13441	Mr. C. K. Dillon The R. Cope Corporation 1600 Northern Boulevard Cadiz, Ohio 43907	Mrs. S. S. Orr Sycamore Valley Ohio 43789
Mr. Alfred A. Sanders Director of Personnel Killigrew Brothers Market Street at Ninth Rome, New York 13443	Kenneth D. Voss, Esq. Voss, Miller & Grant 211 Hunter Building 3000 East Erie Road Dayton, Ohio 45403	Dr. Clifford Q. Drake Mount Hope Hospital Duke and Ostend Streets Toledo, Ohio 43603
Mr. Donald Frazier, Jr. 869 Mohawk Street Utica, New York 13511	Mr. W. John Henderson Secretary-Treasurer Henderson and Sons, Inc. Dover, Ohio 44622	Colonel Kent W. Strom 2947 Pacific Avenue Warren, Ohio 44485
Dr. Melvin H. Jennings 702 Medical Building 1304 Mountain Avenue Vestal, New York 13850	Mr. David Reed Cather Apartment 3-R Mead Apartments 3080 Shore Road Kent, Ohio 44241	Miss Lillian G. Campbell Training Supervisor Lane's Department Store Cove and Third Streets Zanesville, Ohio 43701
Professor N. Blayne Howe 1692 University Drive Ada, Ohio 45810	Mrs. James T. Swythe 946 Ponca Boulevard Lima, Ohio 45805na	Mr. Bevin C. McVail P. O. Box 205 Tulsa, Oklahoma 74011
Mrs. Foster R. Mason Pine Grove Apartments 340-344 Calhoun Street Akron, Ohio 44312	Mr. W. W. Rust Great Western Airways Municipal Airport Newark, Ohio 43055	Mr. V. Alvin Boone Michaelson Corporation 840 North River Road Tulsa, Oklahoma 74106

Set left margin and tabulator stops to start each address on the third space from the left edge of the label.

ILLUSTRATION 76
Sheet Of Address Labels

Speed Building

When you decide what you want to do most in life, your   11
next step is to find the best road to reach your goal. You   23
will want to prepare yourself for your first job by getting   35
the best possible training. Read books and trade magazines   47
that pertain to the business or profession you have chosen.   59
Make a special effort to meet people who are engaged in the   71
field in which you are interested. Such people are usually   83
glad to counsel with any beginner who is really interested.   95

1	2	3	4	5	6	7	8	9	10	11

Brief Timed Writing

A person who has already traveled a road is always the   11
one best qualified to give directions to another person who   23
wants to travel a given road and not get lost or be misled.   35

1	2	3	4	5	6	7	8	9	10	11

Lesson 57

Warm-up Practice

High frequency words and phrases

gas get got had has hat hay hen her him his hit hog hot how
flat form four free from full gain give glad gone good half
fresh front great happy heavy hurry ideal issue joint labor
would like to have, we shall be able, there may be, at last
in the meantime, in order to, in addition to, it will be so

Sentence Writing

Good products are produced by good workmen with good tools.
Trouble is usually produced by those who make nothing else.
A record of past expenses may aid you in planning a budget.
Six crazy kings vowed to abolish many quite pitiful jousts.
Our inventory shows 58 Stock No. 936 and 741 Stock No. 820.

Problem 1. (Form 8-1). March 8, 19-- Mrs. Thomas D. Fenwick   4023 Stuart Drive   San Antonio, Texas   78203   Dear Mrs. Fenwick: $102.67   March 1.

Problem 2. (Form 8-2). December 16, 19-- Miss Rachael B. Garner   Oak Grove Apartments   East Madison and Culver Streets   San Antonio, Texas   78204   Dear Miss Garner: $187.50   December 12.

Problem 3. (Form 8-3). May 20, 19-- Mr. C. Humphrey Darr   11 West Lake Avenue   Carlton, Minnesota   55718   Dear Mr. Darr: The Tell-Rad Shop   805 Superior Street   Duluth, Minnesota   55803   323-2376

Problem 4. (Form 8-4). October 6, 19-- Mr. Vincent K. Prince   Apartment B-14   308 Springdale Avenue   Arlington, Virginia   22204   Dear Mr. Prince: District Television Service   572 Madison Avenue   Alexandria, Virginia   342-6007

Single-space the address.

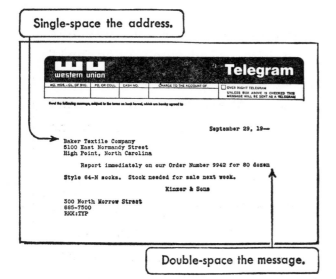

Double-space the message.

ILLUSTRATION 75
Outgoing Telegram

Telegrams. It is good business practice to type all outgoing telegrams—even when the message is to be dictated over the telephone. The typing reduces the danger of errors and omissions.

Kinds Of Telegraph Service

Two types of domestic telegraph service are available—telegram and overnight telegram. A basic interstate rate is charged for each of these two classes of service. When the sender specifies delivery by messenger, an extra charge is added.

Telegram—this type of message provides the fastest service. The minimum charge is for fifteen words.

Overnight telegram—this kind of message is sent during the night for delivery the following morning. The minimum charge is for one hundred words.

Preparing Telegrams

The keynote of the well-worded telegram is conciseness. State your message just as clearly and briefly as possible. You should, however, not sacrifice clarity for the sake of brevity. It is always better to use a few extra words when they add to the clarity or the emphasis of the message.

Punctuation marks, such as the period, comma, semicolon, colon, dash, hyphen, parentheses, question mark, quotation marks, and apostrophe, are neither counted nor charged for. Words, such as *stop, quote, period,* and *comma,* are counted and charged for as one word.

Abbreviations are counted at the rate of one word for each five letters. In most cases no saving is effected by abbreviating a word instead of spelling it in full.

Telegrams written in paragraphs will be transmitted and delivered in paragraphs without charge.

Do not write figures as words. The charge for figures, signs, and letters is at the rate of one word for each group of five or fewer characters. (Thus, *130* is charged as one word, but *One Hundred Thirty* is charged as three words.)

Proper names from any language are counted according to the number of words and initials which they contain. Two or more initials may be written together as a letter group. For example, *Van Dusen, United States,* and *St. Louis* are counted as two words each. *O'Malley* and *DeCosta* are counted as one word each. *New York City,* and *John L. Powell* are counted as three words each.

Technique Improvement

Drill on the third bank of the keyboard

wet eye rot try ire put ore wit ewe rip tie pet rye pot pry
quit were rope true your poet pore wipe tree peer quip writ
quiet worry equip wiper write queer error wrote erupt upper
We tried to tie rope or wire to the top of the rotted tree.
My letter in reply to your query was written two weeks ago.

Speed Building

				Words
The ability to get along with other people happily and				11

The ability to get along with other people happily and   11
without friction is an art you must foster in order to gain   23
success in business. There are few people who get top jobs   35
without that character trait. Ability and training are, of   47
course, important; but the only key which will unlock doors   59
to success in business is real ability to work with others.   71
Nobody can hope to get ahead without the aid and support of   83
others. If people like you, they will usually do what they   95
can to smooth your path on the road to a successful career.   107

```
    1     2     3     4     5     6     7     8     9    10    11
```

Brief Timed Writing

A business executive who headed a large and successful   11
company said that he would pay more for the ability to deal   23
with people than he would pay for any other business trait.   35

```
    1     2     3     4     5     6     7     8     9    10    11
```

Extra Credit. The following paragraph contains all the letters of the alphabet. It is an excellent review. If your instructor asks you to do so, type the paragraph twice with *single* spacing. Space twice after the first writing.

If you prize your friends, never say anything that may   11
injure them or cause them to question your loyalty to them.   23
Mending a broken friendship is an exceedingly slow process.   35

Division Eight—Secretarial Typing

Much of your work in a business office will consist of typing business forms, reports, and records. This Division will help you to prepare yourself for these important aspects of applied typewriting.

You will be given a model and instructions for each problem. Study the model carefully and use it as a guide. The forms and business papers you will use are exact reproductions of forms used in business offices.

In typing all dates, use the current year.

Fill-in Form Letters. Fill-in letters are widely used for some kinds of routine business correspondence. Portions of such letters are multigraphed in proper position on letterheads. The typist inserts only the missing parts.

Study Illustration 74. Contrast the two uncompleted form letters with the letters that have been filled in. You will see at once that good work on fill-in letters demands special care.

Your first concern must be to get the sheet absolutely straight in your machine. Try, too, to make your own typing the best possible match.

After you type the date on a fill-in letter, turn up the sheet to the first line of the body. Set the left margin stop. When you are sure that the alignment is perfect, roll back the letter—line by line—until you come to the first line of the inside address. Remember to count the interlines.

Forms 8-1, 8-2, 8-3, and 8-4 in your Workbook are reproductions of the two fill-in letters shown in Illustration 74.

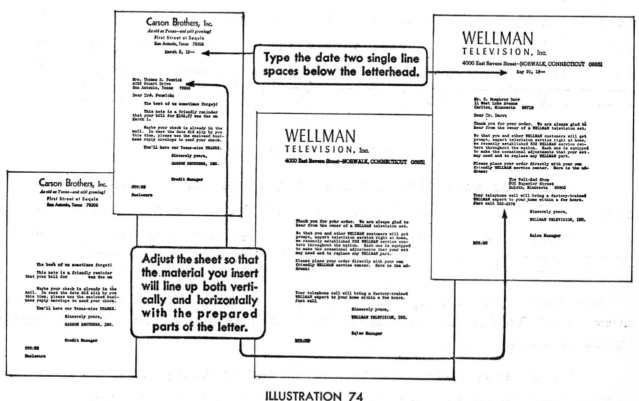

ILLUSTRATION 74

Fill-in Form Letters

How To Divide Words

Up to this time you have been typing line for line just as the copy is printed in your book. Beginning with this Lesson, the copy for Speed Building and for Brief Timed Writing is in printer's type. To keep the right margin of your typing reasonably even, you may find it desirable now and then to divide a word at the end of a line. Avoid dividing words if at all possible to do so.

Read the following article carefully. It gives simplified instruction on the correct division of words at the end of lines. Your instructor may ask you to type the article now or later. If you do type it, use a 60-space line with a 5-space paragraph indention. Double-space your typing throughout. The hyphen, as you learned in Lesson 36, page 45, is typed with the little finger of the right hand.

		Words
To divide a word correctly, you need to know the right		11
way to pronounce it by its syllables because no word may be		23
divided at the end of a line except after a whole syllable.		35
Each of the following five words is shown by its syllables;		47
the spaces within the words show where they may be divided.		59
pre ferred pref er ence rep re sents rec og nize knowl edge		71
If you apply that basic rule for dividing words at the	11	82
end of lines, you will never divide a word of one syllable.	23	94
through strengths breadth breathed freight strained planned	35	106
If one of the syllables in a two-syllable word is just	11	117
a single letter, never divide the word under any condition.	23	129
omit item about against enough equipped study sturdy eighty	35	141
Here is a good rule to apply: Do not divide a word in	11	152
such a way that two letters would go over to the next line.	23	164
also ever envy proper plenty happy plainly plumber stronger	35	176
What about words that include double consonants? As a	11	187
general rule, type the hyphen after the first of the double	23	199
consonants; then begin the next line with the second one of	35	211
the double consonants. If the root word ends with a double	47	223
consonant, you type the hyphen after that double consonant.	59	235
suc ceed traf fic hap pened com menced scat tered ship ping	71	247
press ing express ing tell ing bill ing roll ing enroll ing	83	259
As a general rule, divide a word after a vowel that is	11	270
a syllable by itself. If the word has a suffix, you should	23	282

Paragraph Typing C

These paragraphs contain many figures, symbols, and capital letters.

1   This lot at 3958 West Alexander, as you know, is about 428½ feet wide and 927½ feet deep. A well-known builder is of the opinion that the cost of excavating will be at least $2,700. As of today--August 21--4,931 citizens have signed the petition for the purchase of this lot by the city. The total cost of securing the signatures has proved to be less than 3 1/3¢ a name. Should we now ask Winterling & Ransome to get up a detailed estimate covering the excavating work?

2   The zinc etchings on your Order #3740 are in work. We lettered the heading thus: <u>Diagrams</u> <u>of</u> <u>Slugs</u>. The firm of Newson & Quincy (successors to A. X. Newson) directed us to ship the large blocks to Blacksburg. Shall we send you the 3/8" and the 5/16" blocks? Mr. Newson definitely asked for the 3/16" blocks when he called at 10:30 a.m., February 26. The etchings are being billed at the special price of 20¢ a square inch. There won't be any charge for extra blocking.

3   To write exponents, release the ratchet, turn <u>down</u> the sheet, and strike the letter or the figure to be put in for the exponent; as, $(a \times b)^n$; $(3 \times 3)^2$. After you have typed the exponent, adjust to the writing line. Now and then you may be asked to type sub-numbers. To type sub-numbers, you turn <u>up</u> the sheet a half space, type the sub-number needed, and then adjust to the writing line; as, H_2O_2. When typing copy which includes exponents or sub-numbers, double-space.

carry over the entire suffix to the next line; but when the   35   294
vowel that begins the suffix is pronounced as a part of the   47   306
syllable before the suffix, then divide after that syllable   59   318
and carry the other letters of the suffix to the next line.   71   330
The three lines below show words falling into these groups.   83   342
bene fit tele phone hesi tate privi lege gaso line hero ism   95   354
accept able incred ible marvel ous desir able merchant able   107   366
applica ble amica ble communica ble dura ble indefatiga ble   119   378

Many English words end with the termination pronounced   11   389
as shun. Divide such words by writing the hyphen after the   23   401
syllable which precedes the termination pronounced as shun.   35   413
atten tion inten tion recommenda tion techni cian magi cian   47   425

Do not divide figures, abbreviations, or contractions.   11   436
$12,485.92 $731.60 c.o.d. R. F. D. haven't aren't shouldn't   23   448

There are some compound words which are spelled with a   11   459
hyphen. Make sure to divide such words only at the hyphen.   23   471

When you type a letter or a whole page, avoid dividing   11   482
the word which comes at the end of the first typed line and   23   494
the final word on the last line. Try not to have the words   35   506
at the end of two successive lines divided. In typing, try   47   518
to avoid dividing a word in such a way that only a syllable   59   530
of two letters would come before the hyphen. Take over the   71   542
two letters to the next line and thus avoid using a hyphen.   83   554

Lesson 58

Warm-up Practice

High frequency words and phrases

hug ice ill ink its job joy kid lap law lay led leg let lie
hard have hear held here home hope hour idea into item join
large learn least legal light limit local loose lucky lunch
for some, if you do, with whom, for sending, give me, I can
you are ready, as long as, in spite of, less than, for them

Paragraph Typing B

Each of these paragraphs contains all the letters of the alphabet.

Words

1   Work gets done when people cooperate and work together   11
zestfully and congenially. You do not get efficiency where   23
there is friction. It pays to face each day in a jolly and   35
cheerful attitude and to meet and work with other people as   47
you would have them meet and work with you. The person who   59
examines himself day by day and who determines that he will   71
live up to this ideal will quickly find that people will be   83
sure to go out of their way to meet him more than half way.   95

2   In order to live a useful and truly successful life, a   11 106
person needs to develop both his mind and his heart. If he   23 118
develops just his mind, he can quickly become quite selfish   35 130
and indifferent to others. If he lets his feelings run off   47 142
with him, he will become a shallow sentimentalist. We have   59 154
an old maxim to the effect that we get only as we give. If   71 166
we recognize the truth of that maxim, we shall embrace with   83 178
zeal the opportunities to give which come our way each day.   95 190

3   Genuine sincerity is the quality that lies at the base   11 201
of a joyous and successful life. If you see a salesman who   23 213
does not believe in the merchandise or service he is trying   35 225
to sell, you do not need to look any further to explain why   47 237
he is a failure. Many people, amazingly enough, seem to be   59 249
engaged in the silly attempt to bluff the world. No matter   71 261
how you handicap a person, he will still command respect if   83 273
he has the quality of genuine sincerity shining out of him.   95 285

Sentence Writing

Anyone who spends more than he earns is headed for trouble.
Your life consists in what you are and not in what you own.
Your finest assets lie in a strong mind and a healthy body.
Jack amazed a few girls by dropping the antique onyx vases.
Send 748# of #92 "D & M's" @ 50¢ <u>less</u> 6½% (n/30) via B & O.

Technique Improvement

Drill on the lowest bank of the keyboard

zoo vex cab van box nab mob zip six can vim ban nix man bin
zinc next cram vain born name mock move none buzz vane come
zebra vixen cream venom bench seven blame fuzzy buxom black
Seven dozen boxes of clams will come back by van next month.
The men crammed the burned corn cobs in the six vacant bins.

Speed Building

	Words
One of the great psychologists of modern days once said	11
that the deepest principle in human nature is the craving to be	24
appreciated. Here is an important secret of how to get other	36
people to like you. Fix in the mind of everybody you meet the	48
idea that you think that he is the most important person in the	60
whole wide world. The best possible way for you to make	71
another feel more important is to give attention instead of trying	84
to get attention. When you are talking to another, look him	96
straight in the eye. Do not glance about or allow your attention	109
to wander away from the person to whom you are talking.	120

Brief Timed Writing

When you grant to another person the courtesy of your	11
complete and undivided attention, you show by your actions	23
and your attitude that you are deeply interested in him.	34

Division Eight

Paragraph Typing A

Many of the words in these paragraphs are balanced-hand words.

Words

1   It is the duty of a citizen to work with his neighbors   11
to make the town or city that he calls home a good place in   23
which to live and work. He may lend a hand by carrying out   35
his civic duties, by fighting for the right, and by turning   47
his thoughts to the future. Your town or city owes much to   59
those of its busy citizens who work for the good of all and   71
who have a vivid sense of civic duty about common problems;   83
they gladly give their aid and do work that may irk others.   95

2   The man or woman who wants to make the right amount of   11 106
progress does not permit his or her education to halt or to   23 118
slow down in any visible way when the usual formal training   35 130
comes to an end. With the aid of an intensive course by an   47 142
apt tutor, all of us can make ourselves far more proficient   59 154
than the people who halt their education with the final day   71 166
of high school. Most men who got to the top of their field   83 178
kept right on with their studies and thus kept on learning.   95 190

3   Work is hard when we do not know how to handle it; the   11 201
way to make your work fun is to make yourself proficient in   23 213
the tasks that form the bulk of your work. It also pays to   35 225
map out your work in such a way that you have the best part   47 237
of the day to handle those tasks which embody big problems;   59 249
when you are tired, any big problem looks bigger than it is   71 261
and harder than it is. If you make it a habit to plan your   83 273
work and then to work your plan, you may grow to like work.   95 285

Lesson 59

Warm-up Practice

High frequency words and phrases

lot low mad man map mar may men met mud nap net new nor not
June July just keep kind knew know laid last late left less
Madam March maybe metal model money month motor moved music
at once, thank you for, up to the, if you will, it might be
in their letter, for instance, you would not, at which time

Sentence Writing

An idea that isn't put to work always remains just a dream.
Giving consideration to others will bring happiness to you.
It is usually wise to think that others know more than you.
Jeb Grant memorized quickly and exactly the five new poems.
Send 56 pairs of List No. 893 and 41 pairs of List No. 327.

Technique Improvement

Reaches from the third bank to the lowest bank and from the lowest bank to the third bank

tin tax rub once pin into imp wove yon prim rob turn ice in
move broom crop brown numb crumb mice verve zoom brine mint
excel quince inner equine pact unique woman orbit pounce on
Next winter ninety expert printers expect to be at Praxton.
Every boy in the crew won ten prizes in the unique contest.

Speed Building

	Words
Another secret of how to win friends is to be a friend. A	12
cordial handshake and a cheery smile are the outward signs of	24
an inner feeling of friendliness toward others. When you are	36
first introduced to another person, assume from the very start	48
that he is going to like you and that you likewise are going to	61

Judgment is another characteristic of every successful secretary. 13
Judgment is the outcome of knowledge and experience, for the judgment 27
of a person on a problem or a situation about which he knows nothing 41
is generally worthless. The secretary understands the attitude of her 55
employer on personal and business matters. Out of that wide knowledge, 69
she can arrive at a correct judgment when a problem is presented to 82
her for decision. When she interviews a visitor, she is tactful enough 96
to find out what is wanted; then, with the interests of her employer 110
in mind, she can arrive at a decision on how to take care of the caller. 124
She may be able to do what needs to be done herself; she may decide 137
that someone else in the office can take care of the matter; she may 151
conclude that here is something which her employer would want to 164
take care of himself. Above all things else, the secretary does not jump 179
at conclusions. She has sound judgment because her judgment is based 193
on a knowledge of the facts. 199

When a judge tries a suit in his court, he listens to all the evidence 213
that is presented to him. Both the accused and the accuser have their 227
day in court. It is on the basis of the evidence which is offered that 241
the judge makes a judgment. The secretary does the same thing. She 255
does not take sides; she hears all the evidence; she studies and weighs 269
it carefully; then, in the light of all the evidence and in the light of 283
her own knowledge and experience, she arrives at a judgment on the 296
particular matter with which she is dealing. If you were to talk with 310
a hundred business and professional men who have competent 322
secretaries, those men would tell you that one of the outstanding 335
characteristics of their secretaries is good judgment. 346

Efficiency is still another quality which every successful secretary 360
possesses. An efficient person, in the last analysis, is one who gets 374
things done. An inefficient person is one who is lazy, slipshod, 387
and indifferent. An efficient person, on the contrary, is one who is 401
methodical, alert, and enthusiastic. He does not dawdle over his work, 415
and he does not work haphazardly. The good secretary is a thoroughly 429
efficient business person. She commands the respect of other people, 443
and by her own efficiency she stimulates them to do their work 455
efficiently also. After all is said and done, it is results that count. A 470
person may be ever so willing; he may work ever so hard; but unless 483
he gets results, he is not an efficient worker. The good secretary is 497
efficient because she keeps things moving in the right channels. When 511
friction arises, she goes to work thoughtfully and tactfully to iron out 525
the difficulty because she wants nothing to interfere with efficiency. 539

like him. Lead off with a friendly approach. Do not wait for 73
the other person to take the first step. Look for the good 85
qualities in those you meet and do all in your power to overlook 98
their weak points. You will soon discover that a cordial, 110
friendly attitude toward other people works wonders in winning 122
their help and cooperation in any kind of activity. 132

Brief Timed Writing

Words

Many times a friendly manner will win for you in just a few 12
minutes an important goal that can be gained in no other way. 24

Lesson 60

Warm-up Practice

High frequency words and phrases

now odd off oil old one our out owe own pal pan pay pen pie
life like line list long look loss lost made mail make many
never night north occur offer often order other ought owner
all right, there will be, in favor, in a few days, to write
you can make, if you would like, there would be, to see him

Sentence Writing

There is no substitute for hard work over a period of time.
The one way for you to make dreams come true is to wake up.
There is no power on earth that matches the power of truth.
Fred specialized on the job of making very quaint wax toys.
Leon J. Kraus (1872-1936) suggested this title: Moonbeams.

Technique Improvement

Drill on double letters

ebb accept eddy week off soggy all comma inn soon apple err
pass matter nozzle robber accent ladder keep off beggar ill
summer announce effect oppose terrible recess better dazzle
The error deterred him from attempting a needless struggle.
A terrible ferry accident occurred suddenly that afternoon.

No. 19

The good secretary files letters accurately so that they can be quickly 14
found when they are asked for. When she looks up information in 27
reference books, she gets accurate information and she puts down that 41
information in accurate form. If her employer does a good deal of 54
traveling, she will often need to prepare itineraries of trips for 67
him. She makes sure that the information on which she bases her 80
memorandums is correct and is presented to her employer in such a way 94
that there can be no misunderstanding. Perhaps it is a part of her duty 108
to write up the minutes of meetings of executives over which her employer 123
presides. She writes up those minutes accurately, so that they truthfully 138
present the discussions and the conclusions. The appointment schedules 152
which she makes up for her employer are accurately prepared. The 165
notes she makes of a telephone conversation are accurate notes. 178

Intelligence is the second quality which the successful secretary 191
possesses. People differ greatly in the matter of intelligence. Some 205
are more intelligent than others; they somehow have greater possibilities 220
of profiting from their experiences than have other people. An intelligent 235
person is one who uses his head. He is never content to do things in 249
a routine way. He has a constant urge to broaden his point of view 262
and to do things that are out of the ordinary. One evidence of 275
intelligence is the ability that some people have to see their own work 289
in relation to the whole. There is a story about a successful man who 303
was one day walking down one of the main streets of a city and came 316
to a place where a great cathedral was being built. He stopped and 329
spoke to one workman and asked what that workman was doing. The 342
workman looked up from his task and said that he was mixing mortar. 355
The man walked on a few paces, went up to another workman, and asked 369
him the same question. This workman looked at the questioner and 382
said that anybody who had eyes could see that he, the workman, was 395
carrying bricks. A few paces on the man stopped beside a third workman 409
and addressed the same question to him. This workman, unlike the 422
others, looked up from the task on which he was engaged and replied, 436
in an exultant tone of voice, that he was helping to build a great cathedral. 451

This third workman saw his own task in the light of the whole 463
enterprise. He could look beyond the work that he was doing and view 477
that work as a part of the whole. He gathered inspiration from a vision 491
of the result toward which so many hands and minds were working. 504
In the same way the successful office worker can see his own work in 518
the light of the business as a whole. The ability to tie in your work 532
with the work of others is a mark of real intelligence. 543

Speed Building

You have probably found out that nobody ever gets tired of 12
talking about himself.   People like to discuss all their successes 25
and their problems.   One of the best ways to gain a friend is to 38
give the other person a chance to talk about himself.   When 50
you meet a stranger, it is an easy matter to find out right away 63
what his chief interests or hobbies are. Ask him leading 74
questions that will start him talking about matters in which he 87
has a special interest.   You should make comments or ask 98
further questions to show that you are alert and are interested 111
in what he is saying.   Many people have gained friends and won 123
popularity by simply being good listeners. 131

Brief Timed Writing

If you let the other fellow do most of the talking, you help 12
to make him feel more important.   It is a fact that you can win 25
more friends by listening than by talking. 33

Lesson 61

Warm-up Practice

High frequency words and phrases

pig pin put rag ran raw red rid rip row rub rug run sad sat
mark mean meal meat meet mere mile milk mind miss mood moon
paint paper party peace piece place plain plant plate point
if it is, says that, up to, asking you, due us, to make the
who is, the next day, and be, who do not, he will, who will

Sentence Writing

It is in the minds of men that the defenses of peace begin.
Work becomes hard when we begin to worry and fret about it.
If you cannot make light of worries, keep them in the dark.
Just keep examining every low bid quoted for zinc etchings.
Dux Typing Desk No. 7 is 30 inches high and 36 inches long.

A business letter is a good letter when it achieves the result at which | 14
it is aimed.   Unless it collects the bill, answers the question, makes the | 29
adjustment, sells the goods or produces a mental attitude which leads | 43
to a sale, it is not a good letter, no matter how attractive its arrangement | 58
or how perfect its grammar may be.   To be a successful office worker, | 72
rest assured that one of the qualifications you need to develop is the | 86
ability to write business letters and write them in a human, interesting, | 100
and forceful way.   Letters are the shuttles that fly back and forth to | 114
weave the web of commerce.   Remember that the secretary is a secretary | 128
because she has the ability to sit down at her typewriter and compose | 142
letters that will favorably represent her employer to the outside world. | 156
When she writes such letters, she is doing work that is productive. | 169

There is one other highly important aspect of business life, and that | 183
is the personal contact which the employee has with people both in the | 197
office and outside of it.   The human element is an important factor | 210
in all our relations with people.   The successful office person has | 223
developed the ability to get along with other people.   It is safe to say | 237
that personal traits are always more important than the skills you are | 251
learning and which you will use at least as a beginner.   There are | 264
seven traits which are nearly always put at the top of the list by | 277
employers.   Think of those traits as they apply to the secretary. | 290

Accuracy comes first.   The secretary is accurate in everything she | 303
does; she is accurate in the larger aspects of her work, as well as in | 317
the small details.   She checks and rechecks the business data she | 330
receives or which she herself prepares.   She takes nothing for granted; | 344
she makes sure that the job on which she is engaged is done accurately. | 358
If it is a part of her duty to take care of the personal checkbook of her | 373
superior, she does that work accurately.   She makes out the stubs | 386
accurately; she makes all the additions and subtractions accurately; | 400
she writes all the checks accurately; she goes over the paid checks | 413
returned by the bank and then compares the balance shown by the | 426
bank with the balance in the checkbook; she knows how to make | 438
reconciliation of a checking account.   If she also keeps the personal | 452
accounts of her employer, she keeps those accounts accurately.   She | 465
sets up a system by which she can record all figures correctly.   There | 479
is no quality in business that is more important than accuracy.   Business | 494
is a vast web of related transactions.   If an error is made somewhere | 508
along the line, that error will reproduce itself over and over again. | 522
While you are in school, you will do well to put your mind on the job | 536
of working accurately.   Check everything you do before you hand it in. | 550

Technique Improvement

Drill on double letters

bazaar rubber accrue dotted seem suffer baggage roll common
funny wee apply error add butter puzzle cabbage accommodate
keeps stuff egg deer ball grammar annual food appear terror
Harry Massell referred to efficiency in commercial affairs.
The massed troops stood at attention when the staff passed.

Speed Building

Words

Ever since the world began, there have been differences of   12
opinion. You will have to search for a long time before you   24
can discover any subject on which everybody shares the same   36
point of view. One person will have a certain opinion on a   48
subject. Another will see the matter in an entirely different   60
light. There is certainly nothing wrong with a friendly   71
discussion between two persons who hold opposite views on a   83
question. A great deal of harm can be done when the discussion   96
turns into a bitter argument. It has often been said that nobody   109
can win an argument. You may be able to win your point, but   121
there is a good chance that you will lose a friend.   131

Brief Timed Writing

You are bound to dislike anybody who proves to you that you   12
are wrong and that he is right. Remember this point the next   24
time you are tempted to start an argument.   32

Lesson 62

Warm-up Practice

High frequency words and phrases

saw say sea see set sew she sir sit six son sum sun tan tax
more most move must name near next nine none note once only
power press price pride print prior prize prove pupil queer
to do, with those, for others, I shall be able, it will not
that have, let you, to ship the, on time, if it is, in fact

The person who is deceived the worst is the one who deceives himself. 14
Of his own accord he blinds his eyes to the truth. He lives and acts in 28
an aimless way, and then he wonders why others get along better than 42
he. He wonders why other people have so many good friends while 55
he has few or none; he wonders about many other things, but the trouble 69
is that he does not do anything to make matters better for himself. 82
He talks about luck and about knowing the right people and about having 96
a pull, but it never seems to occur to him that push instead of pull may 110
be the right answer for him. Many men and women who have won 122
success in life had no influential friends to smooth the way for them. 136
They came up the hard way. By the force of character, by absolute 149
honesty, by genuine sincerity, by their willingness to shoulder their own 164
burdens, they won the respect and the esteem of other people. 176

If you want people to think well of you, go to work on the 188
problem. Make yourself pleasant and agreeable; most people have so 201
many troubles of their own that they do not want to hear about the 214
troubles that somebody else has. If you want to stand higher in your 228
class and prepare yourself better for the future, go to work. If, when 242
you are employed in an office, you want a better position and wider 255
opportunities, go to work and keep on working. You dare not allow 268
every little interruption to distract you from the work to which you have 283
set your mind and hands. You have a job to do; you may say to yourself 297
that you do not feel quite up to it today and that you will put it off 311
until tomorrow when you will feel more like doing the job. If so, 324
what you are really doing is pretending; you are just deceiving yourself. 339

To know and to do are two different things. The fact that a person 352
knows what is right does not at all mean that he will do what is right. 366
To do the right thing, he must bring his will power into play; he must 380
compel himself to do the thing which he knows is right; he must refuse 394
to be swerved from the course on which he is embarked. He must 407
understand that anybody who tries to keep him from his work is not 420
his friend, but his enemy. 425

If you really intend to go to work, there is no better place than right 439
where you are; if you do not intend to go to work, you cannot get along 453
anywhere. Going from one place to another will do you no good. 466
Remember that other pastures always seem greener than the familiar 479
home pasture. The trouble is that the average person does not stop 492
to realize all the toil and labor to which the other fellow subjected 506
himself to make his pasture green. The thing to do is to work hard 519
at the task which confronts you right now. 527

Sentence Writing

Remember each day that the only way you can get is to give.
A genuine sense of humor is to life what oil is to a motor.
An ounce of loyalty weighs more than a pound of cleverness.
Jeb quickly drove a few extra miles on the glazed pavement.
Each typist should know the ASTERISK (*) and AMPERSAND (&).

Technique Improvement

Drill on double letters

nabbed accompany added keen suffice struggle call recommend
tonnage maroon oppressed berry press chatter vacuum drizzle
incessant platter muzzle ribbon according peddle seek stuff
The raccoon was bagged and hurriedly dropped into the coop.
I called to offer an attractive cottage for immediate sale.

Speed Building

	Words
The best way to see the point of view of another is to put	12
yourself in his shoes. Many times you will see a friend do	24
something that seems to you to be entirely incorrect. A fellow	37
worker may make a statement that you know is false. You	48
will be tempted at once to tell your friend that he is wrong. It	61
is natural for you to react in that way. Before you do so,	73
however, think a little bit about the other man. Keep in mind	85
that he thinks that whatever he is doing or whatever he is saying	98
is perfectly all right. Try to decide in your own mind the reason	111
for his action. Make a determined effort to understand why he	123
talks as he does. When you have looked at the matter from	135
the point of view of the other person, you will often find the	147
key to his behavior. It is easy to get along with other people	160
when you look for the good in them.	167

Brief Timed Writing

When you try your best to find good in others, you will soon	12
notice that they are also trying to find good in you. It takes	25
only a little effort to get people on your side.	35

No. 16

The third aspect of the individual word to which you need to pay   13
attention is its correct division at the end of a line. There are rules   27
for the division of words which you should master; for instance, you   40
should know that it is always wrong to divide a word in such a way   53
that only one letter comes at the end of a line. The basic rule to   66
remember is that a word may be divided only after a syllable. Unless   80
you are sure about the syllables that make up the word, the only thing to   95
do is to go to the dictionary to find out what the syllables are.   108

All the time and effort you put on learning how to spell words correctly,   123
when to use capitals to begin words, and how to divide words at the   136
end of lines will repay you well. When you have really mastered   149
these aspects of words, your work will stand out above the work   162
produced by the average employee who has not acquired such a mastery.   176

The purpose of all the material you typewrite is to convey thought to   190
someone. That thought is conveyed by means of the orderly and correct   204
arrangement of words in sentences. Not only must the words themselves   218
be correctly spelled and in correct order, but they must also be set off   232
by punctuation marks in such a way that the reader can take in the   245
thought of the sentences as he reads along. Suppose that this page   258
had no periods or other punctuation marks. All the words could be   271
correctly spelled, but the sentences would not make sense. The reader   285
would have to puzzle out the meaning of what he is reading, and he   298
would have a hard time doing so. You surely realize how extremely   311
important it is for you to master the principles that underlie correct   325
punctuation. It is simply not true that everyone punctuates according   339
to his own taste or feeling at the time; on the contrary, there are definite   354
rules which have been set up and which, when they are followed and   367
applied, set off words in sentences in such a way that the meaning of   381
each sentence becomes clear.   387

It is also the responsibility of the stenographer to make sure that   400
the words in a sentence harmonize with one another and that the rules   414
of grammar are applied so that the correct forms of words are used.   427
You have learned that a sentence which has a singular noun as its   440
subject must also have a singular verb for its predicate. It often   453
happens that a singular subject is followed by a phrase that contains   467
one or more plural nouns; in such a sentence an error is often made   480
because a plural predicate is typed. Your employer is intent on the   494
thought; he expects his stenographer to catch up errors he makes in   507
dictation. He also expects her to use the apostrophe correctly in words   521
that call for the use of that much abused and often misused mark.   534

Lesson 63

Warm-up Practice

High frequency words and phrases

ten the ton too top try two use was way who why win yes you
open ours over paid part pass plea poor pull quit rate real
quick quiet quite quote radio raise reach ready refer reply
to give, it was, of the, it was not, more than, there would
as large as, from this, with that, how much, from us, it is

Sentence Writing

Talent tells us what to do, but tact shows us how to do it.
No man can try to aid another without also helping himself.
The desire to get the maximum work out of yourself is rare.
Too few office workers stop to realize their opportunities.
West quickly gave Bert handsome prizes for six juicy plums.
The Mack Company's address is 1827 (<u>not</u> 1872) Queen Street.

Technique Improvement

Balanced-hand drills   Two-letter and three-letter words   Phrases and sentences

to by am ye me us go an so he it of do to am or if is so me
woe rod got urn pan lap eye tub air hay jam ken for sit man
to do so if it is of the but it is and or end of the did or
Tie the end of the fur rug to the cot and pay Doris for it.
Sid or she may fix the cut map and lay it by a big oak box.

Speed Building

	Words
It has often been said that no man can hope to master others	12
until he has learned how to master himself. Before a person	24
can inspire and lead others, he must be the master of his own	36
emotions. There is no emotion that is stronger than fear. A	48
person who enters sales work learns right at the start that he	60

Problem 11. Type this tabulation with 10-space margins on a sheet of plain paper.

Double-space. Leave an extra line between the subheading and the top line of the column headings. Single-space the two-line column headings.

Plan your work so that the dollar sign at the top of a column lines up with the dollar sign in the column total.

Use the current year date for *19 - -* in the subheading and in the heading of the fourth column.

COMMON STOCK
HOLDINGS
December 31, 19--

Shares	Name of Stock	Market Value	19- Dividends
70	Appleton Electric	$ 5,987.50	$ 329.31
125	Cranton Power and Light	13,750.00	825.00
80	Custer Gas and Light	8,400.00	483.00
220	El Monte Light	16,115.00	1,007.19
35	Grant Electric Power	3,198.75	223.91
110	Hudson Utilities	6,022.50	270.01
540	Kennebec Power	56,700.00	3,402.00
75	Le Grand Electric	6,093.75	304.69
50	Meade Gas and Light	6,325.00	347.88
460	Riverside Electric	32,200.00	1,851.50
		$148,698.75	$8,739.80
		$154,792.50	$9,044.49

214

must find out how to conquer his fear. If a salesman is gripped   73
by fear as he enters the office of his prospect, he will not be able   87
to do much of a selling job. The timid person who is afraid to   100
move ahead boldly cannot hope to get far in business. He is   112
doomed to failure from the start. You will find that faith will   125
help you to conquer fear. Have faith in yourself, and others   137
will have faith in you. Believe in yourself, and others will   149
believe in you. Force yourself to do over and over again the   161
things you are afraid to do. Remember that fear will not   172
disappear of its own accord; you have to take positive steps to   185
shake yourself loose from its grip. That effort, painful as it   198
may be at the time, will reward you handsomely.   207

Brief Timed Writing

Words

Will power is the strongest force that you can use in the   11
conquest of fear. No one has ever been able to overcome fear   23
by dodging the things he is afraid of.   31

Lesson 64

Warm-up Practice

High frequency words and phrases

rent rise rush safe said same seem seen send sent shop show
right river rough round route scale scene score sense serve
accept advice advise almost always answer around attach too
you might be, since then, you will, we shall be glad, on us
you can see, please send, to ask us to get the, than others

Sentence Writing

Good service to the public produces good will for business.
You cannot hold down another unless you stay down with him.
It has been proved that anger causes a poisonous condition.
All questions asked by five watch experts amazed the judge.
"Angel-blues" (@ $9.80 a set) are on sale at Tabb's--today.

Problem 10. When you type a tabulation from a penwritten rough draft, be especially careful in finding the longest line of each column. Remember to include punctuation marks and spaces between words in your count.

Type this tabulation with double spacing on a sheet of plain paper. Triple-space below the second line of the heading. Leave five spaces between the first and second columns and five spaces between the second and third columns. In typing the first column, line up the figures at the right.

This tabulation contains all the letters of the alphabet and all the figures.

ITINERARY FOR JUNE 19--
Mr. Gilbert R. Wayne

Date	Hotel	City
1	State Hotel	Columbus, Ohio
2-5	Hotel Lincoln	Frankfort, Kentucky
6-8	Hoosier Hotel	Evansville, Indiana
9	Hotel Robinson	Cairo, Illinois
10	The Wayside Inn	Memphis, Tennessee
11-19	Hotel Dixie	Shreveport, Louisiana
20-21	Southern Hotel	Dallas, Texas
22	Park Plaza Hotel	Fort Worth, Texas
23	Hotel Franklin	Tulsa, Oklahoma
24-27	St. James Hotel	Wichita, Kansas
28	Mesa Hotel	Pueblo, Colorado
29	James Madison Hotel	Denver, Colorado
30	Queen City Hotel	Cheyenne, Wyoming

Technique Improvement

Balanced-hand drills   Four-letter words

quay idle wish oaks rock pelf tick hair auto jams sign kale

duty land bush name firm make girl isle corn lend soap melt

they held when paid kept with turn down rush them idle land

Ruth paid them for the auto soap and then kept the big rug.

An heir of the clan held lake land rich with coal and rock.

Speed Building

	Words
Set up for yourself a high standard of accuracy. Before you	12
turn in a piece of work that you have finished, take just a few	25
extra moments to check it quickly to make sure that no errors	37
appear. The worker who is always making mistakes and has	48
to be asked to correct errors makes a poor impression on the	60
employer. When an error is found in your work, do not try to	72
think of an alibi or attempt to put the blame on some other	84
person. It is far better to accept the blame and admit that the	97
mistake is yours. At the same time you should make up your	109
mind that you will not repeat that mistake. A wise man once	121
said that success does not depend on never making a mistake,	133
but on not making the same mistake more than once. When	144
you are not sure whether some detail of your work is correct	156
and you are not able to find the answer yourself, do not hesitate	169
to seek the aid of someone else who can help you solve your	181
problem. Most people are glad to be helpful.	190

Brief Timed Writing

It is better to make sure that what you are doing is right than	13
it is to guess and then to hope that you have guessed correctly.	26
Only in that way can you keep down errors.	34

Extra Credit. If your instructor asks you to do so, type the following paragraph twice with single spacing. Space twice after the first writing. The paragraph contains all the letters of the alphabet.

An amazingly small bit of extra effort will help you to catch	12
errors that would be adequate cause for the rejection of your	24
work. Careful checking pays dividends.	32

Problem 9. (Form 7-9). This letter is to be typed on an executive-size letterhead. Trim the form in your workbook to the indicated size before you start.

Center today's date. Use the semiblock letter style with mixed punctuation. Type the letter to a line length of $4\frac{1}{2}$ inches. Single-space.

Use the following inside address—typed *below* the body of the letter.

```
Dr. J. Benjamin Collins
Wesley Memorial Hospital
Lake Avenue at 134th Street
Chicago, Illinois    60613
```

Dear Dr. Collins:

I had to leave promptly at the close of ~~the~~ today's meeting, ~~and therefore missed.~~ Thus I missed the pleasure of telling you in person how helpful and how inspiring ∧I found your report. ~~was for me.~~

I have had two occasions ∧recently to use the Carter technique. The patients' response in each case coincided with your own findings. If the ∧clinical records of these cases will be helpful to you in preparing ∧the ~~your~~ report you mentioned, I shall gladly send ~~them to~~ you copies.

You are doing your fellow ~~doctors~~ surgeons an important service. Carter's methods aren't ∧by no means ~~nearly~~ so widely used as they should be.

Cordially yours,

212

Lesson 65

Warm-up Practice

High frequency words and phrases

side size sold some soon sort spot stay step stop sure tell
seven shall share short since sixty small solid sorry space
become before better borrow bother bought change charge our
in the, to this, you are, it will be, has done, that is the
some of, at that time, you could have, no doubt, to be able

Sentence Writing

Burt stated that it is better to wear out than to rust out.
By going to the bottom of things, you may well land on top.
The idea that there is joy in work has been proved by many.
My request for five extra pages was authorized by Jan Lock.
Please ship at once 95 Stock No. 840 and 731 Stock No. 629.

Technique Improvement

Balanced-hand drills   Words of five or more strokes

snake ivory endow prism robot kayak their slept audit laugh
spend neigh digit prowl fight usury chair penal visit bugle
amend turkey antitoxic neighbor enchant profit forms mantle
An authentic map of the island is burnt by the giant flame.
He kept the ancient bicycle by the field of their neighbor.

Speed Building

	Words
It has often been said that time is money. The waste of time	12
means the waste of dollars and cents. Every business employer	24
knows that the office worker who wastes time is also wasting	36
money. People who are always asking others to answer	47
unnecessary questions are guilty of double waste. They waste	59

Problem 8. Sometimes you will be asked in business to make a copy of an incoming letter. If the letter you are to copy is typed, you may follow exactly the placement plan of the original. If, on the other hand, the letter is handwritten, plan the placement of your typed copy just as though you were writing the letter for the first time.

Make a COPY of this letter on a sheet of plain paper. Double-space. Type the letter in the indented style to a line length of five inches. Show the current year date instead of 19--.

Type the word COPY prominently in the center of the top margin. Most offices prefer to have the word spaced out and typed diagonally, thus:

C

O

P

Y

Type /s/ before the signed name to show how the signature appears on the original, thus:

Sincerely yours,

/s/ Elizabeth Mallory

(Mrs. Hugh G. Mallory)

28 Memorial Avenue
Frederick, Maryland 21701
March 14, 19--

Webster Mail Order Company
360 North Exeter Avenue
Jamaica, New York   11426

Gentlemen:

On February 19 I mailed you my order for one electric percolator (Stock no. 7194) and enclosed a check for $19.25. You sent me a card to say that the percolator would be shipped promptly.

It has now been more than three weeks since I placed my order, but the percolator has not come. Is it possible that my order has been overlooked?

Sincerely yours,
Elizabeth Mallory
(Mrs. Hugh G. Mallory)

their own time, and they also waste the time of those who are 71
called on to give the answers.   Before you take the time to ask 84
a question, try first to figure out the answer for yourself.   If 97
you cannot solve the problem alone, then it is surely all right 110
to get the help of another person.   You should always keep in 122
mind the fact that the time you spend in the office does not 134
belong to you.   It is really the property of your employer.   The 147
writing of personal letters and the making of telephone calls to 160
your friends should be left for the hours when you are away from 173
your office desk.   Efficient office workers try to cut the waste 186
of time.   They know that every minute has a cash value. 197

Brief Timed Writing

Words

Time is wasted when a piece of work has to be done twice   11
because the job was not done right the first time.   It is a good 24
rule to make sure that you are right and then go ahead. 35

Lesson 66

Warm-up Practice

High frequency words and phrases

than that them then they this thus took true upon very want
speak spend stamp stand start state still stood style teach
clever cotton county credit damage decide depend desire you
you will be, at any time, thank you, and it has, if you had
can give you, is to be, less than, who may be, he will need

Sentence Writing

Ideals are like stars; you cannot touch them with the hand.
We have obtained judgment against the debtor for the claim.
Friendship is the cement that can hold this world together.
Jay visited back home and gazed upon a brown fox and quail.
The quotation is $759.47, with a trade discount of 33 1/3%.

Problem 7. Type this page of PACKING AND SHIPPING INSTRUC-
TIONS on a sheet of plain paper. Make all changes and corrections indicated.
Use a 6-inch line.

This sheet of instructions contains all the letters of the alphabet.

¶ *Never show prices on any packing slip or shipping list.*

PACKAGING AND SHIPPING INSTRUCTIONS

for shipments to

Monarch Trading Company

~~Packaging~~   *How To Pack*

Numbering ~~of Packages~~

Number the cartons, cases, or other containers for each
~~individual~~ shipment in a single series starting with 1.   Show
our order number on *the outside of* each container.

Record of Contents

similar   Include in each carton or case a packing slip to show an
itemized list of contents.   No packing slip is required for
crates or ~~other~~ containers which *permit the contents to be* ~~contain merchandise that is~~
easily visible. *for each shipment.*

¶ Prepare *l.c.* A shipping list ~~must accompany the first container.~~ Put
sturdy the list in a ~~sealed~~ envelope.   Attach ~~it~~ firmly to the outside of ~~the~~ container *the envelope*.   Such list will show (a) the number of
separate pieces in the entire shipment ~~and~~ (b) the contents
of each container in the entire shipment *, and (c) our purchase order number.*   *number 1.*

~~Shipping~~

Method of Shipping *exact*   *How To Ship*

Use ~~only~~ the *exact* shipping method specified on our purchase
order.   You are authorized to change the transportation line
when necessary to give improved service.   The line ~~shown~~ *named* on
our purchase order is suggested--not required.   You may not,
however, change from air to rail or motor, from rail to motor or air, or from motor to rail or air without our written
authorization.

"Rush" Shipments
Make shipment of orders marked "Rush--Fastest Way" by
motor express, railway express, or parcel post--whichever, *tr.*
in your judgment, is best.   Do not use air freight ~~or~~ air
express without our definite authorization.

, or special delivery

210

Technique Improvement

Drills on one-hand words of two and three letters

we you at ill as pin be ply wet up eat in tax on few my beg
bet ink vex oil car pin get hum far lip sad hip art hop tea
ax are fat tab lo see him no add pi bar mop cat was saw nip
As you see, Burt was in my red car as John ate at West Inn.
As Jo was ill far at sea, we saw Jim get oil on my red car.

Speed Building

	Words
Soon after you start work in an office, you will find that you	12
are learning many things about the business which should be	24
kept secret and not passed along to people on the outside. The	37
best way for you to show your loyalty to your employer is to	49
work at all times with the interests of your company firmly fixed	62
in your mind. You will be working for your company when you	74
keep business secrets to yourself. Every now and then you may	86
be tempted to discuss business affairs with your friends. You	98
will find that the wise course is to avoid all talk of business	111
matters outside of the office. You should be just as careful in	124
your talk with other people who are working with you in the	136
same office. Let us suppose that you have a position in the	148
personnel department. Through your everyday work you learn	160
many facts about those who work with you. You will find out	172
which ones are in line for salary raises and which ones are to	184
get promotions. Such matters should never be made the subject	196
for office gossip. The best way to make sure that secrets are	208
not told is to resolve that you will use care when you talk about	221
any business matters. If you hope to advance in the company	233
for which you are working, you will have to prove to the	244
executives of that company that they can safely confide in you.	257

Brief Timed Writing

	Words
In your work you will get to know many facts that others do	12
not know and which they have no right to know. As a loyal	24
employee, you owe your company the duty to keep such matters	36
confidential and never discuss them with anyone.	46

Problem 6. Type this VACATION SCHEDULE with double spacing. Triple-space after the main heading. Plan the tabulation carefully before you start to type.

VACATION SCHEDULE

Name of Employee	No. of Weeks	First Week Starts	Second Week Starts	Third Week Starts
Carter, A.	2	July 20	July 27	
⅂ϲrowell, [D. L.]	1	August 17		
#Donnelly, K. H.	3	June 1	June 8	August 24
#Elliott, C. R. ~~Eliot, M. J.~~	2 ~~1~~	June 8 ~~July 27~~	August 3	
Erdman, W.	2	July 6	July 13	
Gardner, B. T.	2 ③	July 20	July 27	
Glover, E. E.	2	June 15	August 3	August 10
Jacobson, T. D.	3	July 13	July 20	August 3
~~2 Johnstone, I. R.~~	~~1~~	~~July 27~~		
Justice, O. L.	2	July 6	June 29 tr.	
Leonard, H. K.	1	August 10		
Plummer, V.	2	August 17	August 24	
Saunders, J. Y.	2	July 6	July 13	
Schaefer, N. S.	1	June 1		
Shaffrey, T.	1	August 24		
Wheeler, A. W.	3	June 15	June 22	June 29
Wooda, R. M.	1	October 5		

Lesson 67

Warm-up Practice

High frequency words and phrases

wear week well were what when whom will with word work your
thank there thing think three truth under usual wages would
detail direct dollar eleven enable finish follow forced out
we shall send, I do not, if this is, let us know, this time
he may, who have been, for the past, will be able, few days

Sentence Writing

We should all be more interested in giving than in getting.
Some people confuse freedom to work with freedom from work.
No matter what kind of work you do, take pride in doing it.
We have just quoted on nine dozen boxes of gray lamp wicks.
Send $374.95 to Room 741, 867 Gray Street, Cleveland, Ohio.

Technique Improvement

Drills on one-hand words

were yolk exert union regard homonym tease monopoly greater
noon vacate pump carve kill barber hymn feats loop reversed
look fact pull rate milk scatter jump aggregate lymph exact
We stared as you scattered better cabbage seeds on my hill.
A jump in taxes assessed on car greases affects my garages.

Speed Building

	Words
After you have started your work in a business office, you will	13
soon learn that the progress you make will depend on your own	25
efforts. There are some people who say that nobody can get	37
ahead unless he knows the right people. Pay no attention to	49
such talk about luck or influence. If you will study the careers	62
of those who hold top positions in business, you will soon find	75

Problem 5. (Form 7-5). Type this letter with the changes and corrections indicated. Use the date shown (this year). Type your initials for those of the typist.

COLERIDGE'S, INC.

Fine Groceries - Party Delicacies

Delivery Service

5 KING STREET • LONG BEACH, CALIFORNIA 90805

March 18, 19--

Attention of Accounting Department
J. Hudson Wallace and Sons, Inc.
2360 North Belvedere Avenue
San Francisco, California 94117

Gentlemen

Your statement dated March 15, which we have just received, shows a balance due of $1,351.55. That amount is $373.29 higher than the balance shown on our own records.

It may be that we have misplaced some of your invoices. So far, however, we have been unable to find purchase orders to account for the difference.

The difference of $373.92 consists of the total of four invoices for which we have no record. Here are the invoice numbers and amounts.

Invoice	Amount
R-742	126.90
R-805	73.10
R-816	14.58
R-927	151.60

In case these invoices do cover shipments made to us, please mail us duplicates. Show our purchase order number, please, on each invoice.

Meantime, it is a pleasure to enclose our check for $978.26. *Please credit our account* with this letter *as indicated on the voucher stub of the check.*

Very truly yours,

COLERIDGE'S, Inc.

Office Manager

BMR/ty

Enclosure

that ability and skill are the factors that make for success. 87
There is no use in trying to find a short cut or an easy way. 99

You will show your employer that you have a real interest in 111
your work when you report to the office on time each day and 123
when you show that you are willing to work overtime in order 135
to get an important piece of work completed. Businessmen are 147
also quick to notice the employee who goes ahead with an 158
assignment on his own without waiting for someone else to 169
tell him what to do. A person who takes on added duties 180
usually finds that he will have extra dollars in his pay envelope. 193

Business is also willing to reward a worker who tries to find 205
a new and better way to complete a job. Look beyond the 216
routine and try to think of a more efficient way to do any task. 229

Brief Timed Writing

Words

It is an easy matter to keep right on doing a certain piece of 12
work in the same old way. The worker who wins the favor of 24
the employer is the one who is always looking for a better 36
method of doing the work that needs to be done. 45

Extra Credit. If your instructor asks you to do so, type the following copy twice with single spacing. Double-space after each paragraph. Each of the paragraphs contains all the letters of the alphabet.

No business lasts long unless it renders a service for which 12
people are willing to pay. It is equally true that no employer 25
will hire you to work for him merely because he is dazzled by 37
your charm. Although he will expect you to have an attractive 49
personality, he is going to be primarily interested in what you 62
can do and how well you can do it. You cannot expect him to 74
contract to pay you a regular salary unless he feels that your 86
services will justify the cost to him. 94

Your general attitude during an interview will, of course, be 106
taken into account by the person who talks with you. Other 118
things being equal, he will not be eager to select you for the job 131
if you impress him as being lazy, slovenly, and indifferent. No 144
matter how expert you are, your talents are worthless in 155
business unless you are willing to use them and unless you have 168
the personality to get along easily with other people. 179

Problem 4. (Form 7-4). Type this letter with the changes and corrections indicated. Use the date shown (this year). Type your initials for those of the typist.

HEFFLIN BROTHERS

700 NORTH WASHINGTON STREET
PROVIDENCE, RHODE ISLAND   02907

April 3, 19--

Mr. Hugh B. Clemson, Pres*ident*
Clemson & Livingstone, Inc.
Oxford and Wells Sts.*reets*
Waterbury, Connecticut   06708

Dear Mr. Clemson *:*

(the midst of) You're in a busy season, and I know how quickly the days *(work)* rush by when each one of them is packed with ~~activity.~~ I hope, therefore, that you won't object to a friendly reminder about *(payment)* the plan you outlined in your letter of February 19.

You wrote:

(No)
"I am enclosing our Order #621 for some more *l.c.* Spring stock. You will also find with this letter *tr.* our check for $280.30 to apply against the amount of your Invoice No. R-7092. Our check for the balance will be mailed by March 1.

(s)
"May we have your permission to follow a similar payment plan for our new order? We would make a partial payment within one month of your invoice date and send the balance in two more weeks."

No ¶ The partial payment for the stock shipped on your new order, however, has not yet come. ~~It may be that~~ your check is now in the mail. If not, we'll appreciate your using ~~this~~ envelope to send it to us today.

(the enclosed stamped)

Sincerely yours, *¶ Your check for the balance due on the older invoice was received all right.*

HEFFLIN BROTHERS

Ray W. Rossiter
Credit Manager

ty

Enclosure   *¶ Perhaps*

207

Lesson 68
Spacing With Punctuation Marks

Line of 60 spaces. Set left margin stop.
Type each line twice with single spacing.
Space twice after each 2-line group.

Preliminary Drill

All these words are balanced-hand words. *Keep your eyes on the copy.*

```
aid also am apt audit auto bid big bit blame body both burn
bush busy but by chair city coal corn did dish do dog docks
due dug duty eight element end entitle eye field fight firm
fish flame fog for formal fuel fur girl goals got gown hair
```

Spacing With Punctuation Marks

You need to form the habit of spacing correctly with punctuation marks. Each of the numbered paragraphs in this Lesson and in Lessons 69 and 70 gives a rule. The *typewritten* sentences illustrate the rule. Write the typewritten sentences according to the directions given at the top of the pages.

1. Space twice after a period that ends a sentence.

```
Both men work.  They kept busy.  They did their civic duty.
```

2. Space twice after a question mark that ends a sentence.

```
May I aid them?  Is she to blame?  May they make the audit?
```

3. Space twice after an exclamation point that ends a sentence.

```
What a handy key that is!  Oh, how the anthem enchanted me!
```

4. Space once after a period following an abbreviation when the abbreviation comes inside a sentence.
```
Mr. C. W. West and Mr. Charles R. Boynton are the partners.
```

5. When an abbreviation comes at the end of a sentence that would also end with a period, space twice after the period. Type just *one* period.
```
See Mr. C. B. King, Jr.  His attorney is R. A. Butler, Esq.
```

6. The title *Miss* and the contractions *1st, 2nd, 3rd, 4th, 10th,* etc. are not abbreviations and hence should not have periods.
```
Mr. Wise expects Miss Nelson to arrive by the 7th of March.
```

7. Do not space after the first period in the abbreviations *a.m.* and *p.m.* When you use the abbreviations *A. M.* and *P. M.* (capital letters), space after the first period. Of course, you will always space after the second period in these abbreviations—*once* if the abbreviation stands inside a sentence and *twice* if the abbreviation comes at the end of the sentence.
```
My train finally arrived at 2:30 a.m.  Frank waited for me.
```

Problem 3. (Form 7-3). Type this letter in correct form on the letterhead provided in your Workbook. Use the date shown (current year). Type your initials for those of the typist.

BOND PAINT COMPANY

1643 LAUREL STREET - ERIE, PENNSYLVANIA 16505

center] October 15th, 19--

ter
tr. Mr. Leslie T. Mac Clure
Premeir Supply Company
98 South Commerce Street
Youngstown, Ohio   44507

Dear Mr. McClure: *(a)*

Thank you for your letter. *We appreciate your* ~~You did exactly~~ ~~the right thing in~~ telling us about the complaint you received from one of your good customers.

? Would you like to give us your customers' name *tr.* and address ~~and have us~~ write directly to him? ~~We~~ ~~shall be glad to do so~~ and ~~to~~ mail you copies of ~~all~~ correspondence.   *We'll gladly*

the Most complaints, we find, result from users' disregard of the definite instructions ~~that appear~~ on the label. Each Bond product is manufactured to do a specific job. When that product is used in *tr.* any other way than the way definitely outlined on the label, trouble often develops.   *printed* *ve*

¶ *Does* ~~Please find out whether~~ your customer has some of the paint left from the job that turned out so poorly. If he will send us part of a can, we'll have a chemical analysis made. Ask him to ship by express collect and to address the shipment to me.

¶ *Please find out* ~~Do you happen to know~~ whether your customer used this BOND paint on a new surface or on ~~one~~ that had not been previously treated or painted.   *a surface*

Sincerely Yours,

BOND PAINT COMPANY

l.c.:

Jefferson H. Flynn
Dealer service division

ty

Lesson 69
Spacing With Punctuation Marks

Preliminary Drill

All these words are balanced-hand words. *Keep your eyes on the copy.*

half ham handy handle hang hay he height held hen if is ivy
kept key laid lake land laugh lay lend make man map may men
pans pane panels pays pen penalty problem proficient profit
rich rid right rigid risks roams rock rod row rub rye shake

Spacing With Punctuation Marks

8. In typing sentences, space once after the comma and after the semicolon.

If Mr. Coe will come, May, John, and Joseph will come also.
Keep your eyes on your copy; do not look up; type smoothly.

9. Do not space *after* the opening quotation marks or *before* the closing quotation marks. Space once *after* the closing quotation marks when the quotation stands inside the sentence.

Remember that "ounce of loyalty" which Mr. Lake emphasized.

10. The comma and the period are typed *inside* the quotation marks. The semicolon is placed *outside* the quotation marks.

"Show the men," said Mr. Kurtz, "how they will save money."
I said, "To save time is to lengthen life." Do you agree?
I told her, "This machine saves money"; she agreed with me.

11. If the quotation is a question or an exclamation, type the question mark or the exclamation point before *(inside)* the quotation marks.

Miss Berkley asked them, "Do you know what happened there?"
The goal is surely not to get you to exclaim, "How clever!"

12. If the entire sentence that ends with a quotation is a question or an exclamation, type the question mark or the exclamation point *outside* the quotation marks.

Do you know the maxim, "The dawn always follows the night"?
What an inspiration it is to study your "Ideas and Ideals"!

13. If the entire sentence that is a question ends with a quotation that is also a question, type just one question mark—outside the quotation marks.

Was it they who asked, "What are the dates of the meeting"?

Problem 2. Type this bulletin board announcement in correct form on an 8½ by 11 sheet of plain paper. Use a line length of six inches.

Single-space the paragraphs. Double-space after each heading and after each paragraph. Use a 5-space paragraph indention.

Leave a two-inch top margin.

center] MAKE YOUR IDEAS PAY ~~OFF~~

Can you tell us how we can do a better job? Can you suggest a way to improve ~~some phase~~ *any part* of our operations? Put ~~down~~ your idea on paper and drop it in the suggestion box. You may be in line for extra dollars. @

already Employees have received more than $38,000 in cash for suggestions that we could use. There's ~~plenty~~ more money *to* waiting for men and women ~~who can suggest ways in which we~~ ~~can improve.~~ *with new ideas.*

. New Employees Are Eligible
¶ *Everybody is eligible.* ~~You don't have to be an "old-timer" to enter your sug-~~ ~~gestion.~~ Bill Rush in Maintenance came up with a suggestion *during his first week* that paid him $75.

How To ~~Write Up~~ Your Suggestion *Submit*
put Just ~~give us~~ your idea in your own words. ~~Remember that~~ it's the suggestion--not fancy wording--that counts. Use any size paper. Use either pen or pencil. ~~Be sure, though,~~ to give your full name, your department, and your badge number or ~~your~~ employee number.
stet

You'll Get A Report
tr. Five executives will study your suggestion. If they can not adopt your idea, they'll tell you why.

Keep Trying
l.c. *in Plant A* Last year LeRoy Stoneleigh submitted eight suggestions before one was adopted, but that single idea brought him a check for $125.

No ¶ Laura Bancroft in Accounting gave us seventeen sugges- tions and scored with five. Those five ~~of her~~ ideas earned her a total of $360.

Lesson 70
Spacing With Punctuation Marks

Line of 60 spaces. Set left margin stop
Type each line twice with single spacing.
Space twice after each 2-line group.

Preliminary Drill

All these words are balanced-hand words. *Keep your eyes on the copy.*

```
shape she shelf shield shrub sick sight sign signal sir sit
six slang slap snake snap so soak soap social sow span such
sue suspend than the their them then theory they throw tidy
tight title to town turkey turn usual visit when wish works
```

Spacing With Punctuation Marks

14. Space twice after the colon except when it is used between figures that mean *hours* and *minutes.*

```
The telegram reads thus:  "Ship Order No. 851 at 7:30 a.m."
```

15. Do not space before or after the hyphen that comes inside a word.

```
Your 24-page booklet, "Bay Products," is a first-class job.
```

16. The *formal* dash is typed with two hyphens—no space before the first hyphen or after the second hyphen. The *informal* dash is typed with a single hyphen with one space before and one space after that hyphen.

```
Three of our men--Weston, Parker, and Jamison--will attend.
Both filing methods - alphabetic and geographic - are used.
```

17. Space before (but not after) the left parenthesis mark. Space after (but not before) the right parenthesis mark.

```
Just fill in this form (no postage needed) and mail it now.
```

18. Space before and after the ampersand (&).

```
Mr. Post is the senior member of the firm of Frank & Kagel.
```

19. Do not space between the number sign (#) and the number with which it is used. The number sign used *after* a number means *pounds.*

```
Please ship by fast express 841 Stock #285 to Kretz & Land.
These three cartons weigh 74#, 86#, and 128#, respectively.
```

20. Do not space between the dollar sign and the number with which it is used.

```
The total estimate is $37,500.  She made a deposit of $500.
```

21. Do not space between the per cent sign (%) and the number with which it is used.

```
The discounts from the catalog prices are 20%, 10%, and 5%.
```

22. Type made fractions without a space before or after the diagonal (/). When you type a made fraction with a whole number, space after the whole number.

```
Walter is to multiply 446 7/8 by 19; then divide by 18 5/7.
```

Division Seven—Rough Drafts

Any handwritten copy or any typed copy that has been changed or corrected in longhand is called a *rough draft.* This Division will give you practice in typing from rough drafts. First, however, you must become thoroughly familiar with the standard marks used to indicate changes and corrections.

Mark	Meaning	Example	Example Corrected
⌗	Leave space	S O LD ⌗	S O L D
◡	Close up	GRO CERY	GROCERY
l.c.	Change to lower case (small) letter	Lease	lease
☰	Change to capital letter	corner	Corner
¶	Start new paragraph	¶ Priced	
∧	Insert	quick ⓒ	quick
		including (modern) fixtures	including modern fixtures
ℛ	Remove	ℛ excellent merchandise	merchandise
No ¶	Eliminate paragraph separation	No ¶ Now	
stet	Keep; disregard mark to remove	business a week	business a week
tr.	Transpose	Busniess	Business
		quickly expand	expand quickly
[	Move to left	[by progressive man	
]	Move to right	]WALDRON	

Problem 1. Type in correct form the following copy for a newspaper ad. Use an 8½ by 11 sheet of plain paper. Center your work on the sheet. Double-space. The examples given above come from this problem.

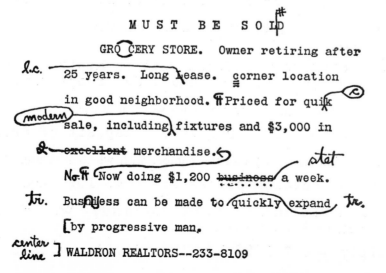

Division Four

Type the drill paragraphs on this page and on the following two pages and the five pages of timed writing articles (pages 107 to 111 inclusive) as your teacher directs. Special drill paragraphs are provided at the beginning of Divisions 4 to 10 inclusive, and timed writing articles are given at the end of Divisions 4 to 9 inclusive.

Paragraph Typing A

Many of the words in these paragraphs are balanced-hand words.

Words

1 When ancient men had an arithmetic problem that had to be figured out, they used the fingers. Each digit on their left hand and on their right hand represented a number from one to ten. If the problem they had to handle was complex, they got aid from a neighbor or a visitor to their own hut.

11
23
35
47
59

2 The fingers of the neighbors and visitors provided the extra digits required for counting big amounts. Units were counted on the fingers of the first person. The fingers of a second person were used for tens. Hundreds were recorded by a third man. Thus did ancient men solve their problems.

11 70
23 82
35 94
47 106
59 118

3 Oriental people taught the world another system. Each digit of the hand was used for a unit. Smooth pebbles were used to count tens. When the problem included hundreds, it was the usual custom to employ a quantity of big rocks. It was later on that the Chinese used sets of knotted strings.

11 129
23 141
35 153
47 165
59 177

4 Rich and busy merchants of the Orient also made use of another handy device. They solved any usual problem with a series of rods on which were sliding beads. The calculator was kept right on the nearest shelf. This figuring aid was the earliest form of the abacus made by the ancient Romans.

11 188
23 200
35 212
47 224
59 236

5 The work of the Romans gave us another early theory of calculating. They spread sand on a flat board and laid out on the panel a field of squares. A rock or some other kind of token was placed in a block as the sign of such-and-such a value. The checkerboard plan was later found in England.

11 247
23 259
35 271
47 283
59 295

Paragraph Typing C

These paragraphs contain many figures, symbols, and capital letters.

1   It was in 1867 that Alaska, the 49th state, was bought from Russia. Congress authorized Secretary of State Seward to invest $7,200,000 to purchase this frozen peninsula. It contains half a million square miles (one-fifth the size of continental United States). A good many people said it was a mighty poor buy and called it "Seward's Icebox" in scorn.

2   Samuel W. Ullman, Henry K. Zimmer, and Thomas D. Lyman are the new executives of the Eastern Furniture Corporation with headquarters at Paterson, New Jersey. Quite some time ago they were associated with Boynton-Maxwell, Inc., Xenia, Ohio. The two new regional managers are Nathan K. Grayson, Harrisburg, Pennsylvania, and R. C. Hallman, Auburn, Maine.

3   Fill our order quickly for 2,475 pounds of No. 134, EF Extra Strong; 9,860 pounds of No. 73, Calendered Gloss; and 16,426 pounds of No. 23/738, your 24-lb. Ledger. I believe the average price of this paper will work out to $15\frac{1}{2}$¢. The paper is for a job that includes a number of zinc etchings. Please wire shipping date; we must be on press by August 5.

4   The catalog price of Stock #68473 is $9.50, subject to discounts of 30% and 10%. Chapter XV, "Population Trends," has been extensively rewritten to include the author's work in this field and has been favorably reviewed in scientific journals by leading critics* in its specialized field. The book is published by Ryan & Elder (formerly Ryan & Treder).

Paragraph Typing B

Each of these paragraphs contains all the letters of the alphabet.

1   If you really want to accomplish something that is out — 11

of the ordinary, you have to work with vim and zeal. It is — 23

the people that put forth extra efforts that always win out — 35

in any contest. Those who jog along in a rut day after day — 47

and who quickly become tired of work get precisely nowhere. — 59

2   Ask yourself whether you have developed real dexterity — 11 — 70

in the matter of inserting sheets into your typewriter. It — 23 — 82

is a joy to observe the zip with which the expert takes one — 35 — 94

sheet out of his machine and feeds in another. Just to sit — 47 — 106

and watch him as he works will give anybody quite a thrill. — 59 — 118

3   It is, as I am sure you know, quite a task to write by — 11 — 129

the use of just short words and at the same time write them — 23 — 141

in such a way that each line you write will come out at the — 35 — 153

same space. The task will tax your mind and calls for very — 47 — 165

much skill, thought, and zest to goad you on in a hard job. — 59 — 177

4   It is quite true that you never see a typist who is an — 11 — 188

expert of great skill gazing about the room while he types. — 23 — 200

He keeps his eyes on the copy he is typing, and he does not — 35 — 212

look at the keys or the paper for fear of losing his place. — 47 — 224

He knows how to put each sheet into his machine in a jiffy. — 59 — 236

5   You surely need to learn how to adjust yourself to any — 11 — 247

situation in which you are apt to find yourself. Determine — 23 — 259

to train yourself to be exact, quick, and alert. Decide to — 35 — 271

do your work with zeal, vigor, and enthusiasm. The quality — 47 — 283

of enthusiasm is the dynamo that makes the wheels go round. — 59 — 295

Paragraph Typing B

Each of these paragraphs contains all the letters of the alphabet.

1   The businessman who knows human nature writes numerous 11
letters of appreciation and congratulation. The people who 23
get those letters are happy to learn that they are not just 35
names and are important enough to get individual attention. 47
They may not write to express their feeling, yet often they 59
quickly seize the chance to tell about the letter received. 71

2   We are all different. What appeals to one as just the 11   82
right vacation would be a terrible bore to another. How we 23   94
invest our time off is for each of us to determine. We can 35   106
add zest to our lives and have new experiences when we take 47   118
the kind of vacation that we most enjoy. Some like a quiet 59   130
time; others do not, yet they all come back with new vigor. 71   142

3   The basic purpose of drill is the formation of habits. 11   153
You become expert as the result of directed practice. Just 23   165
before you start a drill, quiz yourself on what you want to 35   177
achieve. Resolve never to do any typing drill haphazardly. 47   189
Never type in a mechanical way, but keep your mind awake to 59   201
what you are doing; then you will really profit from drill. 71   213

4   To be better than the average in your work, you do not 11   224
have to be a genius. All that you need is what we may call 23   236
the extra ten per cent. If you have ten per cent more zip, 35   248
are ten per cent more creative, and equip yourself with ten 47   260
per cent more training than the average, you are sure to be 59   272
a person who gets more joy and finer rewards from his work. 71   284

Paragraph Typing C

These paragraphs include many figures, symbols, and capital letters.

1   Type the asterisk (*) to call attention to a footnote. The apostrophe (') is used in the possessive form of nouns. You may find it used occasionally to designate <u>hour</u> (<u>hours</u>) or <u>foot</u> (<u>feet</u>). The chief use of the quotation marks is to indicate that the word or words enclosed are direct quotes.

2   The single quotation mark (same as the apostrophe) may be used to mark off a quoted word or words that come inside a quotation. You may find the quotation marks used now and then to indicate <u>inch</u> (<u>inches</u>) or <u>minute</u> (<u>minutes</u>). We may thus, for instance, type 6' 2" to mean <u>six</u> <u>feet</u> <u>two</u> <u>inches</u>.

3   The only correct use of the ampersand (&) is in typing the names of firms or companies that use it themselves; as, Weston & Saylor. The per cent sign (%) is used in bills or in series discounts; as, 30%, 20%, and 10%. In writing the dollar sign ($), do not space after it; as, $27.50, $94.83.

4   Box Truck #245 measures 96" x 48" and is 3' deep. The shipping weight is 95#. Our Traffic Department states that the freight charges (f.o.b. Chicago) will be $37.10. There will be a small extra charge of $12.50 for carting. Please note the 5% discount that is deducted from all list prices.

5   At 9:30 a.m. please deliver to Scott & Moore 137 cases measuring 5' 6" x 7' 3" x 9' 9". Here is Check No. 5735 in payment for the containers. The check has been written for $157.45 ($129.30 for the cases and $28.15 for the amount of the freight charges). Please return the receipted invoice.

Division Seven

Paragraph Typing A

Many of the words in these paragraphs are balanced-hand words.

1 When any man is paid a big salary, it is usual to find 11
that the work he is doing is work which not many men can do 23
with proficiency; such men are worth their big pay. In any 35
field of work some men stand out from most other men in the 47
same field; the usual reason is that they have been able to 59
do the work with more proficiency than the men around them. 71

2 The work that is dismal or downright dull for one girl 11 82
or boy may bring visible delight and joy to another. It is 23 94
vital for each of us to find the work that is right for us, 35 106
for the right work is the usual key to an eventful and rich 47 118
life. Too many boys and girls get into a rut; thus they do 59 130
not make half the pay or the progress that they could make. 71 142

3 Make it a habit to lend a hand to others when they can 11 153
use aid and when you can give such aid to them; the men and 23 165
women who turn down chances to aid others are apt to be the 35 177
ones who do not make many firm or authentic friends. It is 47 189
not right for any of us to be so busy with our own schedule 59 201
that we refuse to halt now and then and lend aid to others. 71 213

4 When a man owns a business, he wants to make a profit, 11 224
for both his work and his time go for naught if he pays out 23 236
more than he takes in. It is odd, then, that so few owners 35 248
do sit down and make a formal analysis of their costs; they 47 260
think that if they are kept busy at their work, that single 59 272
fact signals a tidy profit for them at the end of the year. 71 284

Division Four—Headings and Articles

In this Division you will *apply* the skill you have developed to the correct placement of headings and articles.

From the beginning of your work, you have been automatically centering your typing across the sheet (horizontally). You have set the left margin stop for a 50-space line or for a 60-space line at a point which equalized the white space at the left and at the right. You will now learn the *why* of the art of setting left *and* right margin stops so that your work will always be centered across the page.

The first thing to keep in mind is that on a pica-type machine there are 10 spaces to the inch and on an elite-type machine, 12 spaces to the inch. Study Illustration 40.

1 Inch {

    These six lines have been typewritten in pica type
    in order to give you a picture of the vertical and
    horizontal measurements. You will note that these
    six lines occupy a vertical inch and that each 50-
    space line will make five inches across the paper.
    There are ten pica spaces to each horizontal inch.

Pica

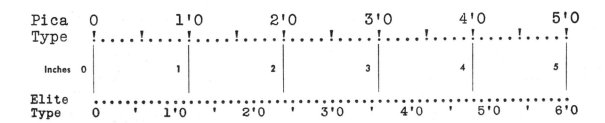

1 Inch {

    These six lines have been typewritten in elite type in order
    to show you the difference between this size of type and the
    pica style. You will see right away that both sizes of type
    occupy the same vertical space--six lines to the inch. Note
    that each 60-space line of elite type equals five horizontal
    inches. There are twelve spaces of elite type to each inch.

Elite

ILLUSTRATION 40

A sheet that is 8½ inches wide thus provides for 85 spaces, pica type, across the page (8½ times 10). The same sheet provides for 102 spaces, elite type, across the page (8½ times 12). Study Illustration 41.

XXXXXXXXXXXXXXXXXXXXXXXXXXXXXXXXXXXXXXXXXXXXXXXXXXXXXXXXXXXXXXXXXXXXXXXXXXXXXXXXXXXXXXXXX

(85 spaces—pica type)

XXXXXXXXXXXXXXXXXXXXXXXXXXXXXXXXXXXXXXXXXXXXXXXXXXXXXXXXXXXXXXXXXXXXXXXXXXXXXXXXXXXXXXXXXXXXXXXXXXXXXXXXXX

(102 spaces—elite type)

ILLUSTRATION 41

If you will stop to think, you will realize right away that your stock 14
in trade is words. Just as the linen salesman has to know about linen 28
and the shoe salesman has to know about shoes, so you have to 40
know about the materials with which you are working. Think of 52
typewriting as a tool which you are now mastering. Just as the carpenter 67
has learned how to use his tools on the wood which is his material, so 81
you need to learn a great deal about your material, which consists of 95
words. Words are like the links in a chain; you may think of a sentence 109
as being the chain. Your problem has to do not only with the words 122
themselves, but with linking together the words in such a way that the 136
sentences are correctly written. 142

The first thing you need to know about a word is its correct spelling. 156
While it is true that there are rules which apply to the spelling of 170
certain classes of words, it is also true that there are many words which 185
you can learn to spell correctly only by careful study. The goal at 199
which you are to aim is to make sure that no typewritten material 212
leaves your hands until you have made certain that it contains no words 226
incorrectly spelled. The more words you have learned to spell properly, 240
the fewer words you will have to look up. Unless you are absolutely 254
sure of the spelling of a word, there is nothing for you to do except to 268
look it up in the dictionary. A misspelled word in a letter stands out 282
like a sore thumb. It is because so many business students never took 296
time to study spelling and never formed the habit of looking up 309
words of which they are not sure that so many businessmen say their 322
stenographers and typists cannot spell. 330

Another aspect of words you need to study is the matter of capitalizing. 344
Of course, you know that the names of people and places should 356
begin with capital letters. In the course of the work of each day the 370
stenographer has to transcribe a good many proper names. The thing 383
that is most personal to you is your name. Just as you want to have 397
your name spelled correctly, so you should understand that the people 411
to whom your employer writes letters want to have their names, too, 424
spelled properly. Often the employer gives the stenographer the letter 438
to which he is replying; then the stenographer can get the correct 451
spelling of the name from that letter. If you do not get the incoming 465
letter, it is right and proper for you to ask for the correct spelling of 480
the name. The same situation occurs in the case of unusual technical 494
words that may be used. Unless you are sure of the word and can find 508
it in the dictionary, ask to have the word spelled for you. Such a 521
request makes a favorable impression on your employer. 532

Margin Stop Settings

Beginning with this Division, you will set the right margin stop as well as the left. Your object always is to set the margin stops so that one-half of each typed line will be to the left of the center of the paper and one-half to the right of the center.

Your typewriter is equipped with a bell which rings about 8 spaces before the end of the typed line. You will, therefore, set the right margin stop 5 spaces beyond the normal end of your typed line. You will then have 8 spaces to type after the bell rings. As a general rule, you won't begin a new word after you hear the bell. Some of your lines may be a space or two short of the normal right-hand margin; others may be a space or two over. The result, however, will be that your typed lines will be about even, and the right writing margin will present a pleasing appearance.

Different makes of machines provide for different ways of setting the margin stops. Your instructor will explain to you how to set the right margin stop on your particular machine. You may also refer to the instructions given below. Find the name of the machine you are using and study the instructions for it.

Royal, Smith-Corona, R. C. Allen, Remington Electric, and IBM. Set your paper guide so that indicator on the guide is at 0. Assume that you are typing on a pica-type machine to a line of 60 spaces. You will, therefore, have 25 spaces (85 — 60) for the two side margins. As 25 is an uneven number, put the extra space into the left margin. Set the left margin stop at 13 and the right margin stop at 78 (5 spaces beyond the normal line which will end at 73). 13 (left margin) + 60 (line length) + 12 (right margin on paper) = 85 (width of paper in pica type).

Now, let us assume that you are using an elite-type machine and are writing to a line of 60 spaces. You will have 42 spaces (102 — 60) for the two side margins. Set the left margin stop at 21 and the right margin stop at 86 (5 spaces beyond the normal line which will end at 81). 21 + 60 (line length) + 21 = 102.

Refer to Illustration 43 on the next page and study Diagram D and Diagram I.

Remington Standard. Set the paper guide so that the readings at both sides of the paper will be the same. Insert the left edge of the paper against the paper guide. When you examine the line scale, you will see that 0 is at the center. All you need to do to center a line of 60 spaces is to set the left margin stop at 30 and the right margin stop at 35 (to provide for the bell).

Underwood. If you are using an Underwood model with a zero marking on the paper guide, insert the paper with the guide at 8½. Set the left margin stop for a pica-type machine at 13 and the right margin stop at 78 (to provide for the bell). 13 (left margin stop) + 60 (line length) + 12 (right margin on paper) = 85 (width of paper in pica type).

Elite type: Set the left margin stop at 21 and the right margin stop at 86 (to provide for the bell). 21 (left margin stop) + 60 (line length) + 21 (left margin of sheet) = 102 (width of paper in elite type).

Turn to Illustration 43 on the next page and study Diagrams D and I.

Centering Headings

In this Division you will develop skill in the centering of headings horizontally; that is, across the paper. Your object is to have the same amount of white space to the left of the heading as to the right.

When you are learning to center headings, clear all margin and tabulator stops. Next, insert the paper correctly. Third, move the carriage to the center of the paper. (By setting a tabulator stop at that center point, you can easily find the centering point whenever you are to center a heading).

Now, backspace once for each two letters in the heading. Start to backspace at the center point. Begin typing the heading at the space to which you have backspaced.

Example 1: You are to center the name WASHINGTON on a sheet 8½ inches wide.

1 WA—backspace once

2 SH—backspace once

3 IN—backspace once

4 GT—backspace once

5 ON—backspace once

The personnel manager has dictated test letters to four applicants for the position that is open. Two of those applicants made transcripts which showed clearly that they do not have the knowledge of the language which this position requires. Those two people are simply told that their work on the tests was unsatisfactory. It is not the business of the manager to go over the letters with the applicants as your teacher goes over your transcripts with you. The other two applicants turned in letters that were reasonably correct. There is not much to choose between them, as far as the transcripts go. They have shown that they can not only take dictation, but can transcribe it with reasonable accuracy. Of course, nobody expects that a beginner will be perfect; the personnel manager knows that somebody in the business must spend time in giving special training on the letter style and language used in the office.

The manager now has two applicants who have shown that they have possibilities. Next comes the job of selecting one of the two for the position. You can easily see that right here is where the matter of personality enters into the picture and casts the deciding vote. The personnel manager must now determine which of the two will fit into the work of this particular office. He has to bring into play his experience and his knowledge of human nature which he has acquired over a period of time. Such traits as loyalty and industry may be determined to some extent by the record of the applicant and by the answers to questions. Before the personnel manager employs one of the two applicants, he must satisfy himself that the one he selects is reliable and can work without constant supervision.

Interviewing applicants, as you can easily see, is a human situation that can never be reduced to a formula. When you have shown that you have possibilities for doing the work required by the position for which you are applying, you still have the problem of making the employer feel that you are reliable; that you have the qualities which will enable you to get along with other people in the office; that you are, in other words, a good risk. When you are employed, it is just as much to the interest of the employer that you make good as it is to your own interest. Every employer tries to keep the turnover among his employees as low as possible. He has to make an investment in each new employee because every new employee has to be trained in the practices and procedures of that particular office. When you get your first position in an office, your point of view should be that now you have a chance to put into practice what you have learned.

14
28
41
54
68
82
95
109
123
137
151
164
177
183
196
210
224
238
250
264
277
290
303
316
330
340
354
367
381
394
408
422
436
450
464
477
490
504
518
530

If the heading consists of two or more words, you will need to take into account the space between words. Backspace the words in the heading in groups of two letters—or one letter and the space. Always start at the center. Begin typing at the space to which you have backspaced.

Example 2: The heading you are to center is the two words CENTERING HEADINGS.

CE—backspace once   HE—backspace once
NT—backspace once   AD—backspace once
ER—backspace once   IN—backspace once
IN—backspace once   GS—backspace once
G and space—backspace once

Centering Point
↓

GIAHGIENC   Read down:
SNDE NRTE   CENTERING
          HEADINGS

↓

CENTERING HEADINGS

ILLUSTRATION 42

On certain machines there are special devices for centering headings. Some Underwood models, for example, have a dual scale on the front of the machine which will enable you to center a heading without backspacing.

ILLUSTRATION 43

Let us have a talk with a personnel manager who has had hundreds 13
of interviews with young men and women who were applying for office 26
positions.   It is a fact that the most important element in any enterprise 41
is its manpower and womanpower.   Anyone who is at the head of any 54
business must take into account the people who work in that business. 68
It is not products or commodities that make a business go, but the 81
people who work together to carry on the activities which produce 94
goods or render service. 99

This matter of interviewing applicants for a position and of selecting 113
a new employee is not easy.   It is true that certain employment tests 127
have been devised; but because people differ so widely, it is not possible 142
to rely entirely on such tests, no matter how carefully they have been 156
devised.   When you buy a product of any kind, you probably know just 170
what the product is and to what use it is to be put; but when you are 184
employing people, you are in the realm of human values. 194

As a sort of case study, this personnel manager has made some 206
observations about interviewing applicants for positions.   As soon 219
as the applicant comes into the office, the manager gets a certain 232
impression.   The applicant is tidy or untidy; he is bold or timid.   When 246
the applicant introduces himself, the manager gets a further impression 260
from the voice and bearing of the applicant.   Always keep in mind the 274
fact that first impressions are likely to be lasting because they come 288
ahead of later impressions.   The position which the personnel manager 302
is talking about is a secretarial position.   The first thing the manager 316
does is to find out whether the applicant can take dictation and 329
transcribe it.   If the applicant, upon being told that she is to take 343
dictation, has with her a notebook and a pen or pencil, she makes a 356
favorable impression.   The manager sees that the applicant has thought 370
about the interview and has come prepared.   If, on the other hand, 383
the manager has to send for a notebook and a pencil, the applicant has 397
lost the chance to make a good impression at this point. 407

As the personnel manager knows, some businessmen, when they 419
dictate letters to an applicant, simply pick up correspondence which 433
may be lying on their desks and dictate replies to those letters.   In 447
other companies special test letters have been devised.   Often those 461
letters have been constructed in such a way as to test understanding 475
of grammar and punctuation, especially the correct use of the apostrophe. 490
Certain words which are pronounced alike or nearly alike are 502
included in the letters.   From the transcript anyone can quickly tell 516
whether the applicant understands the correct use of words. 528

Problem 1. Check the position of the paper guide. Insert an 8½ by 11 sheet. Align the top edge of your paper with the line scale. Clear the margin stops by putting them all the way over to the extreme right and left. Set the line space regulator for double spacing. Set a tabulator key at the center point of your paper. Space down three double spaces from the top edge of the sheet; then center the following heading.

THE AMERICAN WAY

Space down three double spaces. **Tabulate** to the center point of your sheet; then center the following two-line heading with double spacing.

METROPOLITAN SAVINGS BANK

Fayette Street Office

Space down six double spaces from the two-line heading you have just typed. Set the left and right margin stops for a 60-space line. Center the heading, ALPHABETIC PARAGRAPHS. *Triple*-space after the heading; that is, double-space once and then single-space. (When you type an article with double spacing, triple-space after the heading.) Type the three paragraphs with double spacing. Use a 5-space paragraph indention.

Each of the three paragraphs contains all the letters of the alphabet.

ALPHABETIC PARAGRAPHS

Every organization is a joint enterprise. The work of each must be tied in with the effort of all so as to produce harmony and eliminate petty quarrels and general exasperation.

Amazingly enough, some seem to feel justified in trying to keep others down when the exact opposite is the truth. He who pushes somebody else down is quite sure to go down himself.

However much skill and knowledge you eventually acquire, try to realize that the ability to adjust yourself quickly to any existing situation is what will mark you as a civilized person.

When you have completed Problem 1, compare your sheet with page 99. The page was typed on an 8½ by 11 sheet in pica type; then slightly reduced to fit the page size.

No. 12

In the next place, these people who are members of a service club | 13
are there eating together. Most of us eat our meals in our homes with | 27
our families. It is a contrast for us to eat with a large number of | 41
people who have come together in circumstances that differ from those | 55
they find at home. We look forward to a banquet or to a large dinner | 69
not only because of the food that will be served, but also because we | 83
know we shall be with a large number of people. It is a trait of human | 97
nature to want to be with others; and when we eat with others, we | 110
somehow feel that we have something in common with them. In the | 123
ancient world it used to be said that people should eat measures of | 136
salt together so that the function of friendship could be fulfilled, by | 150
which was meant that people ought to share those aspects of life that | 164
give variety and thus make new friends and strengthen old friendships. | 178

Finally, every service club is constantly engaged in projects of one | 192
kind or another in behalf of the community, of crippled children, of | 206
vocational guidance for young men and women, and a thousand and one | 219
other activities which are designed to help those who perhaps have not | 233
been kindly treated by life. You can easily see how the principle of | 247
contrast applies here. The people who make up the membership of a | 260
service club are, for the most part, busy people who have to spend their | 274
time and effort on the enterprise in which they are engaged and on | 287
which the livelihood of a great many other people depends. Here they | 301
have a chance, still working with people whom they have learned | 314
to know, to engage in a kind of activity which is of a wholly | 326
unselfish nature and which has nothing to do with buying or selling. | 340

There is a time for some things and a time for other things; a time | 353
for great things and a time for small things. There are mountains and | 367
there are valleys; there are little streams and there are great oceans; | 381
there are small islands and there are great continents surrounded by | 395
oceans. No matter where we look there are contrasts. To the degree | 409
that we bring the principle of contrast to bear on our own way of life, | 423
to that degree we shall enjoy the flavor of life. We need to learn | 436
how to work because work is the answer to a great many situations | 449
in the world, but it is not the answer to them all. We also need to | 463
learn how to relax, how to play, how to use the principle of contrast | 477
in such a wholesome way that it will contribute toward the development | 491
of all our powers. You can put it down as a fact that you have more | 505
capacity for both work and play than you realize. The job is to keep | 519
them in proper balance and thus get the fullest benefit from them both. | 533
By maintaining that balance, you make yourself a well-balanced person. | 547

THE AMERICAN WAY

METROPOLITAN SAVINGS BANK

Fayette Street Office

ALPHABETIC PARAGRAPHS

Every organization is a joint enterprise. The work of
each must be tied in with the effort of all so as to produce
harmony and eliminate petty quarrels and general exasperation.

Amazingly enough, some seem to feel justified in trying
to keep others down when the exact opposite is the truth. He
who pushes somebody else down is quite sure to go down himself.

However much skill and knowledge you eventually acquire,
try to realize that the ability to adjust yourself quickly to
any existing situation is what will mark you as a civilized
person.

ILLUSTRATION 44

Anyone who has made a study of human nature knows that there is [13] such a thing as taking ourselves too seriously too much of the time [26] or all the time. From nature we learn the principle of contrast; night [40] follows day; rain is succeeded by clear weather; the warm sun of the [54] summer brings out the flowers, and the cold of winter destroys their [68] beauty and fragrance. Life itself is a matter of contrast; thus we have [82] childhood and manhood or womanhood, sorrow and joy, life and death. [95] It is contrast that gives point and meaning to our lives and prevents [109] the boredom that must result when everything goes along in a straight [123] line, so to speak. You remember the old proverb which tells us that [137] variety is the spice of life. Of course, a person can live without spice, [152] but such an existence is likely to be a humdrum piece of business. If [166] the food we eat were not properly flavored, it would be tasteless. [179]

You probably know about the many service clubs that have sprung up [192] in our country during the last few decades. In these service clubs are [206] banded together hundreds of thousands of men and women who are [218] representative citizens in their communities. In such clubs you will find [233] not only leaders in business, but also lawyers and doctors and ministers [247] and engineers and people from almost all other phases of society. [260] People have sometimes wondered why service clubs have achieved such [273] success; why busy men and women are willing to devote so much time [286] and thought and effort to work for the good of their communities. [299]

If you dig deep enough, you will find that the answer has something [312] to do with the principle of contrast. A man who is responsible for the [326] conduct of the affairs of a business must have a serious attitude toward [340] that business. A surgeon who is about to perform an operation must [353] go about his business seriously. A lawyer who is preparing a brief or [367] arguing a case must be on his guard to see that he does not overlook [381] something that is vital. When, however, this businessman or this [394] surgeon or this lawyer goes to the weekly meetings of his service club, [408] he throws aside the serious attitude which must be his while he is doing [422] his work. He sits down at a table with other men; he does not know [435] much, if anything, about the work in which they are engaged, and they [449] know little or nothing about his work. Instead of being a businessman [463] or a professional man, he is now a man among men. He is meeting those [477] men, as they are meeting him, on a purely personal basis. There is [490] likely to be a good deal of joking and amusement of one kind or another, [504] all of which is probably in decided contrast to the rest of his busy day. [519] The first element of appeal which the service club makes lies in this [533] chance for the members to meet with their fellows on a human basis. [546]

Vertical Centering. A sheet that is 11 inches in depth provides 66 lines from the top to the bottom on either a pica-type machine or an elite-type machine. Six vertical lines make an inch.

To center any typing vertically on an 8½ by 11 sheet, follow these steps.

1. Count the number of lines of typewriting and the number of interlines (blank lines).

2. Subtract the total from 66.

3. Divide that figure by 2 (for the top and bottom margins). The figure you get will be the line space at which you will start typing.

Note: The plan given here for vertical centering automatically makes the bottom margin slightly deeper than the top margin—the plan that results in the most pleasing appearance. If you do want the top and bottom margins to be exactly equal, space down one more line before you start to type.

Problem 2. You are to center the following copy on an 8½ by 11 sheet. There are 18 lines of typing and interlines. See Illustration 45. 66 — 18 = 48; 48 ÷ 2 = 24. Center the heading horizontally on the 24th line from the top edge of the sheet. Triple-space after the heading. Set the left and right margin stops for a 40-space line. Double-space. Use a 5-space paragraph indention.

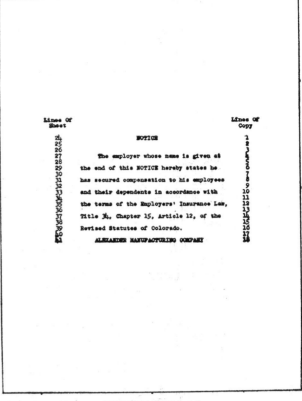

ILLUSTRATION 45
Vertical Centering

NOTICE

The employer whose name is given at
the end of this NOTICE hereby states he
has secured compensation to his employees
and their dependents in accordance with
the terms of the Employers' Insurance Law,
Title 34, Chapter 15, Article 12, of the
Revised Statutes of Colorado.

ALEXANDER MANUFACTURING COMPANY

100

WEBSTER MACHINE COMPANY

1513 EAST LINCOLN ROAD
CLEVELAND, OHIO 44115

October 25, 19--

Mr. David R. Lee, Secretary
Cumberland Chemical Corporation
River Road and Washington Street
Charleston, West Virginia   25302

Dear Mr. Lee:

Yes, we are glad to cooperate with you by providing data about the vacation plan which has been recently adopted by our company for hourly workers. After you have completed your survey, we shall be glad to receive a copy of the report you are planning to publish next month.

Vacation periods for employees who are paid on an hourly basis are as follows:

Length of Service	Vacation
Six to eight months	Three days
Eight to twelve months	One week
One to five years	Two weeks
Five years or more	Three weeks

The vacation pay allowance for one week is two per cent; for two or three weeks, four per cent of straight time earnings for the twelve-month period ending April 1 of the year the vacation is taken.

In case there is any additional information that we can supply to aid you in the preparation of your report, please call on us.

Sincerely yours,

WEBSTER MACHINE COMPANY

Director of Personnel

ABC:TYP

ILLUSTRATION 73
Letter Containing Tabulated Material

Problem 3. On a *half sheet* of paper type the following announcement with double spacing. In the fifth line use the current year date instead of 19--.

The depth of a half sheet, of course, is 33 line spaces. There are six lines to be typed, and there are five interlines; hence there are eleven lines to be provided for. $33 - 11 = 22$; $22 \div$ by $2 = 11$. Space down eleven spaces from the top of the half sheet for the first line. Center each of the six lines horizontally.

NATIONAL SOCIETY OF ELECTRICAL ENGINEERS

Annual Meeting

Thomas Jefferson Hotel

Atlantic City, New Jersey

October 12-16, 19--

MAKE YOUR ROOM RESERVATION NOW.

Problem 4. On a *half sheet* center the following copy horizontally and vertically. Double-space between the heading and the first line. Single-space the paragraph. Use a 60-space line with a 5-space paragraph indention. Type the paragraph line for line. Be sure to set the margin stops correctly, so that the paragraph will be centered horizontally.

When you type an article with single spacing, always double-space after the heading.

THE GIFT OF SINCERITY

You can take from a person every gift but sincerity; let him be blind and deaf and lame; let him stammer in his speech; handicap him in any way you please, just so long as you leave him sincerity. His work will be sure to endure. The world, which is always looking for the real thing, will overlook his weaknesses. There is in the world an immense amount of sham and cant, of front and bluff. So many seem to try to be what they are not. They may think that they are getting away with it, but actually people easily see through them and put them down as insincere. If you want to make yourself worthy of trust and confidence, make sincerity the keynote of all your thinking and acting. Do not try to be what you are not and do not pretend that you know when you do not know.

Letters Containing Tabulated Material

When you type a letter that contains a tabulation, you must not only allow extra vertical line spaces for the tabulated material, but you must also determine the proper horizontal placement of the tabulation.

You have learned that the centering of a tabulation on a sheet 8½ inches wide is planned for the full width of the sheet—85 spaces, pica type; 102 spaces, elite type. A tabulation in a letter is centered within the line length of the letter. For example, if a letter is typed to a 6-inch line, the tabulation is based on a 6-inch width. The tabulated material should usually be indented from the margins of the letter—the same number of spaces from left and right.

You may use either the calculating method or the center-and-backspace method to determine the horizontal placement. Follow the method that your instructor directs you to use.

Study the letter on page 195. It contains a two-column tabulation of four lines with column headings. This tabulation has been centered within the line length of the letter—6 inches.

Problem 16. (Form 6-16). Type the letter in Illustration 73, page 195. Use a 6-inch line. Date the letter today.

Problem 17. (Form 6-17). Type the following letter in the block style and use mixed punctuation. Make a three-column tabulation of the four lines that follow the words *immediate delivery*. Use a 5-inch line. Single-space the letter. Date the letter today.

Mr. Edgar S. Bateman   The Colston Corporation   Milton, Pennsylvania 17847   Dear Mr. Bateman: Thank you for your letter of November 11 and for your interest in the canvas distributing cases that our company manufactures.   It is a real pleasure to send you a descriptive folder that tells why so many business offices everywhere have found Security cases ideal for distributing mail and inter-office communications.   (¶) Here are the prices for the four different sizes that are available for immediate delivery:

No. 95-6	6 Sections	$ 9.75
No. 95-8	8 Sections	11.50
No. 95-10	10 Sections	13.75
No. 95-12	12 Sections	15.95

(¶) The enclosed order form provides a convenient way for you to purchase a supply of these cases for use in your office. Just fill in the form and mail it in the postage-paid envelope that comes with this letter.   Sincerely yours,   SECURITY PRODUCTS COMPANY   Sales Department   RWF: Enclosures 3

Other Heading Styles. There are two other heading styles which you are to learn at this point in your course.

1. *All Capitals Underscored.* The underscoring is often omitted under punctuation marks, such as the comma, that rest on the line. The spaces under marks that are typed above the line of writing, such as the apostrophe and the hyphen, are underscored. Study these examples.

<u>INTERCONTINENTAL BALLISTIC MISSILES</u>

<u>NAMES, ADDRESSES, AND TELEPHONE NUMBERS</u>

<u>LAMB'S TWICE-TOLD TALES</u>

2. *All Capital Letters Spread.* To center a spread heading, tabulate as usual to the center point; then backspace *once* for *each* letter and space in the spread heading. When you type the heading, space *once* after each letter and *three* times after each word. Avoid the spread style if the heading includes punctuation marks.

J A C K S O N   C H E V R O L E T   C O M P A N Y

Problem 5. Center the following copy horizontally and vertically on an 8½ by 11 sheet. Triple-space below the heading. Underscore the heading. Double-space the body of the article. Set margin stops for a 60-space line.

<u>HOW TO GET THINGS DONE</u>

Quite often I hear somebody say, "I'm so busy I don't have time for anything." Whenever I think of the rush and bustle of our lives, I always recall the remark of a well-known humorist: "Every invention during my lifetime has been made just to save time." With a wry smile he continued: "Yet it is a fact that the only commodity that every man, rich and poor, has plenty of is time. Half our life is spent in trying to find something to do with the time we have rushed through the other half to save."

There are two factors--and only two--that lie back of any real achievement. First, we must <u>want</u> to do. Second, we must learn to organize ourselves and our time. There are far too many people who <u>kill</u> time; they don't <u>fill</u> time.

Problem 15. In typing a financial statement, leave from 5 to 8 spaces between the longest line of writing and the first column of figures; from 3 to 5 spaces between the columns of figures.

THE HAMILTON COMPANY

Consolidated Balance Sheet
December 31, 19--

ASSETS

Current Assets:

Cash in Banks and on Hand	$1,012,707.48	
Accounts and Notes Receivable	1,294,677.68	
Prepaid and Miscellaneous	121,839.79	
Inventories	2,955,079.71	
Total Current Assets		$ 5,384,304.66
Investments in Other Companies		34,100.00
Other Assets		808,411.66
Real Estate, Plants, and Equipment (Net)		5,293,417.16
Deferred Charges:		
Prepaid Insurance		59,384.62
Total Assets		$11,579,618.10

LIABILITIES AND NET WORTH

Current Liabilities:

Accounts Payable		$ 485,475.63
Taxes Payable		517,780.14
Total Current Liabilities		1,003,255.77

Net Worth:

Stated Capital (200,000 shares)	$5,000,000.00	
Earned Surplus	5,526,362.33	
Paid-in Surplus	48,000.00	
Capital Surplus	2,000.00	
Total Net Worth		10,576,362.33
Total Liabilities and Net Worth		$11,579,618.10

Problem 6. Center the following copy horizontally and vertically on an 8½ by 11 sheet. Type the heading in the spaced-out style. Double-space below the heading. Single-space the paragraphs. Always double-space between paragraphs. Set the margin stops for a 50-space line.

W O R R Y

Worry is like a rocking chair. It will give you something to do, but it won't get you anywhere. If you can do something about a matter that gives you concern, go right ahead and do it. If, on the other hand, you can do nothing about it, what is the use of worrying?

Most of the things we worry about never come to pass. The only sane way of living is to do in the present what needs to be done and to do it in the most intelligent way you can. Work is the best antidote for worry. A person who is so busy with matters that require his whole attention does not have time to worry.

Determining the Line Length. In your centering work up to this point, you have typed line for line. Usually, however, you will have to decide for yourself how your work should be arranged to give a well-centered effect. You will need to determine in advance *the number of lines* that your typed copy will require. Follow these steps.

1. Count the number of *spaces* that will be required to type a full line in the printed copy. Be sure to count two spaces after each period or other end punctuation mark.

2. Multiply the number of spaces in the line you have counted by the number of complete printed lines. If there is a short line, count the number of spaces in that short line and add that number to your count.

Use the following Guide to determine the line length to which you will type the printed copy, so that your work will be centered.

CENTERING GUIDE

Number of Spaces Required	Set the Margin Stops for a
Up to 500	4-inch line (40, pica; 48, elite)
500 to 1,000	5-inch line (50, pica; 60, elite)
Over 1,000	6-inch line (60, pica; 72, elite)

The Guide is what its name implies—only a *guide*. As you gain experience, you will develop judgment on the matter of varying the line length.

Problem 14. Type the following tabulation on an 8½ by 11 sheet. Box the main heading, the column headings, and the columns. Make the rulings with pen or pencil, unless you are otherwise instructed. Use intercolumns of 5 spaces with pica type; 7 spaces, elite type. Double-space the tabulation. Leave three blank lines between the main heading and the column headings and two blank lines between the column headings and the first line of the columns. This extra space will provide room for the horizontal rulings. Follow the diagrams on page 191 as a guide in planning the horizontal placement.

STADIUMS IN THE UNITED STATES

Name	Location	Capacity	Opened
Soldier Field	Chicago	200,000	1926
Memorial	Los Angeles	140,000	1923
Municipal	Philadelphia	127,000	1926
Municipal	Cleveland	120,000	1931
Stanford	Palo Alto	90,000	1921
Rose Bowl	Pasadena	89,093	1922
Tulane	New Orleans	80,735	1926
California	Berkeley	80,639	1923
Yankee Stadium	New York	80,000	1923
Franklin Field	Philadelphia	78,205	1895
Ohio State	Columbus	76,533	1922
Yale Bowl	New Haven	70,896	1914
Orange Bowl	Miami	70,000	1934
Illinois Memorial	Champaign	69,920	1923
Cotton Bowl	Dallas	67,435	1930
Minnesota Memorial	Minneapolis	65,000	1924
Kezar	San Francisco	60,000	1925
Comiskey Park	Chicago	60,000	1910
Pitt	Pittsburgh	60,000	1925
Harris County	Houston	52,000	1965

Problem 7. Center the following copy horizontally and vertically on an 8½ by 11 sheet. Type the heading in the spaced-out style. Triple-space after the heading. Double-space the paragraph.

T·R·A·I·N·I·N·G

We need to get training that will make it possible for us to earn a living. Training is not something that is routine. The more real thinking you bring to bear on any course of training, the more helpful that training will be to you. Try, therefore, all the time to develop real curiosity about the work you are doing. Every course has some bearing on every other course.

Horizontal Centering

The third line (selected for counting) requires	56 spaces
Multiply by the number of complete lines (6)	✕6
	336
Add number of spaces required to type the last (uncompleted) line	39
	375

As the material contains fewer than 500 spaces, use a 4-inch line (40 spaces, pica; 48 spaces, elite). Refer to the Centering Guide, page 103. Set margin stops accordingly.

Vertical Centering

Pica: 375 (spaces required) ÷ 40 (spaces to the line) = 9 with a remainder of 15. Disregard the remainder and take the next higher whole number— 10 (lines).

Elite: 375 ÷ 48 (spaces to the line) = 7 with a remainder of 36. Disregard the remainder and take the next higher whole number—8.

Placement of Heading

	Pica	Elite
Heading	1	1
Interlines below heading ...	2	2
Lines of typing	10	8
Interlines	9	7
	22	18

Pica: 66 (lines available on a sheet 11 inches in depth) — 22 = 44; 44 ÷ 2 = 22. Type the heading on line 22 from the top of the sheet.

Elite: 66 (lines available) — 18 = 48; 48 ÷ 2 = 24. Type the heading on line 24 from the top of the sheet.

How To Use The Decimal Tabulator

Some typewriters are equipped with a decimal tabulator to aid the typist in arranging tabulations that include money columns. The first key, marked with a period (.), is used to bring the carriage to the decimal point. The second key, marked with a 1, is depressed when the typist wishes to write a figure with one item to the left of the decimal point (6., for example). The third key, marked with a 10, is used for all figures with two items to the left of the decimal point (56., for example).

The fourth key, marked with 100, moves the carriage three spaces before the decimal point and is used for typing hundreds (456., for example). Some typewriters have additional tabulator keys which will move the carriage to a point that is four, five, six, or seven spaces to the left of the decimal point.

As the multiple key tabulator is used chiefly in statistical typing, the typewriter you are using will probably not be equipped with this mechanism.

Boxed Tabulations

Some tabulations, such as price lists or tables of figures, call for the use of horizontal and vertical rules. Horizontal lines separate the main heading from the column headings, as well as the column headings from the items in the columns. Vertical rules are used between the columns.

The rulings may be drawn with pen or pencil before the typing of the table is started, or they may be inserted after the typing has been completed. Some typists prefer to make the rulings on the typewriter.

In a boxed tabulation the column headings and the items in the columns are centered inside their boxes, both vertically and horizontally. Either the heading of the column or the longest item typed in the column—whichever requires the greater number of spaces—determines the width of the column.

Leave at least 3 spaces between columns. If space is available, you may use 5, 7, or 9 spaces for the intercolumn widths. An odd number of blank spaces should be used in order that the vertical rulings may be centered exactly between the columns.

The following diagrams show the longest items in the four columns of Problem 14. The first diagram provides a suggested plan for the horizontal arrangement of the tabulation in pica type. The second diagram is for elite type.

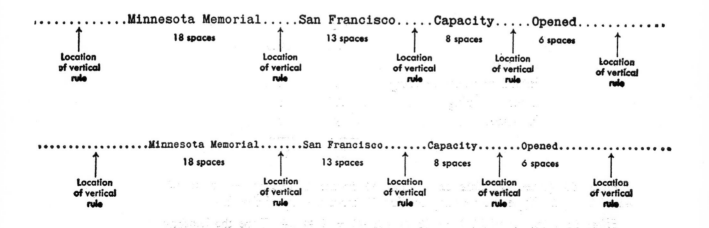

Problem 8. Center the following copy horizontally and vertically on an 8½ by 11 sheet. Underscore the heading. Double-space below the heading. Single-space the paragraphs. Always double-space between paragraphs.

<u>NOT GOOD IF DETACHED</u>

We often see that phrase printed on tickets of one kind and another.

"Not good if detached." In our day nobody can "detach" himself from others. He has to live with, work with, and have his being with other people. The greatest art in life is the art of getting along with other people easily, happily, congenially, and without friction. It is an art that is more important than any other skill we can develop in school or college or anywhere else.

The sensible person keeps his mind open to good influences which will help him to develop his personality. He can solve his daily problems better when he is responsive to the influences that are brought to bear on him than he can if he tries to go it alone.

Horizontal Centering

Count the fourth line of the copy. You will find that this article requires 710 spaces; hence, according to the Centering Guide, you will use a 5-inch line (50 spaces, pica; 60 spaces, elite). Set margin stops accordingly.

Vertical Centering

To determine the number of lines required, make the calculations as they were made in Problem 7. You will find that the copy will require 15 lines, pica; 12 lines, elite.

	Pica	Elite
Heading	1	1
Interline below heading	1	1
Lines of typing	15	12
Interlines (after first and second paragraphs)	2	2
	19	16

Placement of Heading

Pica: 66 (lines available) — 19 = 47; 47 ÷ 2 = 23½. Disregard the fraction and take the next higher whole number—24. Type the heading on line 24 from the top of the sheet.

Elite: 66 (lines available) — 16 = 50; 50 ÷ 2 = 25. Type the heading on line 25 from the top of the sheet.

When the column of figures contains widely varying amounts, you can usually save time by setting the tabulator stop for the lines of the same length that occur most frequently. Then, backspace to the location of the first dollar figure in the longer lines. Thumbspace to locate the shorter lines. Study the column shown here.

Tab
Stop
↓

$ 215.75

134216.19

8236.79

52961.50

456.35

4.45

615489.23

318.26

6.17

Problem 12. Type the following 2-column tabulation. When you set the left margin stop, be sure to allow for the longest line of figures in the first column. In arranging the figures in the second column, set the tabulator stop for the longest line. Allow ten spaces for the intercolumn. Double-space.

VELVET TURF GRASS SEED

Schedule of Prices

Pounds	Price
1	$ 1.35
2	2.66
3	3.93
5	6.45
10	12.70
25	31.25
50	61.50
100	119.75
200	230.50
300	329.25
400	427.60
500	515.75

Problem 13. Type the following 3-column tabulation. Leave 15 spaces between the first and second columns and 10 spaces between the second and third columns. The columns of figures are more easily compared when brought closer together. Double-space.

MONTHLY SALES

Totals For Branch Offices

Month	Last Year	This Year
January	$ 98,116.34	$107,452.76
February	89,329.55	90,421.54
March	145,386.37	145,521.76
April	88,637.17	95,309.67
May	85,392.33	81,229.46
June	91,419.09	89,498.55
July	101,573.87	99,154.21
August	94,621.11	96,735.71
September	87,776.13	88,554.23
October	121,496.11	125,174.98
November	77,409.48	78,945.35
December	96,214.15	97,609.71

Arbitrary Line Length. Most articles and manuscripts are typed to a line length that is arbitrarily determined to provide ample side margins in case penwritten notations are to be made on the manuscript. A common arbitrary line length is six inches. On a pica-type machine, that line length provides for 60 spaces; on an elite-type machine, for 72 spaces. On a sheet that is $8\frac{1}{2}$ inches wide, the two margins will thus total $2\frac{1}{2}$ inches. By setting the margin stops for a 6-inch line, your typing will be automatically centered horizontally.

Articles and manuscripts are usually typed with double spacing. Sometimes, however, you may be asked to triple-space an article—to provide sufficient space for penwritten or typewritten interlineations.

In manuscript typing, it is also customary to leave a top margin of 2 inches (12 line spaces) on the first page of the manuscript, with a bottom margin of 1 inch (6 line spaces) on all the pages.

Problem 9. The following copy represents the first page of a manuscript. Space down 2 inches from the top of the sheet and center the heading horizontally. Type it in all capital letters. Triple-space below the heading. Set margin stops for a 6-inch line. Double-space the copy. Be sure to proofread your work before you take the sheet out of the machine.

In the copy you will find two words that are printed in *italics* (*something* and *thinking*). Underscore those words. Whenever you type from printed copy that contains words in italics, always type those words with underscoring.

In typing copy that is to be set in type by the printer, underscore the typed words that are to be set in italics.

USE YOUR HEAD

A businessman had been writing letter after letter to a certain prospect. The dozen or more sales messages had not produced a single reply. Finally there came a day when the executive called his secretary and said, "Well, we have been fooling around with this prospect long enough. Now I am going to get **something** out of him one way or the other." He then dictated what might best be described as a "snappy" letter. In fact, one might better label it "rude."

After the executive had barked out the last sentence, he noticed a troubled expression on his secretary's face. "Shall we send the letter?" he asked her. He assumed, of course, that the answer would be, "Yes, certainly." Imagine his surprise when she replied, "No."

"Why not?" he demanded. "Because I think your letter is entirely too impatient," the secretary explained.

The letter was redictated. By return mail came the first installment of an order that eventually totaled thousands of dollars.

That secretary had learned the importance of **thinking** about the sense of what is being dictated. Most people, unfortunately for them, are quite content to do their work in a routine way.

Review. Type this paragraph from time to time, as your teacher directs. Set the margin stops for a 60-space line. Use a 5-space paragraph indention. Double-space.

Quite often you should review your control of the letter keys by practice on a paragraph such as this one, which contains every letter of the alphabet. Make such a project a regular part of your training. You want eventually to become an expert typist, and you can achieve your aim if you are willing to pay the price. The only way you can actually realize your ambition is to practice with close attention and concentrate on what you are doing. If you just practice in a thoughtless, listless way, you can rest assured that you will never become an expert typist.

Problem 11. Type the following 4-column tabulation. You will note that the number of digits in the lines of the second and fourth columns is not uniform. Allow ten spaces for each of the intercolumns. Double-space.

LAKES OF THE WORLD

Name	Area in Square Miles	Length in Miles	Depth in Feet
Caspian Sea	168,890	760	3,104
Superior	31,820	350	1,290
Victoria	26,640	200	270
Aral Sea	24,600	280	223
Huron	23,010	206	750
Michigan	22,400	307	923
Tanganyika	12,700	450	4,708
Baykal	12,150	385	5,710
Great Bear Lake	12,000	195	270
Great Slave Lake	11,170	325	2,015
Nyasa	11,000	350	2,316
Erie	9,940	241	210
Winnipeg	9,398	260	70
Ontario	7,540	193	778
Ladoga	7,100	120	730
Balkhash	6,670	300	85
Chad	6,300	130	24
Maracaibo	6,300	100	100

How To Locate The Tabulator Stops When The Figures Contain Decimals

Many tabulations contain columns of figures with decimals.

If all the lines in a particular column of such figures are of approximately the same length, set the tabulator stop for the longest line in the column. Be sure to allow an additional space for the dollar sign. The shorter lines in the column may then be located by thumbspacing from the point at which the stop was set. Study the following column of money amounts and note the point at which the tabulator stop was set

Tab
Stop

$ ↓ 439.52
1732.89
102.13
293.67
1.45
13.29
593.75

Set the tabulator stop for the longest line (second line). Backspace to type the dollar sign in the first line. Thumbspace to type the remaining lines.

No. 1

The most important thing for you to think about is your attitude 13
toward your work and toward other people. You can do a great deal 26
while you are still in school in the way of learning to work and live 40
in a way that will commend you to others. The basic fact to keep in 54
mind all the time is that you cannot live in a world by yourself. 67

The work you do and the way you do it is important; even more 79
important is the spirit and attitude in which you work. There are 92
some people who possess a great deal of knowledge and specialized skill; 106
but their attitude and, indeed, their whole mental makeup are such that 120
they never get a chance to show what they can do, because they do not 134
bring themselves to the favorable attention of others. 145

It is within your power to determine whether people like or do not 158
like you; whether they want to work with you or do not want to work 171
with you. There is something in the attitude of some people which 184
makes us try to avoid having any dealings with them. It is hard even 198
to talk with such people; they have an air about them which somehow 211
makes us uncomfortable when we are in their presence. 221

What has been said, however, does not mean that you have to be 233
all the time deferring to people or taking your cue from them. You 246
are a person in your own right, and you are different from everybody 260
else. You have your own ideas, and you are entitled to express those 274
ideas. It is the manner in which you do that expressing which counts. 288

Now, let us get down to the basic facts of personality. There are 301
people who profess to be able to determine what kind of personality 314
another has just by looking at him or meeting him once. You can put 328
it down as a fact that such people are just deceiving themselves. They 342
are the kind of people who jump to conclusions. 351

It goes without saying, of course, that every one of us makes some 364
kind of impression on the people we meet. That superficial impression 378
is made by the way we dress, the way we shake hands, the light or the 392
lack of it in our eyes, and the hundred and one other physical aspects 406
that are obvious to anyone just at a glance. 415

Everything in life has a physical base. There is an old and true 428
saying that we are what we eat and what we think. The human engine, 442
just like the engine in any piece of machinery, is dependent on its intake. 457
We probably all know people who take better care of the cars they own 471
and drive than they do of their bodies. It is important for each one of 485
us to remember that the human body is much more intricate than 497
any machine built by the hand of man. If the body is neglected or 510
improperly fed, you can be sure that unhappy results will follow. 523

How To Set The Tabulator Stops For Figures

In the preceding tabulation problems the figures in any one column always contained the same number of digits. The typical column of figures in a statistical tabulation, however, contains lines of varying lengths. As all the figures in each column must line up at the right, a special tabulating technique is involved.

Study the 2-column tabulation in Problem 9. You will note that two of the figures occupy nine horizontal spaces (seven digits and two commas), but that one figure occupies only three spaces. In planning a tabulation of this kind, you will save time by setting the tabulator stop in the position that will provide for the greatest number of lines in the column of figures. As eight of the fourteen figures in this column occupy exactly seven horizontal spaces, the tabulator stop should be set to provide for these eight lines. Then, either backspace or space forward from this stop to type the other figures in the column.

Problem 9. Type the following 2-column tabulation. Allow 10 spaces between the columns. Divide the remaining available horizontal space equally between the left and right margins. In

setting the tabulator stop for the second column, follow the instruction you have been given. Double-space. Underscore the column headings.

AREAS OF CERTAIN PARKS

Name	Acres
Crater Lake	160,290
Everglades	271,008
Glacier	997,248
Grand Canyon	645,296
Great Smoky Mountains	461,004
Hot Springs	1,019
Mammoth Cave	50,585
Mount McKinley	1,939,319
Mount Rainier	241,525
Platt	912
Rocky Mountain	252,788
Yellowstone	2,213,207
Yosemite	756,441
Zion	94,241

Problem 10. Type the following 3-column tabulation. As the number of digits in each line in the second column is the same, follow the usual procedure for setting the first tabulator stop. Before you set the second tabulator stop, determine the setting which will be most economical of time. Leave inter-columns of 10 spaces between the first and second columns and between the second and third columns. Double-space.

TERRITORIAL EXPANSION SINCE 1840

Territory	Date	Square Miles
Texas	1845	389,166
Oregon	1846	286,541
Mexican Cession	1848	529,189
Gadsden Purchase	1853	29,670
Alaska	1867	586,400
Hawaiian Islands	1898	6,407
Puerto Rico	1899	3,435
Guam	1899	206
American Samoa	1899	76
Panama Canal Zone	1904	549
Danish West Indies	1917	133

Many of us neglect proper exercise. If we need to go to a store just [14] two or three blocks away, we get out the car. We are likely to think [28] that people who take daily walks are fanatics, when the fact is that [42] just plain walking is excellent exercise. Too many people shy away [55] from any physical exertion. [60]

Now, let us get down to cases. If you went to bed too late last night [74] and got up this morning in an ugly mood, you probably feel like snapping [88] at people or biting off their heads, as the saying goes. You have not [102] prepared your body by proper rest for the work and the contacts of the [116] day that now lies before you, and you face the day with reluctance. [129]

The kind of breakfast you had after the long fast of the night may [142] determine whether or not you have an all-gone feeling around the middle [156] of the morning. Some people eat so much in the morning that their [169] systems get all clogged up, and they are good for little or nothing. [183] The amount of exercise we take and the kind and quantity of food we [196] eat have a large influence on our attitude. [205]

Then there are people who get so excited when they read the morning [218] paper that they become taut, with the result that they are on edge all [232] day long. It is really senseless for anyone to get all wrought up by [246] matters about which he can do nothing or about conditions which he [259] cannot control in any way. Not one person carries the world on his [272] shoulders or is responsible for all that goes on. [282]

If you start the day with the thought that something pleasant is going [296] to happen to you that day, something pleasant will come your way. [309] If you begin the day with the idea that things are going to pot and the [323] world going to smash, you are bound to put yourself into a peevish and [337] disturbed state of mind. If you do not shake off that mood, you are [351] certain to be gloomy and downcast all day. [359]

The past is over and done, and we can do nothing about it. Each day [373] gives us a new opportunity. It is the sure sign of the person who has [387] a healthy mind that he does not keep thinking about the past, which is [401] water under the bridge, but about the future, where he is going to live [415] and move and have his being. Each one of us has sixty minutes in each [429] hour of each day either to use or to abuse. [437]

In one way or another you arrived at school this morning. If you did [451] the work you were asked to do in preparation for the work of today, [464] you rightfully have an inward glow of satisfaction. You have prepared [478] yourself, and now you are ready to go and able to greet your fellow [491] students and your teachers cheerfully. Do not become a fanatic about [505] physical exercise or about diet; keep both in proper perspective. [518]

Braced Headings. A braced heading applies to two or more columns. Such a heading is centered above the group of column headings. One blank line is left between the braced heading and the first line of the column headings. Study the following illustrations.

State Forests		Community Forests	
Number of Units	Total Acreage	Number of Units	Total Acreage
337	3,750,000	9	3,697

Problem 8. Type the following 6-column tabulation. Note that two of the column headings consist of two lines each. Allow an equal number of spaces for the margins and intercolumns. Double-space the tabulation.

AREAS OF STATES

Name of State	Location of Capital	Area In Square Miles		Miles	
		Land Area	Total Area	Length	Breadth
Alabama	Montgomery	51,078	51,609	330	200
Arkansas	Little Rock	52,725	53,102	275	240
Florida	Tallahassee	54,262	58,560	460	400
Georgia	Atlanta	58,518	58,876	315	250
Idaho	Boise	82,808	83,557	490	305
Illinois	Springfield	55,400	56,400	380	205
Indiana	Indianapolis	36,205	36,291	265	160
Iowa	Des Moines	55,986	56,280	300	210
Kansas	Topeka	82,113	82,276	400	200
Kentucky	Frankfort	40,109	40,395	350	175
Louisiana	Baton Rouge	45,177	48,523	280	275
Maine	Augusta	31,040	33,215	235	205
Michigan	Lansing	57,022	58,216	400	310
Minnesota	St. Paul	80,009	84,068	400	350
Mississippi	Jackson	47,420	47,716	340	180
Missouri	Jefferson City	69,270	69,674	300	280
Nebraska	Lincoln	76,653	77,237	415	205
New York	Albany	47,929	49,576	320	310
North Carolina	Raleigh	49,142	52,712	520	200
North Dakota	Bismarck	70,054	70,665	360	210
Ohio	Columbus	41,122	41,222	230	205
Oklahoma	Oklahoma City	69,283	69,919	585	210
Oregon	Salem	96,350	96,981	375	290

We tend to avoid the person who takes himself with deadly seriousness · 14
all the time. When you come right down to it, a sense of humor is · 27
a mark of intelligence. You will usually find that the person who has · 41
a sense of humor also has a sense of values. He makes large allowances · 55
both for himself and for other people. He can stand apart, so to speak, · 69
and look at some of his actions. Often he finds that what he said and · 83
did is slightly on the ridiculous side, and he knows it. · 94

The person without any humor in his makeup is sure he is right and · 107
everybody else is wrong. Such a person is bound to be the butt of · 120
some good-natured fun. Too often, however, he does not get the point · 134
and stalks off in anger. We like nothing better than to deflate someone · 148
who takes himself with deadly seriousness. Such a person, we often · 161
say, is a stuffed shirt; he does not seem to be able to unbend at all. · 175

I once knew a man who had absolutely no sense of humor. With his · 188
face clouded by a frown, he would stride to and fro in his office or in · 202
his home. He had a wide reputation in his field of work, but he was · 216
never known to smile, much less to laugh out loud. He took himself · 229
and everybody else with such extreme seriousness that you felt oppressed · 243
when you were in his presence. · 249

Next to knowing your work, there is nothing like a genuine sense · 262
of humor to help you get your daily work done. There is no point · 275
whatever in taking yourself so seriously all the time. A sense of humor · 289
has the same value in your daily contacts that oil has in machinery. · 303
Every machine has to be lubricated from time to time if it is to run · 317
smoothly and efficiently. In the same way a sense of humor makes the · 331
job easier and more pleasant day by day. When you show people that · 344
you do not take yourself too seriously, they will warm up to you and · 358
work with you cheerfully. · 363

People who take themselves too seriously are likely also to be filled · 377
with nameless fears and anxieties. Half the unrest that exists in the · 391
world, said a great thinker, comes from the vain idea that every person · 405
is bound to be a critic of life and to let no day pass without finding · 419
some fault with the general order of things or putting forth some idea · 433
for what he thinks should be done to improve things. Right there you · 447
have a realistic picture of the person who takes himself too seriously. · 461

Such a person seems to think that he must be forever getting instead · 475
of giving. He lacks a sense of proportion, and he makes mountains out · 489
of molehills. The result is that he is always in a dark mood and has · 503
no interest in the lighter aspects of life. If he could laugh at himself, · 518
he would be far better off, and life would be pleasanter for others. · 532

Problem 7. Type this 5-column tabulation. Allow an equal number of spaces for the margins and intercolumns. Double-space. Underscore the column headings.

INTERCOLLEGIATE BASEBALL LEAGUE
Pitching Records

Name	Team	Won	Lost	Percentage
Snyder	Eastern	9	1	.900
Wilkinson	Central	8	2	.800
Harris	St. Joseph	8	3	.727
Thomas	Western	7	3	.700
Matthews	McKinley	7	3	.700
Gilbert	Jefferson	7	4	.636
Brady	Loyola	5	5	.500
Atkinson	St. Stephen's	4	6	.400
Lewis	Tower Hill	2	3	.400
Mason	Friends	2	4	.333
West	Central	3	7	.300
Kramer	Eastern	2	5	.286
Donovan	Loyola	1	4	.200
Singleton	Tower Hill	1	4	.200
Christopher	Western	0	2	.000
Bates	St. Stephen's	0	3	.000
Olson	Friends	0	3	.000
Young	McKinley	0	4	.000

Long Column Headings. When a column heading contains several words, it should be divided into two or more lines to save horizontal space and to give a more attractive appearance to the tabulation. Study the following illustration of a group of column headings.

Name of Fraternity	Date Founded	Number of Active Chapters	Members
Acacia	1904	31	9,500

You will note that a column heading of two or more lines is single spaced and that the longest line in the heading is used for centering purposes. There is only one blank line between the last line of the column heading and the first line of the tabulation.

To succeed in life is to make a living at work which has a real interest [14] for you. Many men and women who are really interested in their work [28] make a good deal of money. The work in which you are interested [41] may not make you rich. Always remember that the wise and thoughtful [55] person learns to live, and the shrewd man often learns to make money. [69] The man who has learned to live is the happier of the two. [81]

Let us say that somebody asks you to do a certain piece of work. [94] When you are asked to do the work, do not say that you really do not [108] have time for it. If you are honest with yourself, you ought to say [122] that you have no interest in it and therefore you do not care to do it. [136] Your real problem, you see, is to develop a genuine interest in your [150] work. Interest in work is a quality that anybody can develop in the [164] same way that all other qualities are developed. The world that lies [178] around us is often extremely distracting. Some of the things which [191] some people do in their leisure time are really pitiful, if not tragic. [205] Such people have never developed any worthwhile interests in life to [219] which they are willing to give themselves without reserve; hence they [233] are bound to live unsatisfied and unsuccessful and frustrated lives. A [247] person who develops real interests, on the other hand, gives his life a [261] sense of direction; he goes places and does things. [271]

You can put it down as a fact that to achieve genuine success in any [285] field of work calls for a deep interest in that work. Never be satisfied [300] with doing your work in a routine way. Put your mind and your heart [314] into your work every minute of the day. You will not only become a [327] better worker, but you will get from your work a sense of joy and [340] happiness denied to those who are content to go on day after day doing [354] their work in a mechanical and listless way. Of course, you want to [368] make sure that the interests you develop have to do with things that [382] contribute to your mental growth and give you a wholesome outlook [395] on life. Any interests outside of your work that are bad for your health, [410] your mind, and your spirit will react unfavorably on your work. [423]

If you are determined to do so, you can apply these principles right [437] now while you are preparing yourself to do good work in a business [450] office. You can train yourself to develop an interest in your studies. [464] You can avoid getting into a rut in doing your studying and in becoming [478] proficient in business skills. At the same time you can interest yourself [493] in activities that will broaden your contacts with others. You are [506] going to live with and work with and have your being with other people; [520] the more experience you have in living and working with others, the [533] better you will equip yourself for work. [541]

Problem 5. Type the 3-column tabulation in either Illustration 71, page 183, or Illustration 72, page 184. Follow the instructions for the vertical placement and for the horizontal placement of the column headings.

Problem 6. Type the following tabulation. Allow an equal number of spaces for the margins and intercolumns. Type the main heading in all capitals. Type the subheading and the column headings in capitals and small letters. Double-space the tabulation.

POPULAR VOTE FOR GOVERNOR
Votes By Counties

County	Simmons	Watts	Forrester
Addison	3,429	2,874	1,451
Baker	4,513	1,459	1,253
Caledonia	1,567	2,145	1,985
Chester	1,952	3,233	2,293
Essex	2,739	1,245	1,141
Franklin	1,009	1,724	2,277
Grand Isle	3,724	2,986	2,756
Greene	1,409	2,070	3,516
Guthrie	1,053	2,103	1,691
Hamilton	2,927	1,230	2,507
Hancock	1,834	3,151	2,936
Henderson	1,381	1,779	1,066
Howard	1,568	2,794	1,971
Jefferson	2,474	2,532	1,485
Lamoille	1,345	2,443	1,007
Orange	1,973	2,056	1,453
Orleans	2,115	2,525	2,117
Rutland	2,932	2,743	1,956
Tyson	1,177	1,997	1,386
Wayne	2,198	1,872	1,381
Windham	1,642	1,455	2,453
Windsor	1,835	2,366	1,739
York	2,718	1,911	1,214

No. 5

It is a good thing for us to know something about the qualities that   14
make a person a leader; they are the qualities that attract attention   28
and get the right kind of responses from other people. Suppose   41
we do some thinking about the traits of men and women who have   53
personalities that attract favorable attention. You can read personality   68
in the way a person talks, walks, sits, and stands; how he estimates   82
weights, sizes, people, places, and objects. Just as the scientist does   96
not really know what electricity actually is, so nobody can give you an   110
exact definition of personality. We know a great deal about the way   124
electricity acts. In the same way we can arrive at conclusions about   138
personality by noting how a person acts.   146

When you study the traits of people who have achieved places of   159
leadership in any aspect of life, you will find that they are usually   173
people of great vitality. They radiate hope and cheer and optimism.   187
Mental attitude, you may be sure, is just as important as physical health.   202
A person who enjoys his work is a confident person. Confidence is   215
contagious because it easily spreads to others. If you stop to think,   229
you will realize that anything you enjoy doing you do well. People   242
are always attracted to the person who plainly enjoys what he is doing.   256

It is also true that the person who attracts attention couples the quality   271
of modesty with poise. He has about him an attitude of quiet assurance   285
that is always apparent to other people. Such a person is slow to   298
express criticisms and quick to praise good work and right attitudes.   312
He adapts himself easily to any situation in which he finds himself.   326
He knows how to put himself into the place of the man or woman with   339
whom he is dealing and how to say and do the right thing at the right   353
time; hence he does not ever rub people the wrong way.   364

A man or woman of poise conveys an impression of reserve strength.   377
Too many people burn up their energy in fruitless ways. They are   390
worriers, and in many cases they worry about things that never actually   404
happen. If you do your work each day the best you can, you will form   418
the habit of facing the tasks of tomorrow and next week and next month   432
when those tasks present themselves. In that way you develop reserve   446
strength, and you will not be continually working up to the limit of   460
your capacity. The basic trait of people who are leaders lies in the   474
fact that they unconsciously stress the positive and avoid the negative.   488
They look for the best, not for the worst; hence they get the best not   502
only from themselves but from others with whom they live and work.   515
Not only do they do good work themselves; they are also able to get   528
other people to work with them in the spirit of enthusiasm.   540

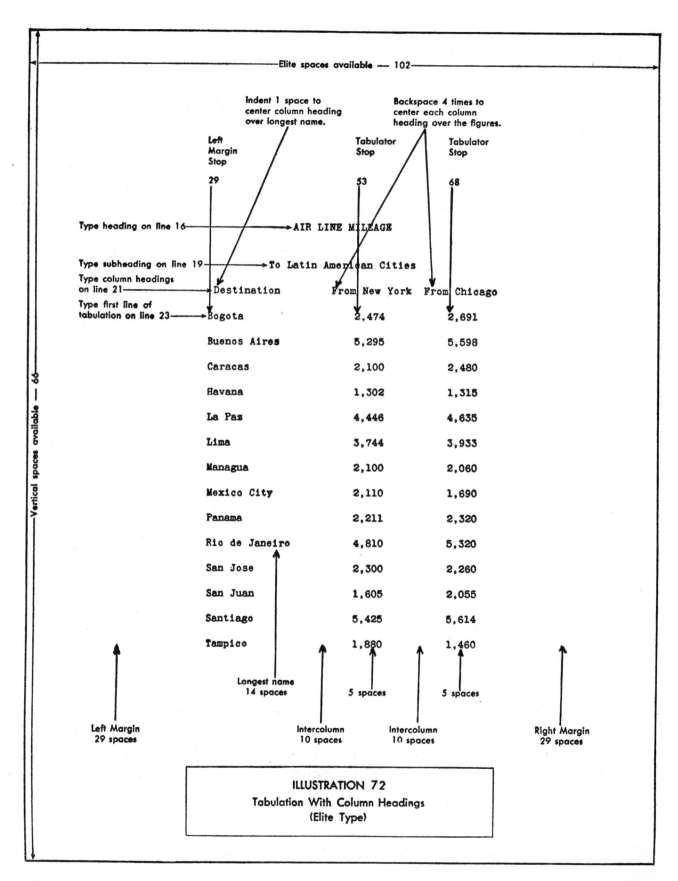

Elite spaces available — 102

Vertical spaces available — 66

Indent 1 space to center column heading over longest name.

Backspace 4 times to center each column heading over the figures.

Left Margin Stop 29

Tabulator Stop 53

Tabulator Stop 68

Type heading on line 16 ⟶ AIR LINE MILEAGE

Type subheading on line 19 ⟶ To Latin American Cities

Type column headings on line 21 ⟶

Type first line of tabulation on line 23 ⟶

Destination	From New York	From Chicago
Bogota	2,474	2,691
Buenos Aires	5,295	5,598
Caracas	2,100	2,480
Havana	1,302	1,315
La Paz	4,446	4,635
Lima	3,744	3,933
Managua	2,100	2,060
Mexico City	2,110	1,690
Panama	2,211	2,320
Rio de Janeiro	4,810	5,320
San Jose	2,300	2,260
San Juan	1,605	2,055
Santiago	5,425	5,614
Tampico	1,880	1,460

Longest name 14 spaces

5 spaces

5 spaces

Left Margin 29 spaces

Intercolumn 10 spaces

Intercolumn 10 spaces

Right Margin 29 spaces

ILLUSTRATION 72
Tabulation With Column Headings
(Elite Type)

Division Five

Paragraph Typing A

Many of the words in these paragraphs are balanced-hand words.

Words

1   A few years ago a famed psychologist was asked to name   11
some of the reasons why so many people in the world are not   23
able to make a success of their lives. The noted authority   35
did not spend more than eight minutes in thinking about the   47
problem. The chairman of the visitors received his answer.   59

2   Each visitor paid close attention as the chairman read   11 70
the reply. The host stated that many men work on the handy   23 82
theory that they are always right. Their only visible goal   35 94
in life is to blame their neighbors and to laugh at others.   47 106
But such people wish to tuck their own faults out of sight.   59 118

3   Some neurotic men wish to duck the work which has been   11 129
assigned to them but feel that they are entitled to profits   23 141
and top pay for the small quantity of jobs that they manage   35 153
to complete. Such people think that results come from some   47 165
sleight-of-hand antics. They have a penchant for shirking.   59 177

4   The psychologist also stated that the habit of putting   11 188
off doing work is another reason for failure. Some persons   23 200
lament the visible quantity of jobs to be done. While they   35 212
laugh at the sight of work to be done, they are idle. Such   47 224
dormant men pay the penalty when others rush ahead of them.   59 236

5   The scientist then explained to his visitors the final   11 247
reason for failure. So many persons have got the idea that   23 259
success comes when slander is practiced. These men make it   35 271
a habit to laud another in public, but they stab him in the   47 283
back with a big dirk when he happens to turn the other way.   59 295

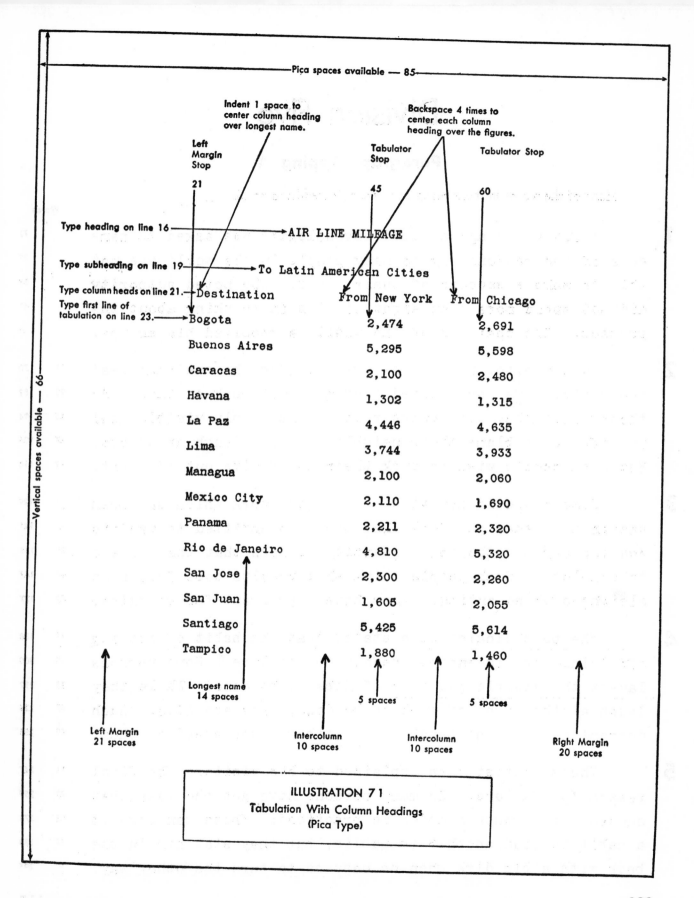

Pica spaces available — 85

Indent 1 space to
center column heading
over longest name.

Backspace 4 times to
center each column
heading over the figures.

Left
Margin
Stop

Tabulator
Stop

Tabulator Stop

21

45

60

Type heading on line 16 ——————→ AIR LINE MILEAGE

Type subheading on line 19 ——————→ To Latin American Cities

Type column heads on line 21. →Destination

Type first line of
tabulation on line 23. ——→

Destination	From New York	From Chicago
Bogota	2,474	2,691
Buenos Aires	5,295	5,598
Caracas	2,100	2,480
Havana	1,302	1,315
La Paz	4,446	4,635
Lima	3,744	3,933
Managua	2,100	2,060
Mexico City	2,110	1,690
Panama	2,211	2,320
Rio de Janeiro	4,810	5,320
San Jose	2,300	2,260
San Juan	1,605	2,055
Santiago	5,425	5,614
Tampico	1,880	1,460

Vertical spaces available — 66

Longest name
14 spaces

5 spaces

5 spaces

Left Margin
21 spaces

Intercolumn
10 spaces

Intercolumn
10 spaces

Right Margin
20 spaces

ILLUSTRATION 71
Tabulation With Column Headings
(Pica Type)

Paragraph Typing B

Each of these paragraphs contains all the letters of the alphabet.

Words

1   When you talk to a man who has reached the top and ask | 11
him to outline some of the reasons for his success, he will | 23
quickly remind you of the extremely important part just the | 35
right brand of smile plays in the battle to get ahead. One | 47
man of note valued his dazzling smile at a million dollars. | 59

2   You will, however, soon find out that there is quite a | 11 | 70
difference between smiles. The smile that wins first prize | 23 | 82
is one involving your eyes. It always pays to exert just a | 35 | 94
little more effort to smile with the eyes. When your smile | 47 | 106
is formed only by your lips, the result is usually a smirk. | 59 | 118

3   You may think it very queer to be told that you should | 11 | 129
practice smiling before a mirror, but you will be amazed to | 23 | 141
see how this exercise will improve your smile. Many actors | 35 | 153
and salesmen know that they are judged by their smiles. No | 47 | 165
one will dispute the fact that a smile is a valuable asset. | 59 | 177

4   The quality of your voice is just as important to your | 11 | 188
success as the kind of smile you exhibit to the world. The | 23 | 200
slow drawl is often the sign of a lazy person. Another way | 35 | 212
to improve your voice is to avoid a harsh, nasal tone. You | 47 | 224
will want to keep on working to improve your tone of voice. | 59 | 236

5   An inquisitive newspaper editor decided to try to find | 11 | 247
out the relationship between vocabulary and success. Eight | 23 | 259
reporters were asked to investigate. Dozens of exceptional | 35 | 271
people reported that they adjudged the correct use of words | 47 | 283
one of the most important qualities of a successful person. | 59 | 295

Study the following working plan:

Total number of lines available 66
   Number of lines occupied by the main heading 1
   Number of lines between the main heading and the subheading ... 2
   Number of lines occupied by the subheading 1
   Number of lines between the subheading and the column headings .. 1
   Number of lines occupied by the column headings 1
   Number of lines between the column headings and the first line of
     the tabulation 1
   Number of typed lines in the tabulation 14
   Number of lines between the typed lines 13
     Subtract from the total lines available 34
     Remainder 32
Divide the remainder (32) by 2 to get the line location of the main heading ... 16

Horizontal Placement Of Column Headings

In Illustration 71, page 183, and in Illustration 72, page 184, the main heading AIR LINE MILEAGE and the subheading To Latin American Cities have been centered horizontally. You have already learned how to determine the locations of the left margin stop and of the tabulator stops to position the columns horizontally. You will now learn how to place the column headings.

Instructions	Column 1	Column 2	Column 3
1. Count the number of spaces in the longest line.	Rio de Janeiro = 14 spaces	2,474 = 5 spaces	2,691 = 5 spaces
2. Count the number of spaces in the column heading.	Destination = 11 spaces	From New York = 13 spaces	From Chicago = 12 spaces
3. Subtract the smaller number from the larger.	14 − 11 = 3	13 − 5 = 8	12 − 5 = 7
4. Divide the result by 2.	2)3 / 1 ½	2)8 / 4	2)7 / 3 ½
5. If the column heading is shorter than the longest line in the column, indent from the left margin of the column the number of spaces obtained in Step 4.	Indent 1 space (disregard the fraction) Destination Bogota		
6. If the column heading is longer than the longest line in the column, backspace from the left margin of the column the number of spaces obtained in 4.		Backspace 4 spaces From New York 2,474	Backspace 4 spaces From Chicago 2,691

Paragraph Typing C

These paragraphs include many figures, symbols, and capital letters.

1   The number sign (#) is also used to designate <u>pound</u> or <u>pounds</u>. When so used, type it after the figure without any space; as, 48#, 139#. The <u>at</u> sign (@) is used in making up bills; as, 200 cartons @ $24.75. The cents sign (¢) may be used now and then with amounts of less than $1; as, 4¢, 9¢.

2   One of the problems in the test was as follows: "What is the total of 34¢, 29¢, 69¢, 47¢, and 58¢?" Nearly every student in the class answered, "$2.27." The correct answer is, of course, $2.37. Very few of the students had learned that @ is the sign for <u>at</u>. Nearly 58% of the class failed.

Contains all the letters and all the figures. **3**   The physical inventory reveals 5,987 flange couplings, 12,643 cold-rolled steel hexagons, 8,024 E-B pillow blocks, 167,849 clamp hub pulleys, and 20,538 oxidized hangers. An adjustment must now be made to equalize that inventory with the stock book records kept in duplicate by the supervisor.

4   "Space-Saver" Cabinets are available in three sizes--a 12-drawer unit, a 15-drawer unit, and an 18-drawer unit. A lock for each drawer will be provided at an extra charge of $2.10. The illustration in the catalog (see page 25) shows the cabinet in use. Your local dealer is Williams & Mason.

Contains all the capitals. **5**   The main office of the International Machinery Company is in New York. It operates factories in Atlanta, Georgia; Zanesville, Ohio; Roanoke, Virginia; Buffalo, New York; and Wichita, Kansas. The officers are D. J. Quincy, President; Herman L. Unger, Secretary; and Edward X. Frank, Treasurer.

Problem 4. Type the following 5-column tabulation. Allow an equal number of spaces for the margins and for the intercolumns. Triple-space below the heading. Double-space the tabulation.

If there are extra spaces after you have made the division, add the extra spaces to the margins.

RELATED WORDS OFTEN MISSPELLED

aggressive	aggressively	aggressor	aggressiveness	aggression
annuity	annuities	annual	annually	annuitant
appellant	appellate	appellee	appellor	appellation
apply	applied	applying	appliance	applicable
commit	committed	committing	committee	commitment
concur	concurred	concurring	concurrent	concurrence
illustrate	illustrating	illustrator	illustration	illustrative
interrogate	interrogator	interrogation	interrogatory	interrogative
occupy	occupied	occupying	occupant	occupancy
parallel	paralleled	paralleling	parallelism	parallelogram
permit	permitted	permitting	permission	permissible
prefer	preferred	preferring	preference	preferable
refer	referred	referring	reference	referee
remit	remitted	remitting	remittance	remitter
suggest	suggested	suggesting	suggestion	suggestible
transfer	transferred	transferring	transference	transferor
transmit	transmitted	transmitting	transmission	transmitter
verify	verified	verifying	verification	verifiable

Placement Of Subheadings And Column Headings

Each of the tabulations which you have typed up to this point has had a main heading centered horizontally on the sheet. In each of the tabulating problems that you will type now, you will also include a subheading and column headings.

As you read the following instructions, refer to Illustration 71, page 183, if you are using a machine with pica type. If your typewriter is equipped with elite type, refer to Illustration 72, page 184.

Vertical Placement Of Subheadings And Column Headings

Note that the tabulation consists of three columns with a main heading, a subheading, and column headings. There are two blank lines between the main heading and the subheading.

There is one blank line between the subheading and the column headings and one blank line between the column headings and the first line of the tabulation.

Division Five—Letters

So far, your work has been concentrated on building skill in the operation of the typewriter. You are now ready to start applying that skill to the typing of business letters. Continue at the same time to build your speed and accuracy by typing special drills and straight copy. Keep up your practice!

The employer is not interested in speed alone. Neither is he interested solely in your ability to arrange typewritten material attractively. He wants a typist who can *produce*—a typist who can turn out rapidly work that meets production standards.

To meet those standards, your letters must be attractively arranged, evenly typed, and free of smudges and smears. Resolve now—right at the start—that you are going to produce letters that are free of finger marks and careless erasures.

Until you develop skill in letter placement, you will be given detailed instructions for each letter. Follow instructions exactly. Later on, you will use your own judgment in arranging letters in the various styles that business uses.

Start by making yourself thoroughly familiar with the parts of the business letter. First, study Illustration 46 at the bottom of this page; then turn over to page 116 and read Style Letter 1 carefully. The body of that letter contains instructions that you will need in your work.

After you have studied Illustration 46 and Style Letter 1, you are ready to type your first letter, according to the instructions given on page 117.

Letterhead. The printed letterhead occupies approximately two inches (12 single line spaces) at the top of the sheet.

Inside Address. The first line of the inside address starts from two to nine lines below the date, depending on the length of the letter. Leave 3 spaces between the state name and the ZIP Code number.

Salutation. The salutation is always typed two single line spaces below the inside address and flush with the left margin.

Company Name. The company name is typed two single line spaces below the complimentary close — usually in ALL CAPITAL LETTERS. Its horizontal position depends on the letter style used.

Identifying Initials. The initials of the dictator and of the typist start at the left margin—usually two line spaces below the dictator's name or title.

Date. The date is usually typed two lines below the letterhead. Occasionally it is typed halfway between the letterhead and the inside address. Its horizontal position varies according to the letter style used.

Body. The body of every business letter starts two single line spaces below the salutation. Most business letters today are single spaced, with double spacing between paragraphs.

Complimentary Close. The complimentary close is always typed two single line spaces below the last line of the body. Only the first word is capitalized.

Dictator's Name (or Title). This line is usually typed on the fourth line below the company name — to allow three blank line spaces for the signature.

DALTON
REALTY COMPANY
2800 BAKER BOULEVARD • NEWARK, N. J. 07109

October 27, 19—

Mr. George R. Martin
2112 North Sixth Avenue
Newark, New Jersey   07112

Dear Mr. Martin:

Your first goal is to learn to recognize the parts of the business letter. Although there are several different letter styles in use, nearly all modern business letters you see will contain the parts illustrated here.

A few other parts are occasionally used. You will study those special parts later in your course. You will also learn later about variations in the positions of some of the parts shown in this letter.

There are certain things about letter arrangement, however, that do not vary. No matter what letter style you use, for example, you will always double-space after the inside address, after the salutation, and after the last line of the body.

There is only one place for the salutation—flush with the left margin and two lines below the inside address. Never indent the salutation.

Sincerely yours,

DALTON REALTY COMPANY

President

NMD:TYP

ILLUSTRATION 46
Parts Of The Business Letter

Working Plans — Problem 3

What is the longest line in each column?   Spaces

    Column 1—Hamilton 8

    Column 2—Correspondence 14

    Column 3—32 W. Washington St. 20

    Column 4—North Odenton 13
                                                           ——
                                                           55

PICA TYPE

Total spaces available in an 8½-inch width ..   85

Total spaces needed for the longest lines ..   55
                                                    ——
      Spaces left   30

Divide by 5 (2 margins and 3 intercolumns) ..   5) 30

          6 spaces allowed for each
          margin and each intercolumn

Left Margin Stop 6	First Tab Stop 20	Second Tab Stop 40	Third Tab Stop 66

.......!..............!....................!.......................!.........
————Hamilton————Correspondence————32 W. Washington St.————North Odenton——————

6   8 spaces   6   14 spaces   6   20 spaces   6   13 spaces   6

ELITE TYPE

Total spaces available in an 8½-inch width   102

Total spaces needed for the longest lines ..   55
                                                    ——
      Spaces left   47

Divide by 5 (2 margins and 3 intercolumns)   5) 47

          9 + remainder of 2

Allow 9 spaces for each intercolumn. Add one extra space to the right margin and one extra space to the left margin.

Left Margin Stop 10	First Tab Stop 27	Second Tab Stop 50	Third Tab Stop 79

..........!..............!....................!..............!.........
————————Hamilton————————Correspondence————————32 W. Washington St.————————North Odenton————————

10   8 spaces   9   14 spaces   9   20 spaces   9   13 spaces   10

DALTON
REALTY COMPANY

2800 BAKER BOULEVARD ● NEWARK, N. J. 07109

October 15, 19--

Mrs. Harvey W. Weston
36 East Maple Street
Newark, New Jersey   07118

Dear Mrs. Weston:

This Style Letter 1 is typed in the semiblock
style, which is one of the most widely used letter
styles in business today. The inside address and
the salutation are both typed flush with the left
margin, but the first line of each paragraph has a
five-space indention.

The five-space paragraph indention used here
is the one you will see most often. There is no
fixed rule, however, about paragraph indentions.
Some offices indent ten spaces. Now and then you
will see a letter in which the paragraph indention
is the length of the salutation.

The style of punctuation used in this letter
is known as mixed punctuation. There is a colon
after the salutation. A comma is typed after the
complimentary close of the letter.

Sincerely yours,

DALTON REALTY COMPANY

President

NMD:TYP

Style Letter 1
Semiblock With Mixed Punctuation
Line length: 5 inches. Words in body: 128

As you gain experience in the typing of tabulations, you will be able to use your own judgment in determining the amount of intercolumn space. When the material to be tabulated consists of only two or three columns, as in Problems 1 and 2, it is usually preferable to plan for intercolumns that are narrower than the left and right margins.

This arrangement brings the columns closer together and makes it easier for the eye to follow.

In planning a tabulation of four or more columns or a tabulation that consists of long words or groups of large figures, you will get a better effect by dividing the available white space equally among the intercolumns and the margins.

Problem 3. Type the following 4-column tabulation. Allow an equal number of spaces for the margins and for the intercolumns. Type the heading in capitals and small letters. Double-space below the heading. Single-space the tabulation.

Before you begin your typing work, check carefully the working plans on page 180 for the horizontal tabulation.

Home Addresses Of Department Heads

Andrews	Shipping	124 Park St.	Catonsville
Bates	Accounting	1455 Exeter St.	Essex
Calder	Personnel	1234 N. Broadway	Middle River
Cross	Legal	911 Lee St.	Woodlawn
Ewing	Credit	1811 Fort Ave.	Aberdeen
Hamilton	Advertising	1516 Baker St.	Catonsville
Hughes	Publicity	211 Hanover St.	Edgewood
Martin	Mailing	1611 Castle St.	Lake Shore
Olson	Maintenance	1143 S. Bond St.	Ferndale
Pierce	Engineering	3119 Milton Ave.	Essex
Pitman	Statistical	15 Paxton Blvd.	North Odenton
Sutton	Order	32 W. Washington St.	Woodlawn
Thomas	Duplicating	1230 N. Elm Ave.	Aberdeen
Turner	Sales	193 W. 21st St.	Parkville
Watson	Printing	2314 Caton Ave.	Marley
Wilkins	Purchasing	342 Oak Rd.	Towson
Woods	Correspondence	450 E. Warren Ave.	Ferndale
Wyatt	Production	1911 Belair Rd.	Essex
Yeakle	Receiving	2132 N. Adams Ave.	Catonsville
Zachary	Filing	203 University Ave.	Parkton

Your Workbook contains five letterheads like the one used for Style Letter 1. The number of the form for each problem is shown immediately after the problem number.

Problem 1. (Form 5-1). Type Style Letter 1.

You will be typing on a letterhead that is the exact size used for most business letters—8½ inches wide by 11 inches deep. Remember that the width of the sheet is 85 pica spaces or 102 elite spaces and that the depth is 66 line spaces.

Clear all stops. Set margin stops for a 5-inch line. In typing the letter, keep the left and right margins approximately equal.

Set a tabulator stop for a 5-space paragraph indention. Set another stop at the exact center of the sheet for the complimentary close and the two lines that follow it.

Type the date on line 14—two line spaces below the letterhead. The date should end at the right margin.

Type the first line of the inside address on line 21 if your machine has pica type; on line 22 if your machine has elite type.

Note that mixed punctuation requires a colon after the salutation, as well as a comma after the complimentary close.

Problem 2. (Form 5-2). Type the following letter in the form of Style Letter 1. It is approximately the same length as the Style Letter. If you arranged the Style Letter properly, the settings you used for that letter and the starting point of the inside address will be the same for this letter.

Use today's date. Use your initials for those of the typist. (Unless you are instructed otherwise, these instructions will apply to all the letters you type in this Division.)

The symbol (¶) in the letter indicates the beginning of a paragraph. The number of words in the *body* is shown at the end.

Try to avoid hyphenating the last word in the *first* line of a business letter. Either type that word in full at the end of the line or carry it over to the second line.

Paramount Printing Company 380 North Tenth Street   Cleveland, Ohio 44125   Gentlemen: When I was in Cleveland last week, I saw a copy of the booklet on home ownership that you printed recently for the Greater Cleveland Realty Group. Except for the last page, that booklet will be perfect for use here in Newark. (¶) Mr. Douglas Strong, who placed the order with you, has graciously given our local association of realtors permission to print from the type now standing.   (¶) Please give me your quotation on the cost of printing 25,000 copies of the booklet for the Newark Realtors' Association, of which I am this year's President. Include in your quotation the cost of setting type for the last page only. (¶) The Newark Realtors' Association will hold a business meeting on Thursday of next week. I should like to have your quotation in time to present it at that meeting.   Very truly yours, DALTON   REALTY   COMPANY Secretary   RND:.

(137 words)

Problem 3. (Form 5-3). Type the following short letter in the form of Style Letter 1. Use a 4-inch line.

Start the inside address on line 23 if your machine has pica type; on line 24 if your machine has elite type.

Notice that the inside address of this letter consists of four lines. The title *President* is typed at the end of the first line. When the name of the person addressed is long and the company name is short, the title may be typed on the second line of the inside address—before the company name. Use the position that gives the better balance.

Remember to show *your* initials as those of the typist.

5. Backspace once for each two letters in these longest words. Spell out the words as you backspace.

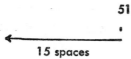

51

← 15 spaces

6. Count the total intercolumn spaces.

10 + 10 = 20

7. Backspace half the total number of intercolumn spaces.

51

←── 10 spaces ──── 15 spaces

8. Set the left margin stop at this point.

Left Margin
26   51

← ──────────────────

9. Space off the longest word in the first column plus the number of spaces between the first and second columns. Set a tabulator stop for the starting point of the second column.

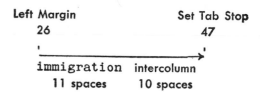

Left Margin   Set Tab Stop
26   47

immigration   intercolumn
11 spaces   10 spaces

10. Space off the longest word in the second column plus the number of spaces between the second and third columns. Set another tabulator stop for the starting point of the third column.

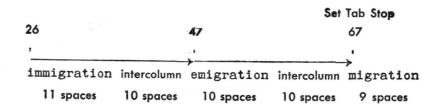

                          Set Tab Stop
26   47   67

immigration   intercolumn   emigration   intercolumn   migration
11 spaces   10 spaces   10 spaces   10 spaces   9 spaces

Problem 1. Type the 3-column tabulation in either Illustration 67, page 174, or Illustration 68, page 175. Use either the calculating method or the center-and-backspace method—whichever your instructor specifies.

Center and type the heading WORDS OFTEN CONFUSED on line 20. Triple-space (one double space and one single space) and proceed with the typing of the tabulation. Tabulate across the page. Never type one column at a time.

Problem 2. Type the following 3-column tabulation with a main heading. You will need to prepare a working plan for both horizontal and vertical placement. Note that the number of spaces in the longest word in each column differs from the count in Problem 1. Allow 10 spaces between columns. Triple-space below the heading. Double-space the tabulation.

MANAGERS AND ASSISTANTS

Atlanta	Snyder	Leslie
Baltimore	Wolfe	Parks
Boston	Jones	Gray
Buffalo	Brandenburg	Owings
Chicago	Oliver	Davis
Dallas	Irving	Young
Denver	Zink	Wilson
Detroit	Mason	Parsons
Houston	Larson	Summerfield
Memphis	Tyler	Perkins
Seattle	Forrest	Adams
Syracuse	Oliver	Hutchinson
Toledo	Robbins	Lee
Tulsa	Mason	Nash
Wichita	Lewis	Harris

Mr. Douglas Strong, President   Mohawk Real Estate Company   3211 Washington Avenue   Cleveland, Ohio 44109   Dear Mr. Strong: Thank you for your letter. I am most grateful for the permission of the Greater Cleveland Realty Group to reproduce your attractive booklet. (¶) Your suggestion about sharing the initial costs of typesetting and art work seems perfectly fair to me. (¶) I don't yet know, of course, whether the project will be approved here. I have asked Paramount Printing Company to quote on making 25,000 copies of the booklet. After I get that quotation, I'll present the plan and see what happens. I'll let you know.   Cordially yours, DALTON   REALTY   COMPANY President   NMD:

(85 words)

Problem 4. (Form 5-4). Use a 4-inch line. Follow the form of Style Letter 1.

Note that a period is used after the abbreviation *Inc.* at the end of the second line of the inside address.

Start the inside address on line 24 if your machine has pica type; on line 25 if your machine has elite type.

Mr. Warren T. Cushing, Manager   Cushing Associates, Inc.   352 West Hudson Street   Newark, New Jersey 07108   Dear Mr. Cushing: Your new lease is ready. Please stop at the office at your convenience within the next ten days, so that we may add the necessary signatures. (¶) This lease includes the added provisions we agreed to in our talk last week. (¶) In case I am out when you call, Miss Barton will gladly help you.   She is authorized to sign

for us.   Sincerely yours,   **DALTON REALTY COMPANY**   Secretary   RND:

(61 words)

Problem 5. (Form 5-5). Type this letter in the form of Style Letter 1. Use a 5-inch line. Start the inside address on line 19 if your machine has pica type; on line 20 if your machine has elite type.

Mr. George L. Burgess, Jr.   788 North Craddock Road   Newark, New Jersey 07112   Dear Mr. Burgess: Forty families who spent last summer in the sweltering heat of the city will be living in cool comfort next August. I hope that your family will be among the fortunate forty. (¶) Several months ago Dalton Realty Company signed an option on one of the most beautiful tracts of waterfront property I have ever seen. Yesterday we bought this scenic spot on the Passaic River—just 45 minutes from your office. It will be developed into an attractive colony of forty summer homes. (¶) The land hasn't yet been subdivided, and plans for a typical home won't be ready for several days. Even a name hasn't been selected. (¶) Am I "jumping the gun" in mailing this letter to you today? I don't think so—not at the modest prices we have in mind. Unless I'm entirely wrong, we'll have swarms of prospective buyers almost as soon as the first foundation is started. The choice sites will go in a hurry. (¶) May I show you the plans when they are ready next week? Please call me today and say "Yes." Next August you'll be glad you did.   Cordially yours,   DALTON REALTY COMPANY   President   NMD:

(185 words)

Horizontal Tabulation By The Center-and-Backspace Method

If your instructor asks you to do so, you may use the center-and-backspace method for setting up the tabulation problems in this Division. The left margin stop is located by setting the printing point indicator at the center and backspacing once for each two spaces in the longest words and in the intercolumns. This method is simply an extension of the backspace method which you have been using in centering headings.

Pica Type

As you read the following steps, refer to Illustration 67, page 174.

1. Clear your margin and tabulator stops.

2. Insert an 8½ x 11 sheet with the left edge at the proper position on the paper guide.

3. Center the printing point indicator at 42.

4. Count the total number of spaces occupied by the longest word in each column.

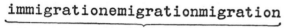
immigrationemigrationmigration

30 spaces

5. Backspace once for each two letters in these longest words. Spell out the words as you backspace.

42

15 spaces

6. Count the total intercolumn spaces.

10 + 10 = 20

7. Backspace half the total number of intercolumn spaces.

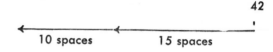
42

10 spaces   15 spaces

8. Set the left margin stop at this point.

Left Margin
17   42

9. Space off the longest word in the first column plus the number of spaces between the first and second columns. Set a tabulator stop for the starting point of the second column.

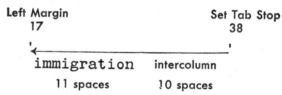
Left Margin   Set Tab Stop
17   38

immigration   intercolumn
11 spaces   10 spaces

10. Space off the longest word in the second column plus the number of spaces between the second and third columns. Set another tabulator stop for the starting point of the third column.

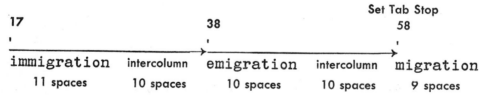
17   38   Set Tab Stop
                                            58

immigration   intercolumn   emigration   intercolumn   migration
11 spaces   10 spaces   10 spaces   10 spaces   9 spaces

Note: When 42 is used as the centering point, the extra space is added to the right. The left margin stop and the tabulator stops are set one space further to the left than they appear in Illustration 67.

Elite Type

As you read the following steps, refer to Illustration 68, page 175.

1. Clear your margin and tabulator stops.

2. Insert an 8½ x 11 sheet with the left edge at the proper position on the paper guide.

3. Center the printing point indicator at 51.

4. Count the total number of spaces occupied by the longest word in each column.

immigrationemigrationmigration

30 spaces

Letter Placement. The following suggestions will help you to produce attractively arranged letters.

Classify each letter according to length—short, medium, or long—and use the correct line length for your letter. The following plan is simple to use and easy to remember.

Letter Length	Line Length
Short (under 100 words)	4 inches
Medium (100 to 200 words)	5 inches
Long (200 to 300 words)	6 inches

Here is an easy guide for deciding where to start the inside address in a single-spaced letter:

In typing letters up to 50 words in pica type and up to 75 words in elite type, start on line 25; raise the starting point one line for each additional 25 words.

Illustration 47 shows how this placement plan works. Study it carefully. Notice particularly how the line length changes and how the starting point is raised as the letters grow longer.

Later in your course you will type some letters that present special placement problems. Don't hesitate to depart from the suggestions given here when your judgment tells you to do so.

The next two pages contain letters for you to set up yourself. Type them in the semiblock style.

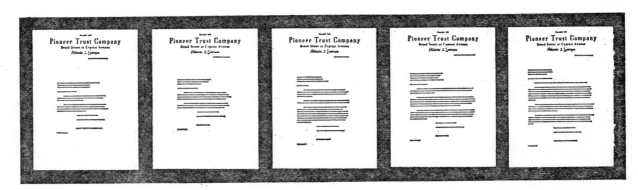

Words	Up to 50	50 to 75	75 to 100	100 to 125	125 to 150
Line	4 inches	4 inches	4 inches	5 inches	5 inches
Start on	Line 25-pica	Line 24-pica	Line 23-pica	Line 22-pica	Line 21-pica
	Line 25-elite	Line 25-elite	Line 24-elite	Line 23-elite	Line 22-elite

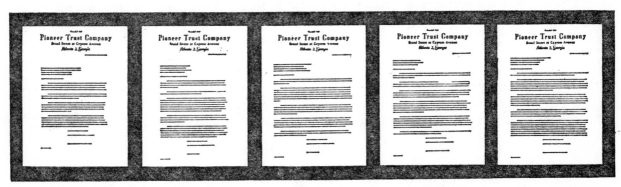

Words	150 to 175	175 to 200	200 to 225	225 to 250	250 and up
Line	5 inches	5 inches	6 inches	6 inches	6 inches
Start on	Line 20-pica	Line 19-pica	Line 18-pica	Line 17-pica	Line 16-pica
	Line 21-elite	Line 20-elite	Line 19-elite	Line 18-elite	Line 17-elite

ILLUSTRATION 47
Letter Placement

Horizontal Placement—Pica Type

If you are using a pica typewriter, study the following working plan and note the positions at which the left margin stop and the tabulator stops are set.

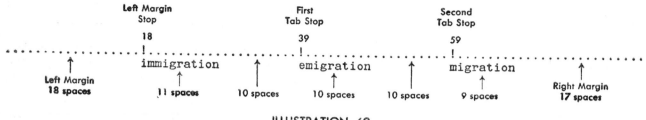

ILLUSTRATION 69
Pica Type

Here are the steps to follow in preparing to type the tabulation shown in Illustration 67, page 174.

1. Clear your margin stops and tabulator stops.

2. Set the line space regulator for double spacing.

3. Insert an 8½ x 11 sheet with the left edge at the proper position on the paper guide.

4. Set the left margin stop at 18. This stop provides for the first column.

5. Set a tabulator stop at 39 for the second column (18 + 11 + 10 = 39).

6. Set another tabulator stop at 59 for the third column (39 + 10 + 10 = 59). As provision has been made for typing the longest word in column three, no right margin setting is needed.

Horizontal Placement—Elite Type

If you are using an elite typewriter, study the following working plan and note the positions at which the left margin stop and the tabulator stops are set.

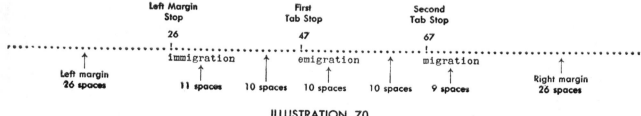

ILLUSTRATION 70
Elite Type

Here are the steps to follow in preparing to type the tabulation shown in Illustration 68, page 175.

1. Clear your margin stops and tabulator stops.

2. Set the line space regulator for double spacing.

3. Insert an 8½ x 11 sheet with the left edge at the proper position on the paper guide.

4. Set the left margin stop at 26. This stop provides for the first column.

5. Set a tabulator stop at 47 for the second column (26 + 11 + 10 = 47).

6. Set another tabulator stop at 67 for the third column (47 + 10 + 10 = 67). As provision has been made for the longest word in column three, no right margin setting is needed.

Problem 6.   (Form 5-6)

Mr. Milton W. McGrail, Secretary   Credit Men's Association   Room 306, Walker Building   Atlanta, Georgia 30318   Dear Mr. McGrail: Yes, I shall be delighted to address the members of the Credit Men's Association at your anniversary banquet.   I have the highest regard for your group and for the superb work that you are doing.   (¶) How long would you like me to talk?   I want to fit my remarks to the time allowed on the program.   (¶) As soon as I hear from you, I'll start getting my notes organized.   Sincerely yours,   PIONEER TRUST COMPANY   President   LNC:

(69 words)

Problem 7.   (Form 5-7)

Stormette Manufacturing Company   274 East Triangle Avenue   Pittsburgh, Pennsylvania 15214   Gentlemen: Your equipment for drive-in banking facilities has been recommended to us.   Please mail us complete descriptive literature.   (¶) Plans are now being made for remodeling one of our branch banks.   We hope to incorporate structural changes that will enable depositors to bank directly from their cars.   (¶) I shall be glad to talk with your representative in this area.   I should like to suggest, however, that he call me first for an appointment.   The architect and some of the other officers can then arrange to sit in on our talk.   (¶) In what banks near Atlanta has your equipment been installed?   We should like, if possible, to see it in operation before we reach a decision.   Very truly yours,   PIONEER TRUST COMPANY   Vice-President   RTR:

(114 words)

Problem 8.   (Form 5-8)

Mrs. Lee W. Claridge   College Vista Apartments   804 South Pine Street   Decatur, Georgia 30030   My dear Mrs. Claridge: Thank you for bringing your questions about your estate to Pioneer Trust.   We shall be glad to help you in any way we can.   (¶) The day when only the wealthy made wills is definitely past.   Even if your estate were only half the amount you mentioned, we should strongly urge you to arrange for its proper distribution by means of a will.   (¶) Unless you do so, the naming of an executor will fall to the court.   Under the circumstances it is true that the court would probably select your son.   One of the distinct advantages of a will, however, is to make certain who the executor will be.   (¶) Another advantage is that the making of a will eliminates some expenses that would otherwise have to be met.   Should the court select your son as executor, for example, it would probably require him to give surety on his administrator's bond.   (¶) Before you do make your will, Mrs. Claridge, we hope that you will also consider the advisability of naming Pioneer Trust Company—rather than any one person—as executor.   I shall be delighted to set aside time any day to talk with you and to explain how we are serving others in this way.   Perhaps you would like to ask your son to come along with you.   (¶) Just tell me the day and hour that will be most convenient for you, and I'll arrange to be free.   Yours very truly,   PIONEER TRUST COMPANY   Vice-President   RTR:

(236 words)

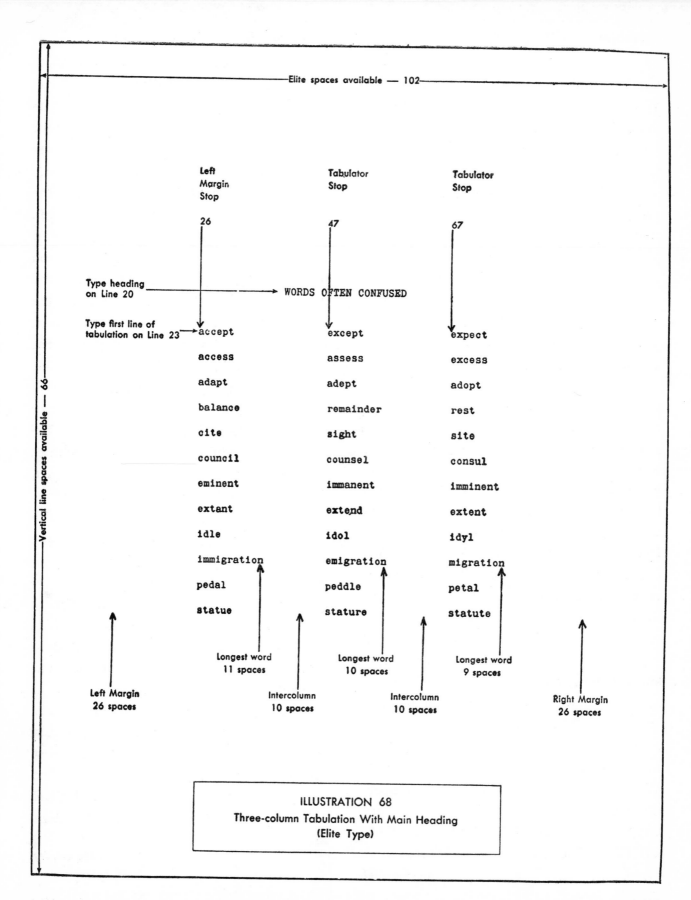

Elite spaces available — 102

Vertical line spaces available — 66

| Left Margin Stop | Tabulator Stop | Tabulator Stop |
| 26 | 47 | 67 |

Type heading on Line 20 → WORDS OFTEN CONFUSED

Type first line of tabulation on Line 23 →

accept	except	expect
access	assess	excess
adapt	adept	adopt
balance	remainder	rest
cite	sight	site
council	counsel	consul
eminent	immanent	imminent
extant	extend	extent
idle	idol	idyl
immigration	emigration	migration
pedal	peddle	petal
statue	stature	statute

Longest word 11 spaces

Longest word 10 spaces

Longest word 9 spaces

Left Margin 26 spaces

Intercolumn 10 spaces

Intercolumn 10 spaces

Right Margin 26 spaces

ILLUSTRATION 68
Three-column Tabulation With Main Heading
(Elite Type)

Problem 9. (Form 5-9)

Miss Louise C. Parker   409 South 21st Street   Atlanta, Georgia 30311   Dear Miss Parker: It surely was a pleasure to learn this morning that you have opened a savings account at Pioneer Trust. Please consider this letter a personal word of welcome. We're proud that you selected us to handle your account. (¶) Your savings account will earn interest twice a year—on April 1 and October 1. I'd like to recommend that you bring your deposit book to us soon after each of those dates, so that we can keep your book right up to date. (¶) As you visit us from time to time to make additional deposits, please ask about the other services at Pioneer Trust that you may find helpful. Many of our depositors, for example, are using special savings plans to provide for Christmas and vacation expenses. By doing so, they are able to keep from disturbing the interest-earning funds in their regular savings accounts. (¶) Any of the tellers will be glad to tell you, too, how you can open a convenient checking account that will permit you to pay all your regular bills by check. (¶) It is good to have this chance to welcome you to the growing group of thrifty people who call Pioneer Trust their bank. Please bring us your questions and your financial problems. We're eager to serve you.   Sincerely yours,   PIONEER TRUST COMPANY   Assistant Treasurer   MRM:

(213 words)

Problem 10. (Form 5-10)

Mr. David S. Dutton   2016 Park Drive   Atlanta, Georgia 30312   Dear Mr. Dutton: Thank you for returning to us promptly your last quarterly statement and the two checks written by another depositor. You will receive a corrected statement tomorrow. (¶) Now and then a depositor will write his account number from memory. That bad habit caused the trouble here. We are writing at once to the depositor who used your number to ask him to verify his own account number on each of his checks. (¶) You will be interested to know that only three account number errors out of several hundred mistakes made by depositors during the last quarter slipped through our error-detection system here. Even though that record is one that few banks can equal, we still want to better it. (¶) It was good of you, Mr. Dutton, to write us as you did. The splendid cooperation of careful depositors like you helps us greatly.   Sincerely yours,   PIONEER TRUST COMPANY   Treasurer   BFR:

(143 words)

Block Style. You will type the next group of letters—Problems 11 to 16 inclusive—in the block style. Make yourself thoroughly familiar with that style by studying Style Letter 2 on page 122. The body of the letter explains the style in which it is written.

You will, of course, continue to use today's date for all your letters unless you are instructed otherwise.

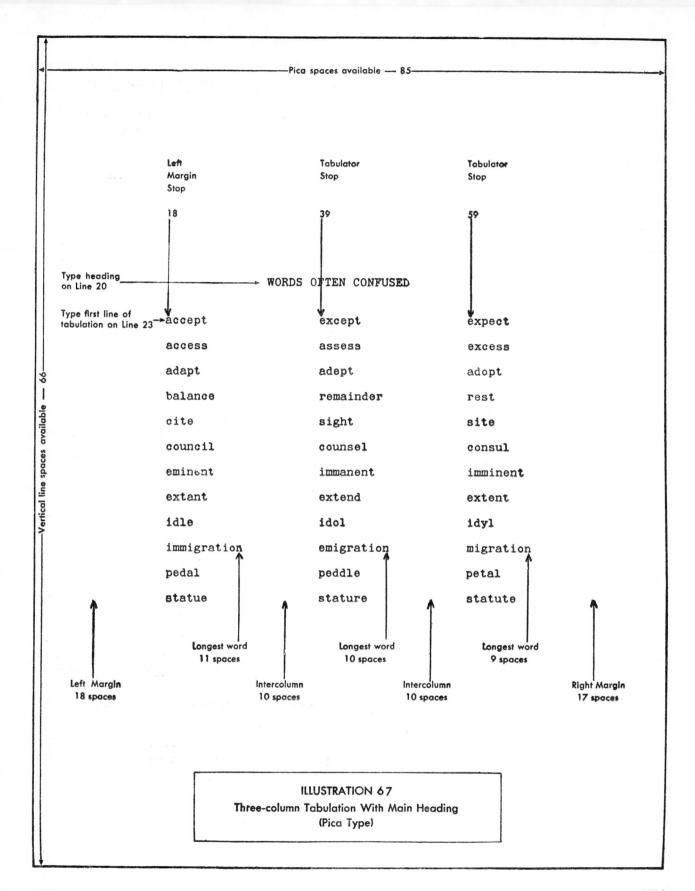

Pica spaces available — 85

Vertical line spaces available — 66

Left Margin Stop — 18

Tabulator Stop — 39

Tabulator Stop — 59

Type heading on Line 20 → WORDS OFTEN CONFUSED

Type first line of tabulation on Line 23 →

accept	except	expect
access	assess	excess
adapt	adept	adopt
balance	remainder	rest
cite	sight	site
council	counsel	consul
eminent	immanent	imminent
extant	extend	extent
idle	idol	idyl
immigration	emigration	migration
pedal	peddle	petal
statue	stature	statute

Longest word 11 spaces

Longest word 10 spaces

Longest word 9 spaces

Left Margin 18 spaces

Intercolumn 10 spaces

Intercolumn 10 spaces

Right Margin 17 spaces

ILLUSTRATION 67
Three-column Tabulation With Main Heading
(Pica Type)

174

SIR KLAY CORPORATION

4607 INDEPENDENCE STREET
LOS ANGELES, CALIFORNIA 90029

Specialists in Ceramics

January 8, 19--

Mr. T. Warren Henderson
1927 North Madison Avenue
Glendale, California   91206

Dear Mr. Henderson:

This letter is typed in the block style with mixed
punctuation. As you will see at a glance, there
are no paragraph indentions when the block style
is used. Each line of the body starts at the left
margin.

The date on this letter is centered horizontally
on the sheet. That position is preferred when the
letterhead design itself is centered. When the
design extends across the full width of the sheet,
the date often looks better typed to end with the
right margin. Either position for the date may be
used with the block style of letter.

The closing lines of the letter--the complimentary
close, the company name, and the dictator's name
or title--are blocked. They start at the center
of the sheet.

Many business offices use the block style because
it does away with paragraph indentions.

Sincerely yours,

SIR KLAY CORPORATION

Joseph R. Winter

TYP

Style Letter 2
Block With Mixed Punctuation
Line length: 5 inches. Words in body: 140

Preparing The Working Plan By The Calculating Method

Illustration 67, page 174, shows a three-column tabulation with its main heading as it would look when typed on a machine with pica type. Illustration 68, page 175, shows the same tabulation typed with elite type. Each tabulation has been reduced slightly.

The heading WORDS OFTEN CONFUSED is centered horizontally. The left margin and the right margin are the same width. The inter-column space between the first and second columns and between the second and third columns is 10 spaces each—to simplify your calculating.

The calculating method for planning a tabulation is simply the process of adding together the spaces occupied by the longest word in each column, adding the spaces in the intercolumns, subtracting the total from the number of available spaces across the width of the sheet, and then dividing the remainder by 2 to determine the width of the left and right margins.

Total available spaces

minus

Total spaces occupied by the
longest words and by the intercolumns

divided by

2 (Margins)

equals

Number of spaces in each margin

By reading the following questions and answers, you will see clearly how this formula is used. If you are using a pica-type machine, refer to Illustration 67, page 174. If you are using an elite-type machine, refer to Illustration 68, page 175.

	Pica	Elite
What is the total number of spaces in an 8½-inch width?	85	102
What is the longest word in the first column? *immigration*		
How many spaces will you need for this word?	11	11
What is the longest word in the second column? *emigration*		
How many spaces will you need for this word?	10	10
What is the longest word in the third column? *migration*		
How many spaces will you need for this word?	9	9
What is the total number of spaces needed for the three words?	30	30
How many spaces will you need for the intercolumns?	20	20
Total spaces needed for the longest words and for the two intercolumns	50	50
How many spaces are left?	35	52
Divide 2 (margins) into the spaces left	2) 35	2) 52
Number of spaces for each margin	17½ (18)	26

Problem 11. (Form 5-11). Type Style Letter 2. Note the identifying initials—those of the typist only. The dictator's identifying initials may be omitted when his name is typed. Follow this practice in typing letters that show the dictator's name in full.

Problem 12. (Form 5-12)

Glover Personnel Agency   Second National Bank Building   67 Canfield Boulevard   San Francisco, California 94107   Gentlemen: Planned expansion of our research facilities will call for adding to our present staff one ceramics engineer and one refractories engineer. We want to fill both positions within two months. (¶) Do you have on file the names of any qualified applicants? Yours very truly,   SIR KLAY CORPORATION   Webster H. Hunt

(41 words)

Problem 13. (Form 5-13). A company name, especially when it identifies a line of products by the same name, is often typed in ALL CAPS. Note the use of such capitalizing in the following letter.

Mr. L. W. Straith, Purchasing Agent Broderick Brothers Corporation   8612 South Hopkins Boulevard   Minneapolis, Minnesota 55423   Dear Mr. Straith: Your copy of the new SIR KLAY catalog is being mailed to you today. Please watch for it. (¶) This new catalog—the largest we have ever issued—replaces Catalog No. 85 and supplements. We hope that you will refer to it often and that you will always think first of SIR KLAY when you need ceramics materials and equipment.   Sincerely yours,   SIR KLAY CORPORATION   M. Jackson Wells

(59 words)

Problem 14. (Form 5-14)

Mr. Harold D. Cutler, Manager   Hillsville Artware Company   850 North Mesa Avenue   Fort Worth, Texas 76109   Dear Mr. Cutler: Yes, please do send us samples of faded ware returned to you by your customers. We shall gladly put them through laboratory tests to help you pin down the cause. (¶) This problem of fading, especially in the case of all overglazed dinnerware, has been with the industry a long time. Until modern detergents and mechanical dishwashers came into widespread use, however, materials suppliers gave it little attention. Now, fortunately, there are colors, foils, glazes, and decals on the market that will solve the problem. (¶) The details on firing and materials that you included in your letter will help a lot. Can you also send us several samples from stock to compare with the faded ones? Although they aren't necessary, they may help us to give you a speedier report. (¶) A separate analysis of the colors themselves can be made later if you wish. In the meantime, we may be able to eliminate color chemistry as the cause simply by studying the uniformity of fading. (¶) You will get our report by air mail within a week after we receive samples for testing.   Sincerely yours,   SIR KLAY CORPORATION   S. T. Ruxton

(181 words)

Problem 15. (Form 5-15)

Mr. Carter W. Neal   Neal, Wadsworth & Starr   20 West Grace Street   Portland, Oregon 97215   Dear Mr. Neal: This letter is a cordial invitation to you to be our

Division Six—Tabulating

Every typist in a business office is called on from time to time to set up information in tabulated form. Some types of material, such as statistical data, can be more easily read and understood when arranged as tabulations.

Careful planning in advance will enable you to produce neat and attractively arranged tabulations. "Be sure you are right; then go ahead" is the slogan you should follow when you begin work on a problem in tabulating.

Your goal is to produce a tabulation that is well placed, both horizontally and vertically. The side margins should be approximately the same width. The blank spaces between the columns (called *intercolumns*) should generally be equal. If your tabulation has a main heading or a main heading and a subheading, those headings should be properly centered.

Vertical Placement

You have already learned that there are 6 vertical line spaces to an inch A sheet of paper that measures 11 inches from top to bottom will, therefore, provide a total of 66 line spaces.

The following table shows how the vertical placement in Illustration 67, page 174, was planned. Refer to the illustration as you follow these steps.

Total number of lines available	66
Number of lines occupied by the heading	1
Number of lines between the heading and the first word in each column	2
Number of typed lines in the tabulation	12
Number of lines between the typed lines	11
Subtract from the total lines available	26
Remainder	40

Divide the remainder (40) by 2 to get the line location of the heading—20.

Horizontal Placement

There are two methods that you can follow in planning the horizontal placement of your tabulations. The first method involves calculating. The second is the center-and-backspace method. Both methods will be explained in detail. In typing the tabulation problems in this Division, use the method that your instructor specifies.

You will now study a simple tabulating problem to see how an experienced typist would go about arranging the tabulation attractively on an $8\frac{1}{2}$ x 11 sheet. First, you will follow the steps in the calculating method. Next, you will see how the same tabulation may be set up by the center-and-backspace method.

guest at the very first conference of its kind ever held in America. You will get the complete program later this month. Meantime, please circle on your calendar April 26 and April 27—the two days when we hope you will be in Los Angeles. (¶) Here is the story behind this unusual invitation. (¶) Three years ago SIR KLAY pioneered on the West Coast in the manufacture of porcelain enamel architectural panels by starting production in the corner of one building. Now we have grown out of that corner and into a separate plant. Production goes up daily as contractors in and around Los Angeles flood us with orders. (¶) Note those words "in and around Los Angeles." The fact that men elsewhere on the Coast haven't seen this exciting new building material bothers us. You can't know the true beauty, the economy, or the adaptability of SIR KLAY panels until you see them—and they're too big to carry into your office. Isn't the perfect solution for you to come to Los Angeles in April at our expense? (¶) More than 100 other men in the construction field—architects, contractors, and engineers—will be our guests then. You will tour the plant. You will hear prominent Los Angeles architects and builders explain how SIR KLAY panels work for them. Best of all, you'll see scores of buildings in which these panels have been used. (¶) Please watch for your reservation card and your advance copy of the program. We do hope that you will be able to come. Sincerely yours, SIR KLAY CORPORATION John V. Easterling

(271 words)

Problem 16. (Form 5-16)

Transson Industries, Inc.   6938 Birmingham Road   Detroit, Michigan 48212 Gentlemen: Thank you for your order for six EXPRO spray guns. They were shipped to you this morning by parcel post. (¶) You will notice that since you placed your last order, there has been a small change in the design. The EXPRO spray gun now comes with an improved "Comfort Grip" handle that has been specially molded to cut down hand fatigue. The working parts remain the same as those used in earlier models. (¶) "Comfort Grip" handles, incidentally, are available at $2.75 each as replacement parts for your older EXPRO equipment.   Very truly yours, SIR KLAY CORPORATION Harris W. Leonard   *(90 words)*

Full-Block Style. You are to type the next group of letters—Problems 17 to 20 inclusive—in the full-block style (sometimes called the *extreme block style*). The body of Style Letter 3, page 125, explains the style. Study it carefully before you do any typing.

Style Letter 3 is typed with open punctuation. Note how that style of punctuation differs from the style you have been using.

One letter in this group, like many modern sales letters, contains quotations. If you are not thoroughly familiar with the rules for spacing when quotation marks are used, review them now. You will find the rules on page 90.

You will be asked to estimate the number of words in two of the letters in this group.

Count the total number of words in three full lines of the letter which you are to type; find the average number of words in a line by dividing by 3; then multiply the quotient by the number of lines in the letter.

Paragraph Typing C

These paragraphs include many figures, symbols, and capital letters.

1   To write the <u>minus</u> sign and the <u>times</u> sign, strike the hyphen and the small <u>x</u>, respectively; be sure to space both before and after, thus: 187 - 65; 436 x 93. Sometimes you may need to type the <u>degree</u> sign. To write it, release the cylinder, turn down the paper, and then strike the small <u>o</u>. Finally, turn up your paper and adjust to the writing line.

2   May he get three copies (1 original, 2 carbons) of our Purchase Order SE-48? It is the order for four (4) plastic desk trays, 8½" x 12¼", listed at 93¢ each, and for six (6) bronze base lamps, 2' high, at $15 each, less the usual 10% discount for cash in fifteen (15) days. The original is to go to Ray Supply Company, 59 Bonner Road, Cincinnati, Ohio.

3   A <u>number</u> is a mathematical aggregate of units that may be expressed either by figures or spelled out in words; as, 36 or thirty-six. A <u>figure</u> is a symbol we use to express a whole number or a fraction; as, 2, 8, ½, and ¼. A fraction not on the keyboard is typed with a diagonal; as, 2/5, 6/7. Especially on checks, the amount of 75¢ is typed as 75/100.

4   Today we interviewed Mr. William L. Royster, who has a large plant at 3857 North 14th Street, Xenia, Ohio, and who does business under the name of Winfield Utilities Company. We inspected the carload of #69 steel shafts shipped to his plant on October 14 and found that 28 of the shafts have in them defects which render impossible their use on this job.

RUST, LAWSON & COMPANY, INC.
18 HENRY STREET, CHICAGO, ILLINOIS   60615

*A*dvertising
*C*onsultants

November 16, 19--

Mr. B. R. Haig, Manager
Dowell Brothers Company
9285 Commonwealth Avenue
Boston, Massachusetts   02123

Dear Mr. Haig

This letter is typed in the full-block style with
open punctuation. Notice that every part of the
letter starts at the left margin.

When open punctuation is used, there is no colon
after the salutation and no comma after the complimentary close. The only lines that have end
punctuation are those in the body of the letter.
You know, of course, that a period must still follow an abbreviation even though the abbreviation
falls at the end of a line in the address.

Letters in the full-block style may be typed with
either mixed punctuation or open punctuation. Now
and then open punctuation is also used with other
letter styles. Most people feel, however, that it
harmonizes best with the full-block letter.

Although the full-block style has not yet won the
same wide acceptance as either the semiblock style
or the block style, it is winning friends all the
time. Many typists prefer it because it helps to
speed up their work.

Cordially yours

RUST, LAWSON & COMPANY, INC.

Jeff D. Lawson

TYP

> Style Letter 3—Full-Block With Open Punctuation
> Line length: 5 inches. Words in body: 166

Paragraph Typing B

Each of these paragraphs contains all the letters of the alphabet.

Words

1   If you ask any successful man just exactly why he made   11
good, he will quite likely reply it is because he likes his   23
work; indeed, he loves it. His mind and heart and soul are   35
wrapped up in it. He exercises all his mental and physical   47
energies and puts them into his work in a most amazing way.   59
There is nothing anywhere you can substitute for hard work.   71

2   If you are determined to get work done, avoid allowing   11   82
tasks to hang over you. Just start on a job which needs to   23   94
be done, and you will finish before you realize it. Do not   35 106
let yourself think that a piece of work will take more time   47 118
than you can give it now. Go quietly to work, even if some   59 130
extra effort is needed. Keep your current work cleaned up.   71 142

3   In analyzing a problem, get all the facts that bear on   11 153
the situation. If you are hazy about the facts, you cannot   23 165
expect to get the right solution. A quick judgment that is   35 177
made to get an immediate decision is to be avoided. Do not   47 189
make decisions which are based on prejudice. Do not permit   59 201
emotion to color your judgment, but proceed on facts alone.   71 213

4   If you do not know the alphabet, you are going to have   11 224
a mighty hard time learning the principles of indexing. It   23 236
is true that specialization in this field is for just a few   35 248
people, but you need to realize that everybody who is to go   47 260
into business should acquire exact and precise knowledge of   59 272
how filing is done and how it serves its important purpose.   71 284

Problem 17. (Form 5-17). Type Style Letter **3**.

Problem 18. (Form 5-18). Note the salutation in the following letter. The use of *Dear Sir* is correct when the letter is addressed to a person whose name is unknown.

Program Director   Station WMEM-TV Memphis, Tennessee 38115 Dear Sir One of our clients will use daily spot announcements during April on several television stations. Your station is one of those now being considered. (¶) Please let us know whether you have spots open that month. We want to arrange for one afternoon announcement and one evening announcement. (¶) When you reply, please include a schedule of your rates. Yours truly RUST, LAWSON & COMPANY, INC. William R. Cecil

(57 words)

Problem 19. (Form 5-19)

Mr. R. V. Wilkinson, President   Keesler Manufacturing Company   5112 South Border Street   Chicago, Illinois 60609 Dear Mr. Wilkinson   Back in the early 1900's, when Grandpa MacTavish was president of his company, he used to do a lot of fretting about the company's annual report. (¶) "The trouble is, lads," he would complain to his board of directors, "this thing is all outgo and no return." (¶) If that comment sounds familiar, you'll want to hear about a telephone call we had the other day from another MacTavish—grandson of the fellow we just quoted. The grandson, who is every bit as dollar-conscious as the old boy ever was, is now president of the company. He's a client of ours. (¶) "I just want to tell you," he said,

"that you folks were right and Grandpa was wrong. The new kind of annual report you made for us is bringing us more good will—dollar for dollar—than any other kind of advertising we ever bought." (¶) Did your last annual report actually pay for itself in the public relations job that it did for you? If you feel that it didn't, please let us show you—without obligation—how we can help you get your money's worth next year. (¶) Fair enough? Just ask your secretary to call STevens 8-4039 and tell us when you will have a free half hour next week. Cordially yours RUST, LAWSON & COMPANY, INC. G. Wilbur Rust

(Estimate the number of words.)

Problem 20. (Form 5-20). Note the city address of this letter. Although you should always spell the name of a *state* in full, use the abbreviation *D. C.* for *District of Columbia*.

Mr. Henry D. Detlinger   Detlinger Mailing Service 2963 Twentieth Street, N.W. Washington, D. C. 20012   Dear Mr. Detlinger We have used lists from a number of mailing list suppliers. I think you're entitled to know that the results we got from the use of one of your lists last month have been the best in our experience. (¶) What you have been telling us about the thoroughness and accuracy of your coverage has been borne out by performance. Cordially yours RUST, LAWSON & COMPANY, INC. Jeff D. Lawson

(Estimate the number of words.)

Indented Style. You are to type the next five letters—Problems 21 to 25 inclusive—in the indented style with close punctuation. Style Letter 4, page 127, explains that letter style and the use of close punctuation. Study the letter carefully.

Division Six

Paragraph Typing A

Many of the words in these paragraphs are balanced-hand words.

Words

1   The young man or woman who picks a goal and then forms — 11
an authentic plan to make the goal is more apt to go to the — 23
top than the boy or girl who does not fix his or her eye on — 35
any goal. It is thus both wise and prudent for us to focus — 47
our eyes on some goal, but it does not pay to rush into the — 59
decision; time spent in fixing the goal is time well spent. — 71

2   It pays to sit down now and then and give some thought — 11 — 82
to the future; if a man is going down the wrong road, he is — 23 — 94
not apt to land where he wants to land. Most of us do make — 35 — 106
goals for our own lives, but so many of us fail to make any — 47 — 118
note of the signs that mark the right turns on the roads to — 59 — 130
those goals; thus the goals elude us despite our hard work. — 71 — 142

3   When work is done in a big rush, there is more risk of — 11 — 153
making a mistake than there is when the work is done in the — 23 — 165
usual way. The way to cut down the element of risk is thus — 35 — 177
to map out the work so that there is enough time both to do — 47 — 189
the work and then to check it; most of us do make mistakes, — 59 — 201
and it is wise to form the habit of checking work for them. — 71 — 213

4   Men and women today laugh at the theory that the world — 11 — 224
is flat, for they know so much more about the shape and the — 23 — 236
nature of the world than did the people who lived but a few — 35 — 248
centuries ago. It is likely that some of the theories held — 47 — 260
by many of us today may also make wiser people laugh in the — 59 — 272
future; but a theory, right or wrong, often leads to truth. — 71 — 284

169

Nelson and Wister
- INSURANCE -
49 South Capitol Street
Harrisburg, Pennsylvania 17103

LIFE · AUTOMOBILE · ACCIDENT · FIRE · CASUALTY · RETIREMENT · THEFT · TORNADO · HEALTH

March 20, 19--

Mr. Leslie R. Hayden, General Manager,
        Supreme Fidelity Insurance Company,
            500 West Iroquois Street,
                Hartford, Connecticut   06117.

Dear Mr. Hayden:

This letter is typed in the indented style. When you use this style, you will indent each line of the inside address except the first line. You will also indent each of the lines following the complimentary close. The most frequently used indention is five spaces.

The punctuation of this letter is known as close punctuation. There is, you will notice, a period at the end of the last line of the inside address and a comma at the end of each preceding line. A colon follows the salutation, and a comma follows the complimentary close.

The practice of putting a period at the end of the date line is still followed in some offices using close punctuation. Most persons today feel, however, that no end punctuation is needed for the date, for the company name, or for the dictator's name or title.

Because the indented style tends to slow down letter production, it is now used mostly in those offices that place a high value on conservatism.

                        Sincerely yours,

                        NELSON AND WISTER

                        S. John Nelson

TYP

Style Letter 4—Indented With Close Punctuation
Line length: 5 inches. Words in body: 170

A patriot is one who loves and supports his country. The love of 13
native land has produced some of the great poetry of all time; it has 27
caused men to endure unbelievable toil and sacrifice; it has given hope 41
and courage when days were dark and when the outlook was uncertain. 54
There are really only two kinds of countries in the world. They are, 68
first, the countries that are governed by the people themselves through 82
their chosen representatives and, second, those that are governed by 96
dictators who have seized power for themselves and who hold that 109
power by a constant reign of terror. In our country we believe profoundly 124
that the state exists for the benefit of the people; that its purpose is 138
to serve the needs of all the people. 145

To be a citizen of our land is one of the greatest blessings that anyone 159
can imagine. All of us who live here have opportunities and advantages 173
such as are unknown in many other parts of the world. We have a 186
heritage to which we can look back with pride. We need to remember 199
that we ourselves did not work for the freedom we have. It has been 213
handed down to us by our forefathers, who were men that came to this 227
land to find freedom of worship and conscience; men who felled the 240
trees and cleared the forests; men who tilled the land and built homes 254
in the wilderness; men who conquered the forces of nature and of 267
opposition of all kinds; men who fought and bled and died for their 280
beliefs; men who built this nation on the foundation they laid. 293

Coupled with those privileges are duties and obligations. Many of 306
us have become so accustomed to the benefits that flow from our 319
citizenship that we are apt to lose sight of our responsibilities. Our 333
first responsibility is to be loyal to the ideals which the great men of 347
the past have handed down. We ought so to steep ourselves in the 360
spirit that actuated them that we shall come to share their deep 373
convictions about the rights of men as human beings. It is not enough 387
to study history with the mind; our hearts and feelings must be engaged. 401
It is always feelings and emotions, not cold intellect, that move men 415
to lay down their lives for their convictions. Until we become charged 429
with that deep feeling which marks the attitude of the true citizen, we 443
are likely to remain listless and unconcerned and occupied only with 457
the small round of our daily lives. We are willing enough to share the 471
privileges we have, but often we do not develop that driving force which 485
makes us willing to assume the obligations and perform the duties that 499
make those privileges possible. Rights always bring with them duties, 513
just as privileges always go with obligations. If we neglect our duties, 528
we cannot expect to have rights and privileges. 537

Problem 21. (Form 5-21). Type Style Letter 4.

Problem 22. (Form 5-22)

Mr. Howard R. Davis, 92 Linden Avenue, Steelton, Pennsylvania 17092. Dear Mr. Davis: This letter will confirm our talk on the telephone today. (¶) We are immediately increasing the amount of fire insurance on your home at 92 Linden Avenue by $2,000 to bring the total amount to $12,000. The usual coinsurance clause will apply to the additional amount. (¶) It is good to know that you have made this decision, Mr. Davis. In case you do have a serious fire loss, the added protection will be well worth the small extra cost. Sincerely yours, NELSON AND WISTER Mark L. Wister

(78 words)

Problem 23. (Form 5-23)

Miss Mary Louise MacClure, Fairview Apartments, 20 East Oak Street, Hershey, Pennsylvania 17033. Dear Miss MacClure: Thank you for completing so promptly and so thoroughly the report of the automobile accident you had last week. (¶) Please go ahead with the necessary repairs to your car. When the work is finished, mail the bill to us to help us get you a fast settlement. Sincerely yours, NELSON AND WISTER Mark L. Wister

(47 words)

Problem 24. (Form 5-24)

Mr. Francis M. Kelly, Manager, New Era Casualty Company, 2320 Appleton Street, Buffalo, New York 14215. Dear Francis: Many thanks for your letter and for the good news it contained. This coming Tuesday will suit us perfectly. We'll be looking for you around eleven o'clock. (¶) Mark has asked me to tell you that the Keystone Club, of which he is president this year, meets on Tuesday at noon. He wants you and me to be his guests that day if your schedule will permit. Cordially yours, NELSON AND WISTER S. John Nelson

(66 words)

Problem 25. (Form 5-25)

Mr. Lawrence B. Watkins, 483 East Cottage Road, Harrisburg, Pennsylvania 17109. Dear Mr. Watkins: Your Detroit Mutual endowment policy matures this summer. The next quarterly premium, in fact, will be the last one required under that contract. (¶) I do want to congratulate you. So many people who start endowment policies are unwilling to make the sacrifices often necessary to carry them through to maturity. (¶) Several options will be open to you when this policy matures. I have always felt strongly that one duty of an insurance agent is to explain carefully what those options are. That duty, it seems to me, is more important now than ever before; the economic picture today is so different from the one that existed when the contract was written. (¶) Could we spend a half hour together one evening soon? If you will call me here at the office, I'll gladly make a date to stop around at your home and help you work out the wisest course for you. (¶) Our telephone number is 3927. Sincerely yours, NELSON AND WISTER S. John Nelson

(Estimate the number of words.)

Now that we have talked about change, it is well for us to understand that the basic traits of good character do not change. On the physical side, the world has made great advances, but it is open to question whether the human race has made advances in a spiritual way. Above the body and above the mind stands character, which is the sum of the qualities we have in mind when we speak about the force and courage that a man has. Education must give us much besides book learning and skills in order to be really good. We need to remember that no keenness of mind, no polish, no cleverness in any way make up for the lack of the great solid qualities. We need to learn self-restraint and self-mastery; we must learn how to accept responsibility and yet act in cooperation with other people. More important than knowledge and skill are these commonplace, everyday qualities and virtues.

If the experience of the present and of the immediate past means anything, changes in the world around us will proceed at an ever more rapid pace. What we need to do is to adapt ourselves to those changes and at the same time hold fast to the everyday qualities for which there are no substitutes and which alone enable us to steer a true course in a sea of swirling change. There is an old saying that a person should not be the first to discard the old or the last to adopt the new. Like many other sayings which have come to us through the stream of time, this one has much truth in it. Notice, however, that the maxim does not say that we should never discard the old and never adopt the new. It simply advises caution; it tells us to be on our guard to make sure we adopt the new only when it has been shown to be better than the old. The old homely qualities of friendliness, of honesty, of loyalty to ideals are not subject to change. When they are changed to hatred, to dishonesty, and to disloyalty to those ideals that make for real progress, then we take a backward step.

We may, therefore, sum up the matter by saying that there are good changes and there are bad changes. Education should produce good changes in us; that is, changes that constantly increase our knowledge and skill and that open our minds so that we can adapt ourselves to changes without being crushed by them or rendered futile and ineffective. We can, if we are resolved to do so, constantly grow in our adherence to right ideals of conduct and to ideals of loyalty to our friends and to our work and to the free institutions which are our heritage from the sacrifices of our forefathers. We can apply constant stimulus to our minds while we still hold fast to the everyday qualities and virtues which underlie all true service and all true satisfaction.

	Words
	14
	28
	41
	54
	68
	81
	94
	107
	121
	135
	149
	162
	174
	187
	201
	215
	229
	243
	257
	271
	285
	299
	313
	328
	342
	357
	370
	385
	391
	404
	417
	431
	444
	459
	473
	488
	502
	516
	529
	541

Double-spaced Letters. Although few offices double-space all their letters, some employers still prefer to have short letters double spaced. You need to learn how to arrange such letters.

A fairly reliable rule is to use the same placement plan that you would use for a letter with twice as many words that is to be single spaced. For example, the inside address of a 40-word letter that is to be double spaced would start on the same line as an 80-word letter that is to be single spaced.

Use your judgment to modify the "rule" in order to fit the particular letter you are typing.

You will usually find that a 4½-inch line is better than a 4-inch line for double-spaced letters under 50 words. A very short line tends to give the double-spaced letter a tall-and-lean appearance. The letter shown in Illustration 48 was typed to a line length of 45 pica strokes (4½ inches).

Type the letters on this page with double spacing. Use the indented style with close punctuation.

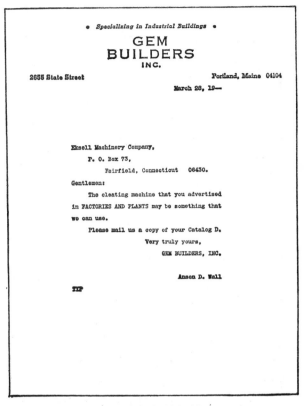

ILLUSTRATION 48
Double-Spaced Letter

Problem 26. (Form 5-26).

Builders' Supply Company, 88 Liberty Street, Concord, New Hampshire 03303. Gentlemen: Please mail us a current statement of our account with you. We should also like to have a copy of your Invoice No. B-5028. (¶) Have you received the check that we mailed you last week for Invoice No. B-4827? Very truly yours, GEM BUILDERS, INC. Carter L. Moore

(39 words)

Problem 27. (Form 5-27). Note the use of underscoring in this letter. Punctuation marks and spaces between words should not be underscored.

Miss Betty W. Clary, 181 Hastings Road, Portland, Maine 04106. Dear Miss Clary: Thank you for applying for the position that we listed in Monday's Morning Herald. (¶) I should like to have the pleasure of talking with you in person. I'll appreciate your calling me tomorrow, so that we may set a time for an interview. Sincerely yours, GEM BUILDERS, INC. Gerald C. Bane

(42 words)

Problem 28. (Form 5-28)

Koffer Heater Company, 9000 West Riverview Street, Youngstown, Ohio 44507. Gentlemen: Do you have a sales representative or agent in New England? If so, please let us know promptly how we can get in touch with him. (¶) We are preparing to bid on a building that will require a heavy duty central heating system. Before we do so, we want to investigate the KOFFER heater. Very truly yours, GEM BUILDERS, INC. John F. Cole

(54 words)

No. 8

We are all aware of the fact that change is the order of the day.   The   14
one fact that we know definitely about tomorrow, about next month,   27
and about next year is that they will be different from today, from this   41
month, and from this year.   In some periods change seems to proceed   54
at a faster pace than during other periods.   No one who does any   67
thinking can live in the world of today without feeling the throb of   81
change.   Forces are at work which nobody wholly understands.   93

It is plain to every thinking person that he must meet changes in   106
his world by changing his own attitudes and points of view.   Some   119
animals that lived in the past were unable to adapt themselves to   132
changes in their surroundings; hence they did not survive.   Human   145
beings are gifted with intelligence, which has enabled them not only   159
to survive, but to harness many of the forces of nature.   Ships sail   173
over the ocean; airplanes fly through the air; submarines ply beneath   187
the waters; messages are transmitted through the ether; rockets and   200
missiles are projected into the wide reaches of outer space.   To a   213
considerable extent, therefore, man has conquered time and space and   227
has made them serve his own ends.   234

The scientists tell us that the composition of the human body changes   248
every seven years.   The basic purpose of the education you are getting   262
is to produce changes in your mind and in your outlook.   You can have   276
the best teachers in the world and the best equipment money can buy;   290
but you yourself will determine how you will profit by the opportunities   304
you have.   If your mind is not open, if you do not adapt yourself readily   319
to the changes that are constantly going on in your world, you will not   333
make the most of your opportunities.   If you find yourself doing a   346
certain thing in a certain way for no other reason than that you did that   361
thing in the same way last month or last year, examine yourself to   374
see whether you really have an open mind that is receptive to new   387
influences and changed conditions.   No one can make you change your   400
attitude or point of view; change in outlook is the direct outcome of   414
personal thought and effort.   420

You can measure the degree of your determination to make changes   433
in many ways.   Ask yourself whether there has been a change for the   446
better in the speed and accuracy with which you typewrite and whether   460
you are becoming more careful all the time in checking your work, in   474
finding errors, and in doing corrective practice to overcome those errors.   489
Every time you make a better record on straight copy typing than you   503
have made before, you have also made a change for the better.   You   516
surely realize that to improve yourself, you have to think and work.   530

Enclosure Notation. Type an enclosure notation below the identifying initials and flush with the left margin. You will find both double spacing and single spacing used in business. Follow the double-spaced style shown in Illustration 49 in typing enclosure notations for your letters in this course. Double spacing after the identifying initials helps the reader's eye to find the enclosure notation quickly.

---

in the enclosed business reply envelope.

Sincerely yours,

LOTT CHEMICAL COMPANY

Sales Manager

TGR:TYP

Enclosure

---

the two booklets that come with this letter.

Sincerely yours,

LOTT CHEMICAL COMPANY

Sales Manager

TGR:TYP

Enclosures 2

ILLUSTRATION 49
Enclosure Notations

When there is one enclosure only, simply type the word *Enclosure* (or the abbreviation *Enc.* if preferred by the office in which you work). When there are two or more enclosures, type the word *Enclosures* followed by the appropriate figure, thus: Enclosures 2

In some offices important enclosures are identified in this way:

Enclosure--Check No. 876

Enclosures

1. Agreement
2. Proxy

Start the inside address of a letter with an enclosure notation one line higher on the sheet than you otherwise would.

Problem 29. (Form 5-29). Type the following letter in the semiblock style with open punctuation. Add the proper enclosure notation.

Mr. Webster V. James   Gaynor Textile Mills, Inc.   4630 South Gulf Street   Mobile, Alabama 36608   Dear Mr. James What happens to a water repellent after dry cleaning? (¶) Hold your answer, please, until you read the laboratory report that comes with this letter. We honestly think that it will bring you the most exciting news of the year. (¶) This report is our first announcement of LOREX, a water repellent that has been in development in the Lott laboratories for more than two years. Before we said a word about the project, we wanted to make sure that LOREX would do what no other water repellent on the market can hope to do. We're convinced that it will. (¶) Note the almost unbelievable results of tests on fabrics treated with LOREX—a spray rating of 90 to 100 after ten rugged dry cleanings. Then note the fabrics used for these tests—viscose, acetate, and mixtures of natural and synthetic fibers, which are the materials that are hardest to treat with old-time water repellents. (¶) Mr. Stephen Joslin, your Lott representative, will spend part of next week in our laboratories. When he visits you next month, he will bring you first-hand details of the job that LOREX can do for you. (¶) Meantime, while quantity production of LOREX is just getting under way, let us tell you more about how this sensational new silicone product works. Your letter in the enclosed business reply envelope will get a same-day answer.   Sincerely yours LOTT CHEMICAL COMPANY   Sales Manager   TGR:

(228 words)

No. 7

A famous football coach made a talk to a group of students. He | 13
began his talk by saying that some people seem to think that the will | 27
to win is a bad thing. He continued by saying that he wanted somebody | 41
to tell him why it is a bad thing. Life, like football, consists of rivalry | 56
and competition. The person who wins is the person who competes | 69
successfully. The successful lawyer is the one who wins cases; the | 82
successful surgeon is the one who saves lives; the successful salesman | 96
is the one who sells; the successful businessman is the one who makes | 110
enough money so that he can give good service to his customers and | 123
have something left over to invest in his business and expand its service; | 138
the successful office worker is the one who does his work efficiently | 152
within the allotted time and is always on the alert to increase his service. | 167

The plain fact of the matter is that there is no reward for the person | 181
who loses. Be sure that there is nothing wrong, but everything right, | 195
with the will to win. The only penalty should be that the person who | 209
wins unfairly ought to be put down. Set up a definite goal for yourself | 223
that is not too far in the future; then do whatever is called for day | 237
by day to reach that goal. You will find that when you do your work | 251
today in the way it ought to be done, the door of opportunity will open | 265
for you. There is just as much opportunity today as there ever was. | 279
There are problems to be solved in the distribution of the services and | 293
commodities which our modern age has brought into being. There are | 306
ways of simplifying the process of getting goods and services to people, | 320
so that more and more of us can enjoy the fruits of invention. | 332

The one basic fact you need to learn is that you have to work with | 345
other people in anything you do. It is an old and true saying that no | 359
one can live unto himself alone. The greatest art in the world is the | 373
art of getting along with other people easily, happily, congenially, and | 387
without friction. The basic factor in good management in business is | 401
to be found in the human art of getting people to work together to reach | 415
the goal that management has set. Men and women are valuable to | 428
any school or college or business only to the degree that they are able | 442
and willing to work together toward a common end. A person who | 455
cannot or will not cooperate with others is a drag on the whole enterprise. | 470
Day by day keep your eyes wide open for ways in which you can cooperate | 484
with others. Remember that the way to cooperate is to cooperate; that | 498
is, you have to show by your whole attitude that you want to work | 511
with other people. When you help them, they will help you; then the | 525
group of which you are a part moves forward to the goal that has been | 539
set. If one person fails to do his share, all the others suffer. | 552

Attention Line. Type an attention line two single line spaces below the inside address and two single line spaces above the salutation. The preferred position is flush with the left margin on all letter styles except the indented. The attention line in an indented letter may be centered or typed to line up with the paragraphs.

You will find several kinds of attention lines in business use. Two of the most widely used styles are shown in Illustration 50. Here are three others that you will sometimes see.

Attention: Miss Frances F. Brown
Attention of Miss Frances F. Brown
ATTENTION--Miss Frances F. Brown

Notice that the correct salutation of a letter with an attention line is *Gentlemen.*

Take the attention line into consideration when you plan letter placement. You will usually get good placement by raising the inside address one line above the normal starting point.

Military Date Style. Many business offices use the date style adopted by the armed forces and by Government offices. This style places the date of the month before the name of the month and omits the comma. Here are two dates properly typed in the military style.

12 September 19--

5 March 19--

Problem 30. (Form 5-30). Type this letter in the block style with mixed punctuation. Use the current date and type it in the military date style.

Clark Manufacturing Company   2300 South Newport Street   St. Paul, Minnesota 55110   Attention Traffic Manager   Gentlemen: Effective today, your shipments to Denver and Cheyenne can be delivered within three days when you ship by D. S. O. (¶) This new service is made available through arrangements just completed with Plateau Motor Express Company. Any Denver or Cheyenne shipment that

Hilton Manufacturing Company
350 East 41st Street
Richmond, Virginia   26207

Attention Mr. J. M. Cunningham

Gentlemen:

Graydon Truck Lines, Inc.
Sunset Street at Ninth
Pasadena, California   91102

Attention of Mr. Herbert L. Algar

Gentlemen:

ILLUSTRATION 50
Attention Lines

you give to D. S. O. will be transferred the following morning in Omaha to Plateau vans for door-to-door delivery within 36 hours. (¶) Try us tomorrow! Let us help you give your Denver and Cheyenne customers the fastest service they have ever seen.   Yours very truly,   D. S. O. MOTOR LINES   Superintendent CLB:

(83 words)

Problem 31. (Form 5-31). Type this letter in the block style with mixed punctuation. Use the current date and type it in the military date style. Notice that the letter has an enclosure.

Boone Brothers, Inc.   26 North Tyler Street Des Moines, Iowa 55301 Attention Miss Ida M. McGovern   Gentlemen: Your new rate schedule for D. S. O. shipments to Omaha is enclosed with this letter. Please destroy all earlier schedules. (¶) Schedule 83 for Minneapolis, St. Paul, and Duluth continues in effect. In case you do not have copies now, please let us know. We'll be delighted to rush them to you. Yours very truly,   D. S. O. MOTOR LINES   Terminal Manager   STL:

(Estimate the number of words.)

131

No. 6

Like many other people, I have often watched with great admiration 13
the work of speed demonstrators. Their typing is done with such 26
apparent ease that one tends to forget about all the work that lies back 40
of their skill and speed. It is the old story of the art that conceals art. 55
If we knew all about the program of training which these experts had 69
followed, we would find that the person who is a master typist has the 83
will and the determination to reach the heights of speed to a degree far 97
above that of most typists. The willingness to practice day in and day 111
out and to keep on typing calls for character development such as 124
not many people are willing to go through with over a period of time. 138

In addition to the qualities of persistence and determination, there 152
are certain other factors that experts have found are necessary to get 166
high speed with accuracy. The machine should be on a desk or a table 180
that is about thirty inches from the floor. The exact height, of course, 195
is determined by the stature of the typist. The chair ought to be about 209
seventeen inches from the floor to the seat. Another real aid to fast 223
typing is the use of blocks or strips which are used to fasten the 236
machine to the desk, so that the machine will not do any sliding or 249
moving while the typing is being done. When the machine stays put, 262
the typist will not lose time in pulling the machine back to its proper 276
position. Correct insertion of the paper and quick and accurate return 290
of the carriage on a manual typewriter are other mechanical factors 303
that add to the development of high speed. Special exercises typed 316
before the typist begins to type from straight copy or from any other 330
kind of copy play the same part that fingering exercises play for the 344
pianist. They limber the fingers and help to put the typist into the 358
mood for fast typing. 362

To build high speed, you need to follow a rigid practice routine. A 376
vital part of that routine is keeping records. After you have typed a 390
piece of copy and have done the recording, you will do well to type 403
the first sentence of the article evenly and continuously several times. 417
Follow the same procedure with the other sentences. The expert 430
carries on that process up to and past the point of fatigue. There is 444
such a thing in typing, as in foot racing, as getting your second wind. 458
When you have typed all the sentences in this way, you then type the 472
entire article again. When you have finished, make a record of the gross 487
words typed and the net speed. Attention to your physical and mental 501
state, unlimited persistence and real work, complete command of the 514
operating parts of the machine, and systematic practice and keeping 527
of records are the factors that enter into building high speed. 540

Subject Line. Type the subject line below the salutation; leave one line space above and below the subject line. Do not type a period at the end of the subject line.

Study Illustration 51. The preferred starting point for the subject line is the same point used for starting paragraphs. That plan saves time. The subject line may also be centered.

Type a colon after the word *Subject.* In offices that use the Latin words *Re* or *In re* instead of *Subject,* the colon is usually omitted. You will, of course, follow the established office style.

A subject line—like an attention line—has bearing on the placement of the letter. Remember to provide for it in your plan.

```
Houseman Brothers, Inc.
48 West Haven Street
Providence, Rhode Island    02902

Gentlemen:

     Subject:  Invoice No. 5583

     What are your time discount terms on this
```

```
Mr. Gifford M. Best
Connecticut Broadcasting Company
426 Division Street
Bridgeport, Connecticut    06602

Dear Mr. Best:

Subject:  Video Association Convention

The third annual convention will be held at the
```

ILLUSTRATION 51
Subject Lines

Dictator's Name and Title. In the letters you have typed so far in this course, you have used either the dictator's name *or* his title. It is perfectly proper, however, to use both the name and the title in the same letter. The two most frequently used arrangements are shown in Illustration 52. Notice that the name precedes the title in either case.

When the company name is quite short, the dictator's name and title should be on separate lines. When the company name is long, the second arrangement shown in Illustration 52 gives the better balance.

```
Cordially yours,

WRDX-TV


Morris Lansing
Station Manager
```

```
Cordially yours,
CONNECTICUT BROADCASTING COMPANY


M. D. Rock, General Manager
```

ILLUSTRATION 52
Dictator's Name And Title

Problem 32. (Form 5-32). Type the following letter in the semiblock style with mixed punctuation. Note the subject line.

Carter Research Associates   25 North Hunt Avenue   Boston, Massachusetts   02108   Gentlemen: Subject: Your Viewer Survey   By official action of the Board of Directors at yesterday's meeting, I have been asked to commend your organization for the thorough, practical, and efficient job you did in conducting the recent viewer survey for us. It is a genuine pleasure to do so. (¶) Let me also add my own special praise for the personnel of the team you assigned to this project. Every one of us on the station staff enjoyed working with Mr. Charles Kurt and his two assistants, Miss Dorothy Guthrie and Mr. Frank Justice. Cordially yours,   WRDX-TV   Morris Lansing   Station Manager

(88 words)

Problem 33. (Form 5-33). The following letter has a subject line and an enclosure notation. Note, too, the five-line inside address. Type the letter in the semiblock style with mixed punctuation.

have similar materials been prepared for the promotion of your fall styles/ we are particularly interested in obtaining mats of complete ads for style no 60 and style no 93/ please send us as quickly as possible any that are now ready

sincerely yours   j rollins and sons

katherine b ashcraft

(69 words)

Problem 70. (Form 5-70)

king and voss clothing company   940 commerce street   elizabeth new jersey 07206   attention of mr j t bates   gentlemen

our check for $571.82 is enclosed with this letter

the voucher stub on the check shows our calculations in arriving at the amount/ have we allowed the correct amount of credit for the two defective suits that you instructed us to return to you on march 13

in case the amount of this check is not exactly right to pay our account in full, please write us at once

sincerely yours   j rollins and sons

ross d marquette   chief accountant

(enclosure)

(Estimate the number of words.)

Problem 71. (Form 5-71)

miss elizabeth r morris   976 north linden street   bryn mawr pennsylvania 19010

dear miss morris

right after you telephoned this morning, we checked with our delivery department to find out what happened to your coat/ just as you guessed, our driver had the parcel on the truck on thursday and brought it back to the store because you weren't home

our delivery days to bryn mawr are tuesday and thursday/ we have requested the driver to deliver your coat before 12 45 or after 4 30 on this coming tuesday/ in case you aren't home, he now understands that he is to leave your coat with mrs hughes at 978 north linden street

sincerely yours   j rollins and sons

marjorie d baxter

(96 words)

Problem 72. (Form 5-72)

mrs lawrence k mallory   apartment 481 park drive apartments   2569 logan avenue philadelphia pennsylvania 19112

dear mrs mallory

it is a genuine pleasure to enclose with this letter your credit card for quick, convenient shopping/ please sign it and keep it in your purse for use the next time you are in the store

your charge account at j rollins and sons also makes shopping by telephone a delight/ simply call main 4-7000 and ask for extension 38/ the order-taker will need only your name and your account number to arrange for prompt delivery

your card authorizes you to charge as much as $500 to your account/ when you plan a special purchase that will run your account over that amount, any floor supervisor will gladly help in arranging for the additional credit

please come to see us often

sincerely yours   j rollins and sons

daniel l watson   chief of credit department   *(enclosure)*

(Estimate the number of words.)

Mr. Robert McVale, Jr.   Director of Personnel   Dixon and Howe, Inc. 721 Jefferson Street   New York, New York 10008   Dear Mr. McVale: Subject: Mr. Vance J. Nesbitt   Your name has been given to us as a reference by Mr. Nesbitt, whose New York City address was 680 Van Glett Street, New York 14, New York. He is now living in Elmwood, Connecticut. (¶) We'll greatly appreciate your telling us something about Mr. Nesbitt's work with you. His application indicates that his service with you lasted about ten months. What were his duties while he was in your employ? (¶) His work here would throw him into close association with a relatively small group of fellow workers. We want to take every precaution to select a man who can work congenially and harmoniously with that group. In case Mr. Nesbitt evidenced personality faults during his service with you, we shall be most grateful to you for telling us frankly what you feel those faults are. (¶) Please use the stamped envelope marked "Personal" that comes with this letter.   Cordially yours,   WRDX-TV Morris Lansing   Station Manager

(Estimate the number of words.)

Carbon Copy Notation. The carbon copy notation is typed at the left margin below the identifying initials, unless the letter also has an enclosure notation. When there is an enclosure notation, the carbon copy notation is typed two line spaces below it.

Note: Several styles are in use. Study the styles in Illustration 53, all of which are acceptable.

Problem 34. (Form 5-34). This letter has a subject line and a carbon copy notation. Type the letter in the semiblock style and use open punctuation. Make two carbons—one for the file and one extra copy. Show the carbon copy notation on the original and both carbon copies. Study the instructions on page 134, "Making Carbon Copies."

When the carbon copy notation is to appear on the carbons but not on the original copy, insert the corner of a slip of paper between the ribbon and the original copy of the letter.

Mr. Everett E. Hess, Manager   Hess Building Supply Company   6 Dowling Street Port Arthur, Texas   77640   Dear Mr. Hess   Subject: Model 9 Drill The factory inspection report, which we have just received, indicates that this drill had a defect in the metal housing. Cost of repair time would exceed replacement cost. (¶) Please issue your customer a replacement without cost. We are instructing the factory to scrap the defective drill.   (¶) Please get a receipt from the customer on one of your forms or letterheads. If you will return this letter with the receipt attached, we'll gladly issue a credit memo or send you a new drill for stock.   Sincerely yours   SURREY CORPORATION N. P. Geller, Manager   Copy to Mr. J. C. Black

(84 words)

```
MRH:TYP

Copy to Mr. R. T. Reed
```

```
MRH:TYP

Enclosure

cc Mr. M. H. Jarman
```

```
MRH:TYP

Copies to
Mr. George R. Taft
Miss Helen Michael
```

ILLUSTRATION 53
Carbon Copy Notations

Alphabetic Unarranged Letters

Each letter on this page and on the next page contains all the letters of the alphabet and all the figures.

You are to type these letters in the semiblock style with mixed punctuation, unless you are instructed otherwise.

Capitalize and punctuate where necessary. A diagonal line (/) indicates the end of a sentence within a paragraph.

Read through each letter before you start to type it. Watch especially for attention lines, subject lines, and enclosure notations.

Problem 66. (Form 5-66)

mrs dennis j wilton 1003 oliver street philadelphia pennsylvania 19119 dear mrs wilton

thank you for your check for $142.96, which we received this morning

we realize that your recent and quite unexpected medical expenses must have played havoc with your budget

your plan to send us the remaining balance of $58.27 by the end of this month is perfectly satisfactory
sincerely yours j rollins and sons louis n bryson

(48 words)

Problem 67. (Form 5-67)

holbrook millinery company 48 custer street toledo ohio 43609 gentlemen

when will the 65 dozen stock no 1482 included in our order no 3007 be shipped

the other items we ordered were received three weeks ago/ when you made shipment, you explained that the remaining item would be delayed just a few days

we must now request you to make immediate shipment or cancel that part of our order
sincerely yours j rollins and sons suzanne m klein

(60 words)

Problem 68. (Form 5-68)

altamont hosiery mills 408 south 23rd street durham north carolina 27701 attention of credit department gentlemen

the monthly statement you mailed us a few days ago lists one invoice of which we have no record/ the number you give is no 9-7156

please check to see whether the amount of that invoice is properly chargeable to us/ in case you find that it is, we'll appreciate your mailing us quadruplicate copies/ meantime, payment of all items except that one invoice has been authorized
sincerely yours j rollins and sons walter s poole

(67 words)

Problem 69. (Form 5-69)

mr herbert h dinsmore director of advertising underwood shoe company 2847 moreland avenue st louis missouri 63113 dear mr dinsmore subject advertising of fall styles

when we introduced your line several months ago, you supplied us with suggested advertising copy and newspaper mats in several sizes/ we found those materials exceedingly effective

Problem 35. (Form 5-35). Type this letter in the semiblock style with open punctuation. Make two carbon copies. Notice that the letter has an enclosure. Be sure to show the identifying initials, the enclosure notation, and the carbon copy notation at the bottom of the letter.

Mrs. Benjamin G. Wakely   211 University Road   Houston, Texas   77004   Dear Mrs. Wakely   Your Houston dealer has referred to us your letter about your SURREY "Kom-pakt" Washer. It is a pleasure to enclose with this letter the leaflet of hints and instructions that you requested. (¶) Yes, the motor on the model which you have should be oiled about twice a year. Model 500, which is the only SURREY washer with a sealed-in unit, has been on the market just a few weeks. (¶) Simply remove the two screws on the top. You can then easily lift off the metal cover to expose all working parts. Add three or four drops of light oil to the oil holes at each end of the motor. Those places are marked "A" and "B" on the enclosed leaflet. (¶) Do not over-oil. In case some excess oil does drip down the side of the motor, just wipe it off with a dry cloth. (¶) No other parts of your SURREY washer need lubrication. The gears are packed in grease that will last indefinitely. With normal care your washer will give you years and years of trouble-free service.   Sincerely yours   SURREY CORPORATION   T. L. Grey, Service Division   Copy to Mr. Craig Billings

(181 words)

Making Carbon Copies. Business letters are typed with at least one carbon copy. That one copy is kept for the office file. Additional copies are often needed for salesmen, customers, company officials, and branch offices.

Here are suggestions that will help you to meet the standards of the business office.

1. Use inexpensive plain paper or special light-weight "copy" sheets for carbon copies. Remember that the letterhead is for the original only.

2. When you are making more than three or four carbon copies, use light-weight carbon paper. Use more serviceable standard-weight carbon paper when you are making from one to four copies.

3. Assemble the carbon pack by starting from the back. If you are going to make two carbon copies, for example, lay the second carbon sheet on your desk, put a sheet of carbon paper on top of it—carbon side down; then build up the pack by adding the first carbon sheet, another piece of carbon paper, and the letterhead (face up).

4. Tap the carbon pack lightly on your desk to get all the sheets straight before you insert the pack into your machine.

5. When the pack consists of several sheets, use the paper release to insert it. Re-engage the release after you have the pack properly started.

6. Use a folded strip of paper or an envelope to keep bulky carbon packs straight until the pack is in your machine. Drop the folded strip or envelope over the top edge of the assembled pack and feed it into your machine with the pack; then remove it.

7. Clip off the corners of the carbon paper you are using. When you remove the pack from your machine, you can then grip the pack in one corner and shake the carbon paper free.

8. Learn to work with the carbon pack so that you keep your fingers clean and the letterhead free of smudges.

Here is another method which is often used—especially when only one carbon is to be made.

1. Insert the letterhead and the copy sheet.

2. Turn the cylinder two or three notches, just enough to hold the sheets firmly.

3. Drop in the sheet of carbon paper, with the carbon side toward you.

4. Turn up the pack to writing position.

INTERNATIONAL RADIO CORPORATION
INTERPLANT CORRESPONDENCE

TO: Mr. Grant H. Miller--Philadelphia

DATE: 25 September 19--

FROM: Mr. Clyde B. Randall--Wheeling

SUBJECT: Company Correspondence

Stationery for interoffice correspondence is quite generally 8½ inches wide. The depth varies. Some companies use half sheets that measure 5½ inches deep for brief messages and full-size sheets for longer messages. Other companies select an intermediate size, such as 8½ inches by 7¼ inches, and use additional sheets when the message requires more than a page.

One reason for using special stationery for messages within the company is economy. Interoffice stationery is cheaper in quality than the company letterheads. Appearance is subordinated to rapid production.

As you may have noticed, the name of the person addressed is typed first on both this sheet and on the half sheet on which you have been working. That position is preferred for the name of the addressee because it speeds up the sorting of the day's mail for distribution.

There is no need for you to type the full address of the person to whom the message is directed. When the company has offices in several cities, however, typists are often asked to show the city name after the addressee's name. Sometimes a similar note is made of the writer's location.

The rules of the company for which you work will determine whether you do or do not indent the paragraphs. In any case you should use single spacing, with double spacing between paragraphs. Separate the first line of the message from the subject by spacing down four lines.

Contrast the arrangement of the four lines at the top of this sheet with the arrangement used on the half sheets you have typed. When the form is designed as this one is, set a tabulator stop for the four top lines and type them to line up at the left. Set margin stops for a six-inch line.

Style Letter 10

Interoffice Message On Full Sheet

Postscripts. A postscript is sometimes used on a business letter to emphasize a point that the writer considers especially important.

When you study Illustration 54, you will notice that the postscript starts two single line spaces

---

    We are looking forward eagerly to the
pleasure of meeting you.

                    Sincerely yours,

                    THE CARTER PLAZA

                    Resident Manager

WLO'Brien/typ

    Your reservation will be held until
6 p.m. unless you notify us otherwise.

    We are looking forward eagerly to the
pleasure of meeting you.

                    Sincerely yours,

                         THE CARTER PLAZA

                         Resident Manager

WLO'Brien/typ

Enclosure

        P. S.   Your reservation will be held
until 6 p.m. unless you notify us otherwise.

We are looking forward eagerly to the pleasure of meeting you.

Sincerely yours,

THE CARTER PLAZA

Resident Manager

WLO'Brien/typ

Enclosure

cc Mr. Harrison Clifton

Your reservation will be held until 6 p.m.
unless you notify us otherwise.

ILLUSTRATION 54

Postscripts

below the last normal line of the letter. It is indented the same number of spaces as the paragraphs in the body. In some offices the letters *P. S.* are used; in others, they are omitted.

A postscript has considerable bearing, of course, on the placement of the letter. Provide for it by raising the starting point of the inside address. Letters with postscripts often look better, too, when you use a longer line than you otherwise would.

Dictator's Name at Left. Pay particular attention to the way the dictator's name and the typist's initials are shown in Illustration 54. This style is coming into greater use, and you will want to be familiar with it.

When you do substitute the dictator's name for his initials, type the name without periods or spaces. Use small letters for your own initials.

Problem 36. (Form 5-36). This letter has an enclosure notation and a postscript. Type it in the semiblock style with mixed punctuation. Follow the style of identification used in Illustration 54.

Mr. Norman D. Brooks   6528 West State Street   Albany, New York 12204   Dear Mr. Brooks: After you left on Wednesday, the maid found in your room one plain gold cuff link, which she turned in to the Lost and Found Office. (¶) Please let us know whether this cuff link is yours. If it is, we'll be delighted to send it to you right away. (¶) Just write "It's mine" or "It's not mine" at the bottom of this letter and mail the letter in the enclosed envelope. Sincerely yours,   THE CARTER PLAZA   Resident Manager   WLO'Brien/   (Postscript)   It was fine to have Mrs. Brooks and you with us last week. Please plan to come again—soon.

(72 words)

Interoffice Letters. Style Letter 9 shows a letter addressed to another person in the same company as the writer. Read it carefully.

Problem 63. (Form 5-63). Type Style Letter 9. Use today's date instead of the date shown.

Problem 64. (Form 5-64). Type this interoffice memorandum in the form of Style Letter 9.

To Mr. Arthur Linder, Jr.   *Subject* Annual Report   *From* Mr. F. F. Greer
The Annual Report, now in preparation, will contain this year a short summary of the improvements we have made in operating methods. I have just turned over to our advertising agency a list of the topics to be covered. (¶) One of them is the new work-flow plan that you set up in the Traffic Department. That system has now been in operation long enough for us to see clearly that it is producing substantial savings. (¶) At my suggestion you will be visited soon by a member of the agency staff to get the pertinent facts about that plan. I know you will help in every way you can. Meantime, I do want you to have this advance notice, so that you can assemble whatever data you feel the agency will need.

Problem 65. (Form 5-65). Style Letter 10 on the next page is an interoffice communication typed on a full-size sheet. The body of the Style Letter tells you more about the use and the arrangement of such letters. Read it; then type the letter. Show the current date in the military style.

PARAMOUNT OIL COMPANY

INTEROFFICE MEMORANDUM

TO: Mr. D. M. Rogers   DATE: January 16, 19--

SUBJECT: Interoffice Memorandums   FROM: Miss G. Ellwood

Interoffice memorandums are messages between different offices, branches, or departments of the same company. The form on which the message is typed may be called a "company memorandum" or an "interoffice communication." It may also have a specific title that is in keeping with the business in which the company is engaged.

Use the same line length for all messages. This form, you will notice, was designed for a six-inch line. The margin set for the name typed at the top after To is also the left margin of the message.

No salutation or complimentary close is used. Identifying initials are also usually omitted. The dictator just initials the message by hand.

Style Letter 9—Interoffice Memorandum On Half Sheet

Problem 37. (Form 5-37). This letter also has an enclosure notation and a postscript. Type it in the semiblock style with mixed punctuation. Follow the style of identification shown in Illustration 54.

Note the underscored words. Although underscoring slows down production, it is often used in sales letters to attract the reader's attention.

Mr. Donald R. Crandon   82 South Larch Drive   Philadelphia, Pennsylvania 19122   Dear Mr. Crandon: When you hear the word <u>bargain</u>, what comes instantly to your mind? Do you think of a department store basement, of a close-out sale, of odd lots and remainders? (¶) And when somebody mentions <u>vacation</u>, do you think of heavy expenses, costly entertainment, and a flat pocketbook?   (¶) If so, this letter brings real news.   (¶) Here at THE CARTER PLAZA the month of April is the time of the year when <u>bargain</u> and <u>vacation</u> team up to mean something special. From the first day to the last day of April, the rates for rooms at THE CARTER PLAZA are exactly <u>half</u> the rates charged all winter. Luxury suites priced at $28 in February and March dip to $14 a day. Regular $12 rooms are only $6, and regular $10 rooms are down to a modest $5.   (¶) We'll let the folder that comes with this letter tell you the whole story. When you've read it, plan to come to THE CARTER PLAZA in April.   Sincerely yours,   THE CARTER PLAZA   Resident Manager   WLO'Brien/   Enclosures 2   P. S. Your reservation card needs no stamp. Just fill in your name and address, tell us the day to expect you, and mail the card.

(163 words)

Erasing

When you must erase, take time to make a good erasure. Learn to follow these steps.

1. Move the carriage to the extreme right or to the extreme left to keep erasure particles from falling into your machine.

2. Raise the paper bail.

3. Turn the cylinder until the spot where you are to erase is far enough away from the line of writing to give you working room.

Rolling the cylinder upward—away from you—three or four lines will usually give you the best position. To erase near the bottom of the sheet, roll the sheet down until the error comes into position from the back of the cylinder.

4. You may hold an erasure shield against the paper to protect the area around the spot you are going to erase. Use the smallest possible opening on the shield. Be careful to keep your fingers from touching the sheet itself.

5. Use an eraser with a sharp, clean edge. Erase with gentle strokes. Don't wear a hole in the paper and don't rub so hard that the paper will slip. Brush away the erasure particles.

6. Turn the cylinder back to the line of writing and return the carriage to the spot you erased. Check alignment.

7. Strike the correct key with a light stroke; then, if necessary to get a good match for your other typing, backspace and strike it again.

Erasing on Carbon Copies. If you are making carbon copies, put a file card or any other piece of light cardboard between the original and the first sheet of carbon paper. Erase the original first and then move the protecting card back for each carbon copy. Use a soft eraser on carbon copies.

When you roll the cylinder upward or downward, grasp the carbon pack with the left hand, so that the sheets will not slip.

Arbitrary Letter Placement. A large office with a great volume of routine correspondence will sometimes sacrifice ideal appearance in its letters to get maximum production. Typists are instructed to set margin and tabulator stops at definite points and to use those same stops for all letters.

The first line of the inside address of all letters is the same distance from the top edge of the sheet. Sometimes that point is indicated on the letterhead by a small printed dot.

When such specific instructions are given, you will usually find that the line length is set at 5½ inches—55 pica spaces or 66 elite spaces. The inside address generally begins on the sixteenth or the seventeenth line from the top of the sheet.

Other details of letter style in such an office will also be arbitrarily determined for you by precise office instructions. One position—and only one position—will be right for each part of the letter, and you will be required to use that position in all the letters you type.

Problem 62. (Form 5-62). Type this letter to an arbitrary line length of 5½ inches. Follow the style of Illustration 66. Type the date on the twelfth line from the top of the sheet. Start the inside address on the sixteenth line from the top of the sheet.

Caslon Manufacturing Company 800 Santa Maria Boulevard Los Angeles, California 90017 Gentlemen: Today the Isenhart Motor Lines delivered to us a shipment of 34 cartons marked with our Purchase Order No. 418-529 and your Invoice No. 5002-A. (¶) The bill of lading specifies 37 cartons. A check against our purchase order shows that the missing cartons contained 156 gross of your Stock No. 3164—an item that we need at once. (¶) Please ask your local office of the carrier to put an immediate tracer on the shipment. In case this part of the shipment cannot be located within 36 hours, please make duplicate shipment. (¶) The office of Isenhart Motor Lines here reports that no cartons consigned to us are being held on the Tacoma dock or in the Tacoma warehouse. Very truly yours, STAR AIRCRAFT COMPANY Chief of Purchasing Division MLPastor/

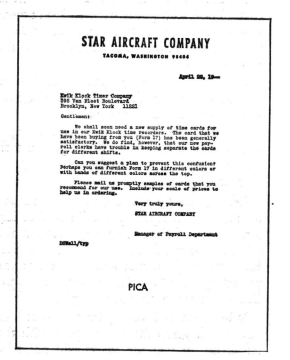

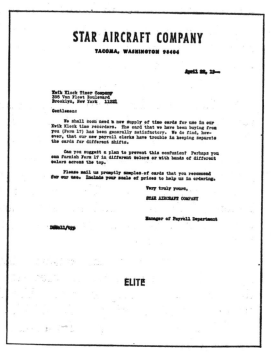

ILLUSTRATION 66
Arbitrary Letter Placement

Omitting the Company Name. Some office managers feel that a letter has a more personal touch when the company name is omitted from the conclusion. A letter typed in this style is shown in Illustration 55.

Problem 38. (Form 5-38). Type the following letter in the full-block style with open punctuation. Show your own initials in small letters. This letter has an attention line and an enclosure notation.

Gold Streak Van Lines   516 West Mission Road   Fresno, California 93708 Attention of Mr. F. F. Hughes   Gentlemen   When it comes to buying special equipment, you're probably like most people we know. You want to see what you're getting before you hand over your money. (¶) Take cargo refrigeration units. Have you been hesitating to install them in your vans because the factory is back East and the only way to buy is from a picture? If we were in your shoes, we'd probably hesitate too. (¶) We said as much recently in a letter to Poole Manufacturing Company, maker of special heating and cooling units for van cabs and cargoes. How come, we wanted to know, there isn't a place on the Coast where fleet operators can see for themselves what your units will do? (¶) "No reason why not," their sales manager wired. "Will you accept dealership?" (¶) And so—with pleasure and pride—Matthews Motors announces its dealership of what we believe to be the finest transport air conditioners made in America. The six units illustrated in the enclosed folder are now on display in our showrooms. You'll be thrilled, we promise, at what the right unit can do for your vans. (¶) Please come in to see for yourself.   Sincerely yours Barclay F. Matthews   General Manager

(190 words)

ILLUSTRATION 55
Letter With Company Name Omitted

Problem 39. (Form 5-39). This letter has a postscript. Type the letter in the full-block style with open punctuation. Use small letters for your initials. Use three lines for the inside address.

Miss Mary T. Tracy   Pinedale California 93652   Dear Miss Tracy   The two tires that you left with us last week for recapping are now ready. They are being held for you at the Service Manager's desk. (¶) You may get your tires at any time. In case you would like to have them mounted, however, please come between 8 a.m. and 4 p.m. (¶) It is always a good idea to have wheels checked for balance and alignment before mounting new or recapped tires. We'll gladly make that check for you while you wait.   Sincerely yours   George D. Monroe   Parts Department   *(Postscript)*   Are you now using SAFE-TEE tubes? They are good life insurance!

(82 words)

Simplified Letter. The Administrative Management Society is sponsoring a variation of the full-block style called the *simplified letter style.*

Here are the features of the *simplified letter.*

1. All parts of the letter start at the left margin—just as in the case of the full-block style.

2. The letter has no salutation and no complimentary close.

3. The letter always shows a subject. That line is typed in ALL CAPITALS, and the word *Subject* is omitted.

4. The inside address is typed so that it will show through a window envelope. Adjacent parts of the letter are well removed from the inside address to keep them from appearing in the "window."

5. The inside address starts at least three (usually four) line spaces below the date.

6. There are at least two line spaces above the subject and at least two line spaces below the subject.

7. The dictator's name is typed in ALL CAPITALS at least five lines below the last line of the body of the letter.

8. The letter is single spaced, with double spacing between paragraphs.

Advocates of the simplified letter point out that the content of the letter should also be "simplified" by making it informal in tone.

Problem 61. (Form 5-61). The following letter is the same one shown in Illustration 65. Type it in the simplified style. Use today's date.

Type the date on line 11 and the first line of the inside address on line 16. Triple-space after the inside address and triple-space after the subject. Use a five-inch line length for the body.

Mr. G. H. Caton, President   Sparta Tool Company   975 North Maple Street   Memphis, Tennessee   38103 FIGHTING FIRES IS HIS BUSINESS You now have—right in Memphis—the services of a man trained to stop fires before they do damage. He is Mr. Bruce W. Haines. You can get his advice quickly and without charge or obligation. (¶) Just telephone LAfayette 4-0028. (¶) That number

ILLUSTRATION 65
Simplified Letter

calls the new Memphis branch office of Holland Brothers. Possibly you know Bruce Haines. He grew up in Memphis, where he has made a host of friends all over town. We are delighted to tell you that he has taken the position of Manager of our new office. (¶) One of these days soon he will drop around to see you. When he does, please let him check over your plant and your offices for fire hazards. If there is a danger spot, he'll find it. (¶) Bruce comes to us with a mighty fine record as a safety engineer. He may be too modest to tell you that he also turned in the best performance we've ever seen when he took the special training course out here in our Detroit laboratories. (¶) You'll like Bruce Haines—and you'll find that he knows his business. STANLEY HOLLAND

Addressing Envelopes

1. Double-space a three-line address.

2. Single-space an address that has more than three lines.

3. Type the envelope address in the block style.

4. Punctuate the envelope address in the same way that the inside address is punctuated.

5. Use at least three lines for the address.

6. Spell the city name in full. (A permissible exception is a name that starts with *Saint*. You may use either *Saint Paul* or *St. Paul*—but not *Phila.*, *N. Y. C.*, or *Pbgh.* Never use the word *City* as a substitute for the actual city or town name.)

7. Be sure to type the ZIP Code number at the end of the last line of the address. No comma is required between the state name and the ZIP Code number.

8. Avoid abbreviations for state names unless you are required to use them by definite office instructions. In any case, be sure that the abbreviation is the one authorized by the Post Office Department. There are no authorized abbreviations for *Alaska, Hawaii, Idaho, Iowa, Maine, Ohio,* or *Utah.*

WATSON BROTHERS
186 McClure Street
ROANOKE, VIRGINIA 24005

Mr. Clyde J. Higgins
Middleburg
North Carolina   27556

THE **DOLE** CORPORATION
2163 RANDOLPH AVENUE
BROOKLYN, NEW YORK 11208

Mrs. James G. Dallas
430 East 28th Street
New York, New York   10017

Gordon Little, Inc.
Crawford
Kansas 66940

Miss Gladys C. Sanford
280 West Pine Street
Greenville, Iowa   51343

R. GARBER & SONS
SALT LAKE CITY, UTAH 84102

Mr. J. Douglas Cline, President
Cline Manufacturing Company, Inc.
4798 North Jefferson Street
Los Angeles, California   90002

ILLUSTRATION 56
Addresses On No. 6 3/4 Envelopes

Problem 55. (Form 5-55). Type Style Letter 8, page 156.

Problem 56. (Form 5-56). Type this letter in the form of Style Letter 8.

Mr. Norman L. Sumter   Room 524   Clark Memorial Hospital   Denver, Colorado 80204   Dear Mr. Sumter: I am glad to tell you that I have been successful in getting your case postponed for sixty days. (¶) There are still a few details that I should discuss with you, but there is no hurry. I suggest that you call me after you come home from the hospital and feel up to a short talk.   Sincerely yours, M. S. MacFarland

(56 words)

Problem 57. (Form 5-57). Type this letter in the form of Style Letter 8.

J. M. Treadman & Sons, Inc.   62 Commerce Street   Denver, Colorado   80208 Gentlemen: One of my clients is planning to purchase the Home Grocery Store at 593 Victory Road, Denver. A condition of the proposed sale is that my client would take over all debts of the business. (¶) Please let me know how much the store now owes you. The owner is Mr. Paul D. Knox. (¶) I am enclosing a stamped envelope for your reply. My client and I will keep in strict confidence any information that you furnish.   Sincerely yours, Gordon R. Willard   Enclosure

(76 words)

The addresses of letters 58, 59, and 60 are to be typed below the identifying initials at the left margin. See Style Letter 7. Write all three letters in the semiblock style with mixed punctuation. The dictator's initials are RKH. Type those initials and your own initials on each letter.

Problem 58. (Form 5-58)

Dear Mr. Jarrett: The partnership agreement that you asked me to draw up for you is now ready. (¶) Although you and your partner could sign without my being present, I'd like to have the chance to go over some of the legal aspects with you. I am hoping, therefore, that we can all sit down together for a final review of the papers. (¶) Can you and Mr. Porter be in my office this coming Monday afternoon at four o'clock? If so, please give my secretary a ring on the telephone.   Sincerely yours,   Mr. Ira M. Jarrett   Jarrett Printing Service   Englewood, Colorado 80111

(87 words)

Problem 59. (Form 5-59)

Dear Dr. Russell: This letter will acknowledge receipt of your claim for $538.92 against the estate of the late Francis H. Moore. (¶) It now looks as though final settlement of Mr. Moore's estate may be delayed several weeks.   Sincerely yours, Dr. T. Dudley Russell   1470 West Mesa Street   Denver, Colorado 80206

(35 words)

Problem 60. (Form 5-60)

Dear Fred: Yes, I'll be happy to serve on the Rules Committee for the coming year. It will be all right for you to submit my name at the meeting in Tulsa. (¶) During the past few weeks I have been working on an involved case, and I feared for a time that I would have to miss the trip to Tulsa next month. Happily, we now expect a settlement within ten days. (¶) It will be good to see you again.   Cordially yours, Frederick B. Keene, Esq.   Court Square Building   Santa Fe, New Mexico 87501

(78 words)

Typing the Address on a No. 6 3/4 Envelope. The standard-size small envelope for business use is known as the "No. 6 3/4." It measures 6 1/2 inches by 3 5/8 inches.

The first line of the address should fall slightly below the center of the envelope. Type that line two inches (12 line spaces) from the top edge when the address is to be double spaced. Type the first line of a single-spaced address on line 13. Start about 2 1/2 inches from the left edge.

Envelope Addressing Problems. Type the following addresses on No. 6 3/4 envelopes. Set the paper guide at the proper position and leave a left margin of 25 pica spaces or 30 elite spaces.

Block Style

1. Mr. Calvin R. Twain, Jr.   502 Rockridge Avenue   Decatur, Illinois   62521

2. Miss Susanne T. Davidson   1149 West 168th Street   New York, New York   10027

3. Mrs. Henry V. Lyons   Chinook Washington   98614

4. Dr. Daniel W. Ashwood   312 Medical Arts Building   80 Connecticut Avenue, N. W.   Washington, D. C.   20008

5. Mr. Alvin E. Barrett, Treasurer J. Roscoe & Sons Company 5614 West Oak Street   Philadelphia, Pennsylvania   19131

6. Sherwood Distributing Company Mount Holly   South Carolina   29463

7. Mrs. Anthony M. Sheridan   Grandview   Oregon   97833

8. Mr. N. W. Lansburg, President   Kingston Mills, Inc.   Kingston, Georgia   30145

9. Professor Albert W. Dudley   Department of History   Riverdale College Riverdale, Kansas   67130

10. Miss Caroline D. Shields   Parkview Apartments   40 North Bristol Avenue Columbus, Ohio   43202

Chain Feeding Envelopes. You will find that you can feed No. 6 3/4 envelopes more quickly and more easily into the *center* of the platen than you can with the paper guide at the usual position. When you are to address a large number of envelopes at one time, therefore, move the paper guide to the right and set the left margin accordingly.

Your next step is to arrange your working materials. Stack the unaddressed envelopes face up at the left of your machine and near the front of your desk. Put the list of names at your right.

As you remove addressed envelopes from your typewriter, turn them face down in a separate stack at your left.

One way to get high production in addressing envelopes is to type the envelopes in an "endless chain." Here are the five steps.

1. Insert the first envelope at the back and turn the cylinder forward until the top edge of the envelope comes even with the alignment scale.

2. Insert the second envelope at the back between the cylinder and the bottom of the first envelope.

3. Turn up the cylinder and address the first envelope. As you do so, the second envelope will feed part way into your machine.

4. Insert the third envelope at the back between the cylinder and the bottom of the second envelope.

5. Twirl the addressed envelope out of your machine. This motion will bring the second envelope approximately into typing position, and the third envelope will start to feed in from the back. After you address each envelope—and before you take it out of your machine—add another unaddressed envelope to the chain.

Practice in Chain Feeding. The only way to master chain feeding is through practice. A good way to start is to take the ten envelopes you just addressed and practice forming them into a chain without typing on them.

After you have learned to form the chain, get ten more envelopes to address.

Higgins, Willard & MacFarland

ATTORNEYS-AT-LAW

138 Seminary Avenue, Denver, Colorado 80202

January 22, 19--

Mr. James M. Warren
2693 North Tenth Street
Salt Lake City, Utah   84104

Dear Mr. Warren:

Use the same line length for all letters typed on letterheads this size. Adjust the letter vertically on the sheet to get proper placement.

This letter is typed in pica type to a line length of $3\frac{1}{2}$ inches. It thus has a left margin of one inch and a right margin of one inch.

Note the position of the date. Type the date on a small letterhead from two to four line spaces above the rest of the letter.

Sincerely yours,

Gordon R. Willard

typ

Style Letter 8
Semiblock Letter On Half-Size Letterhead
Words in body: 79 Date: line 12
Inside address: Starts on line 16.

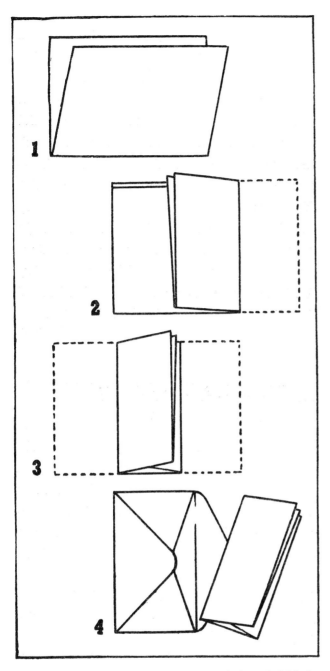

1. Put the letter face up on your desk and fold the bottom edge of the sheet up to within a quarter of an inch of the top edge.

2. Fold the right-hand third in toward the center.

3. Fold the left-hand third toward the center to within a quarter of an inch of the other crease.

4. Insert the letter in the envelope so that the last crease is at the bottom of the envelope.

ILLUSTRATION 57

Folding A Letter For Insertion In A No. 6 3/4 Envelope

Folding a Letter for a No. 6 3/4 Envelope.

When a business letter has been *properly* inserted into the envelope, the reader can open it and start reading the letter without having to turn or twist the letterhead.

Illustration 57 shows the right way to insert a letter in a No. 6 3/4 envelope. Study the four steps carefully; then practice them until you can do the folding and inserting without looking at the diagrams.

Special Situations in Envelope Addressing.

Sometimes an envelope needs to show directions for delivery or to carry some other special notation. Here are the accepted ways of typing such notations. As you study them, refer to Illustration 58 on the next page.

In care of. Type the *In care of* notation as the second line of the address—directly below the name. Sometimes c/o is used.

Attention line. Type the attention line as the second line of the address or type it separately in the lower left-hand corner of the envelope.

Mail directions. Type the words *Registered, Air Mail,* or *Special Delivery* (capitals and small letters underscored or ALL CAPS) in the upper half of the envelope—usually on the eighth line from the top edge. You may start such words at the center of the envelope or type them below the space for the postage stamp.

Special instructions. Type *Hold for Arrival, Personal,* or *Please Forward* in the lower left-hand corner of the envelope.

Typists in some offices are instructed to set off the city and state names in a single-spaced address by double spacing before the last line. Other offices instruct typists to capitalize the city-state line to make that line stand out in the address. See Illustration 58.

Envelope Addressing Problems. Type the following addresses on No. 6 3/4 envelopes. Use the block style with open punctuation.

Type the first eight addresses with standard spacing. Double-space before the city-state line in the last two addresses.

Unless you are instructed otherwise, you may type the mail directions in the style and position you prefer.

Problem 51. (Form 5-51). Type Style Letter 7, page 154.

Cut the forms for Problems 51, 52, 53, and 54 to executive size before you type on them.

Problem 52. (Form 5-52). Type the following letter in the form of Style Letter 7.

Dear Mr. Lee   Just a few minutes ago Mr. Starr brought me your dealership contract for signature.   I can't remember when I have signed a business paper with more pleasure than I signed this contract. (¶) I am certain that the sales volume of Erdman products is in direct ratio to the alertness of the dealer.   In New England, the South Atlantic states, and all through the Middle West, sales last year were the best in history.   As Mr. Starr has told you, the picture on the West Coast was disappointing.   I thoroughly agree with him in placing the blame squarely on our inadequate and inefficient representation. (¶) Your organization is the best one I know to do the job that needs to be done.   I am convinced, therefore, that we have entered into a relationship that will be highly profitable to us both. (¶) I look forward, Mr. Lee, to the pleasure of meeting you in person.   I have tentative plans to be in California in August.   If those plans materialize, I hope that we can spend several hours together while I am in San Francisco.   Cordially yours

Mr. Vernon W. Lee, President   Lee Distributors, Inc.   50-58 Santa Cruz Road   Oakland, California 94604

(181 words)

Problem 53. (Form 5-53). Type the following letter in the form of Style Letter 7.

Dear Mr. Lancaster   I am delighted to have the opportunity to recommend Mrs.

Louis R. Barnett to you for the position you described in your recent letter. (¶) Mrs. Barnett started with us about five years ago in the general office stenographic pool.   She was soon advanced to secretarial work.   During her last two years here—until her husband was transferred to your city— she served as my personal secretary. (¶) If you have not employed Mrs. Barnett by the time this letter reaches you, I strongly urge you to do so.   She is one in a million. Cordially yours   Willard Lancaster, Esq. Keel, Lancaster & Scott   40-46 Legal Building   Richmond, Virginia 23203

(93 words)

Problem 54. (Form 5-54). Type the following letter in the form of Style Letter 7.

Dear Allan   Thank you for asking me to talk to the men of the Forward Club. (¶) The date that you suggest is not a good one for me.   I have agreed to be in New York all that week to work with our Regional Sales Manager. (¶) Although I am forced to decline your invitation this time, I do hope you will ask me again.   Cordially yours   Mr. Allan B. Herbert 72 South Harrison Street   Evansville, Indiana 47705

(62 words)

Half-Size Letterheads.   Letterheads even smaller than the executive size are also used in business.   The most popular of those smaller sizes measures $5\frac{1}{2}$ inches wide by $8\frac{1}{2}$ inches deep.   Style Letter 8 on the next page has been typed on a letterhead of that size.   Study it carefully.

When you type on a half-size letterhead, use a $3\frac{1}{2}$-inch line for either pica or elite.   In setting margin stops, remember that the sheet is only $5\frac{1}{2}$ inches wide.

Rockwell's, Inc.
30 Elm Street
Akron, Ohio 44303

Mr. Howard G. Bethune

In care of Mohawk Hotel

Concord, New Hampshire   03303

Hold for Arrival

STRATHMORE
TEXTILE MILLS
AMERICUS
GEORGIA 31709

Mr. Bernard Schwartz
Broadwood Corporation
Fifth Avenue at 21st Street

New York, New York   10015

PERSONAL

H. Kennedy Lane
● ELECTRICAL ENGINEER ●
50 CARTER BUILDING
DES MOINES, IOWA 55302

<u>Special</u> <u>Delivery</u>

Russell Engineering Company
Attention of Mr. Mark N. Willis
829 South Fremont Street
Charleston, West Virginia   25303

CRAIG HARDWARE COMPANY
18 SOUTH FIRST STREET
DALLAS, TEXAS 75204

AIR MAIL

Accounting Department
Clifton Implement Company
2000 West Fulton Street
LEXINGTON, KENTUCKY   40501

Attention Mr. R. C. Lund

ILLUSTRATION 58

Special Envelope Notations

1. Mr. Ira L. Maddox, Jr.   In care of Hotel Metropolitan   San Francisco, California   94108   Hold for Arrival

2. Special Delivery   Harper Optical Company   Attention of Mr. Daniel C. White   Douglas Street at Third   Denver, Colorado   80209

3. Cooper, Hall & Tremaine, Inc.   Attention of Personnel Department   Flatbush Building   7152 South Rotterdam Street   Brooklyn, New York   11227

4. Professor Lee W. Stephenson   c/o Benjamin Henry Harrison University   Winona, Mississippi   38967   Please Forward

5. Registered   Fisher Brothers, Inc. Attention of Miss Shirley Haines   Triangle Building   St. Louis, Missouri   63102

6. Mrs. Andrew V. Ogilvie   403 New Hampshire Avenue, N. W.   Washington, D. C.   20010   Personal

7. Air Mail   Mr. Robert Gillespie, Jr. In care of Hotel Governor Hay   Third Avenue and Spanish Street   St. Augustine, Florida   32084   Hold for Arrival

8. Special Delivery   Mr. Richard T. Beckwith, President   Gould Furniture Corporation   Dover, Delaware   19901

9. Nolan Cinder Block Company   Attention of Mr. Martin D. Bryant   5006 Key Highway   Alexandria, Virginia   22304

10. Air Mail   Miss Joyce K. Sigmund In care of Mrs. Earl G. Saxton   Wendover Apartments   780-790 Walsh Road   PATERSON, NEW JERSEY   07506

ERDMAN MANUFACTURING COMPANY

WARD AND HOWE STREETS
EVANSVILLE, INDIANA 47703

Philip W. Forrest, *President*

January 22, 19--

Dear Miss Hastings

   The letterhead on which this letter is
typed measures 7¼ inches wide by 10½ inches
deep. It is referred to as the "Executive"
or "Monarch" size. Many business executives
use it to mark off their own correspondence
from the general company correspondence.

   Use a maximum line length of five inches
on this size letterhead. Letters with 75 to
150 words usually look best when typed to a
line length of 4½ inches. You may continue
to use a line of four inches when the letter
is quite short.

   The inside address on a letterhead this
size·may be typed in the regular position or
below the letter, as shown here. Whenever
you type the address at the bottom, you will,
of course, start the salutation high enough
on the sheet to allow room for the address.

   Type the identifying initials four lines
down from the complimentary close.

                    Cordially yours

ty

Miss Grace J. Hastings
629 College Place
Dodge City, Kansas   67801

Style Letter 7—Semiblock On Executive-Size Letterhead
Line length: 4 ½ inches. Words in body: 147
Salutation on line 20 from top of sheet

Addressing No. 10 Envelopes. The standard large-size business envelope is called the "No. 10." It measures 4 1/8" by 9 1/2". You will notice that it is deeper, as well as longer, than the No. 6 3/4 envelope.

On a No. 10 envelope start the address on the 15th line space from the top edge. Put the paper guide at the proper position and leave a left margin of 40 pica spaces or 48 elite spaces.

Study the No. 10 envelopes shown in the illustration.

Other envelope sizes are sometimes used for special purposes. After you have had experience in addressing No. 6 3/4 and No. 10 envelopes, you can readily place the address on other sizes. Just remember to start slightly below the center of the envelope and to leave a little more white space at the left of the address than at the right.

Envelope Addressing Problems. Type the following addresses in the block style on No. 10 envelopes. When the address has an attention line, type that line in the lower left-hand corner of the envelope.

Use regular spacing on the first eight envelopes. Leave one blank line space above the last line in addresses 9 and 10.

Unless you are instructed otherwise, you may type mail directions in either of the accepted styles or positions.

1. Miss Lorraine B. Kreamer   503 Argonne Drive   St. Joseph, Missouri 64501

2. Mrs. Gordon F. Curtis   Round Mountain   California 96084

3. Air Mail   Mr. W. Harry Buckman   Western Glazing Company   West Mason and Guild Streets   Tacoma, Washington 98404

4. Mrs. Sidney M. Knox   c/o Mrs. Edward A. Johns   41 Park Boulevard   Port Richmond   Staten Island, New York 10345

5. Special Delivery   Knight & Wesley, Inc.   740 East Norton Street   Baltimore, Maryland 21202   Attention of Mr. Samuel D. Wesley

6. Del Monte Laundry, Inc.   57 Henderson Street   Las Vegas, Nevada 89101   Attention: Mr. Mitchell T. Hughes

7. Mr. A. Robert Dawes   In care of Central Hotel   Scranton, Pennsylvania 18504   Hold for Arrival

8. Registered   G. R. Tyson and Sons, Inc.   5000 South Broad Street   Richmond, Virginia 29208

9. Mr. Charles A. Kennedy, President   Kennedy Clothing Company   131 Conestoga Street   York, Pennsylvania 17405

10. Northern Distributors, Inc.   Industrial Building   500-540 North 22nd Street   Milwaukee, Wisconsin 53207   Attention of Mr. Carroll Hastings

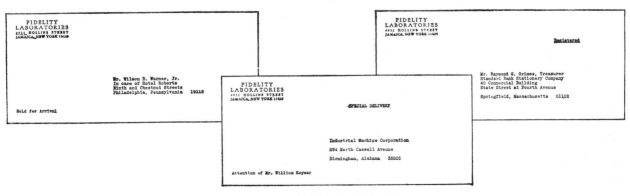

ILLUSTRATION 59
Addresses On No. 10 Envelopes

Signature Styles For Women. An unmarried woman may include *Miss* in her signature. If her first name is decidedly feminine, however, the reader of the letter will usually understand that she should be addressed as *Miss* in the reply. If, on the other hand, her first name is uncommon or is likely to be confusing, the use of *Miss* with her name is both courteous and helpful.

When the writer of a letter is to be addressed as *Mrs.*, that fact should always be indicated in her signature.

Study carefully the following signature styles. Note the use of parentheses. Observe, too, that the proper title—*Miss* or *Mrs.*—never appears before the penwritten signature *when the name is typed*.

Unmarried Woman	Married Woman	Widow
Sincerely yours, *Helen W. Laird*	Sincerely yours, *Velma C. Mason* *(Mrs Paul D. Mason)*	A widow may continue to use the signature style she used while her husband was living. She may also use one of the following styles.
Sincerely yours, *Helen W. Laird* Helen W. Laird	Sincerely yours, *Velma C. Mason* (Mrs. Paul D. Mason)	Sincerely yours, *(Mrs) Martha N. Benner*
Sincerely yours, *(Miss) Marion D. Nolan*	Sincerely yours, *Velma C. Mason* Velma C. Mason (Mrs. Paul D. Mason)	Sincerely yours, *Martha N. Benner* (Mrs. Martha N. Benner)
Sincerely yours, *Marion D. Nolan* (Miss Marion D. Nolan)		

Problem 50. Type the following letter on a sheet of plain paper. Follow the form of Style Letter 6. Type your own home address at the top of the letter and your own name at the bottom. Sign the letter.

Bartow Office Supply Company 626 East Waldron Street Camden, New Jersey 08105 Gentlemen: Please fill my order for one metal typewriter table—Stock No. M-3948. (¶) The price quoted in your Catalog B is $14.75. My personal check for that amount is enclosed. (¶) Please make shipment express collect. I shall pay the transportation charges upon delivery. Very truly yours, Enclosure

(42 words)

Letter Typed on Executive-Size Letterhead with Address below the Body. The next letters you write will be typed in a style often used by professional men and business executives for their personally dictated letters. Style Letter 7, page 154, explains this letter style and gives suggestions for placing letters on executive-size stationery. Study it carefully.

In typing on an executive-size sheet, you will need to have different margin stop settings from the settings you have used in typing on a sheet that is $8\frac{1}{2}$ inches wide.

Monarch Envelopes. A letter typed on an executive-size letterhead should be mailed only in an envelope of matching size.

Fold the executive-size letterhead in the same way you fold a full-size sheet for insertion in a No. 10 envelope. See Illustration 60, page 143.

Folding the Letter for a No. 10 Envelope.
Illustration 60 shows the proper way to fold and insert a letter in a No. 10 business envelope. Study it carefully.

Practice the three steps until you can fold and insert letters without referring to the diagrams.

Using Window Envelopes. A window envelope is a business envelope with a "cut-out" through which the address on the enclosure **may** be read. Window envelopes are widely used **in** business to mail bills, checks, and other business papers. They are also sometimes used for correspondence.

Illustration 61 shows the correct way to fold a letter for insertion in a No. 10 window envelope.

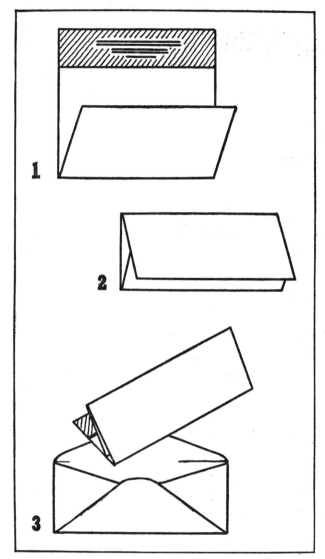

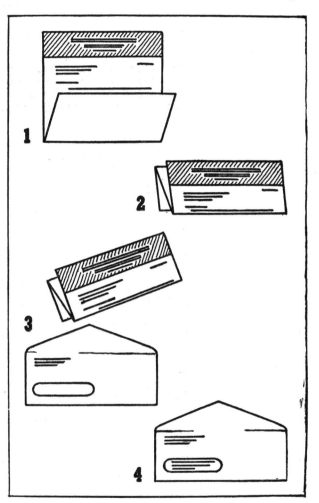

1. Lay the letter face up on your desk. Fold up the bottom third. Take time to make sure that the fold is *straight;* then crease the sheet.

2. Fold down the upper part of the sheet to bring the top edge within a quarter of an inch of the first crease. Check to see that the fold is even; then make a second crease.

3. Insert the letter in the envelope so that the letter-head is at the top and is facing the back of the envelope.

1. Lay the letter face up on your desk; then fold up the bottom third of the sheet.

2. Pick up the letter and turn it face down on your desk; then fold back the upper part of the sheet so that the complete address will show through the window.

3. Insert the letter in the envelope so that the letter-head is at the top and is facing the front of the envelope.

4. Check to make sure that the complete address shows through the window.

ILLUSTRATION 60

Folding A Letter For Insertion In A No. 10 Envelope

ILLUSTRATION 61

Folding A Letter For Insertion In A Window Envelope

941 Rockland Avenue
Baltimore, Maryland   21215
August 18, 19--

Mr. Eric A. Otis, President
Keystone Aluminum Corporation
2830 East Spruce Street
Philadelphia, Pennsylvania   19107

Dear Mr. Otis:

When you type a personal-business letter on plain paper, always include your complete address along with the date. Let the longest line of your address end with the right margin.

You may use either the semiblock style or the block style for your personal-business letters. Mixed punctuation is preferred--especially in letters of application.

Arrange your letter so that the top margin is slightly narrower than the bottom margin. Leave from two to four line spaces--depending upon the length of your letter--between the date and the first line of the inside address.

Your typed name in the conclusion of the letter is optional. Unless your penmanship is above average, however, you will be doing your reader a favor by typing your name.

A man never types or writes Mr. before his name. The use of Miss or Mrs. in the signature of a woman is explained on the next page. Study the examples of signature styles given there.

Sincerely yours,

Marvin L. Richards

Style Letter 6—Personal-Business Letter
Line length: 5 inches. Words in body: 162
First line of home address: Line 11
First line of inside address: Line 18

Typing Two-Page Letters

1. Type the letter with single spacing to a line length of six inches.

2. Type the second page on a second (or continuation) sheet, which is a sheet of plain paper that matches the letterhead in size and quality.

3. Use the same side margins for the second page that you use for the first page.

4. Leave a bottom margin on the first page of from one inch to one and a half inches.

5. Before you start to type the first page, put a light pencil mark about an inch and a half from the bottom to warn you when you get near the end of the sheet.

6. Do not number the first page.

7. Finish the first page with a *complete word.*

8. When a paragraph breaks at the bottom of the first page, type at least two lines of that paragraph on each page. Don't divide a two-line or a three-line paragraph.

9. Type a reference line or heading for the second page. Include the name of the person or company addressed, the date, and the page number. Several widely used styles are shown in Illustrations 62 and 63.

10. Type the second-page reference line or heading at least one inch from the top of the sheet. The top margin should be approximately equal to the left margin.

11. Triple-space before continuing with the body of the letter.

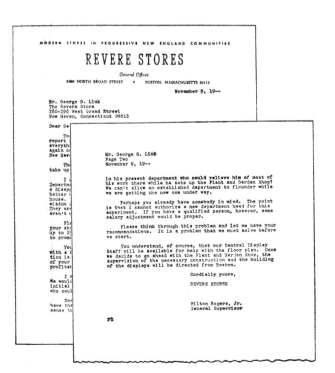

ILLUSTRATION 62
Two-Page Letter

Carver Instrument Company—Page 2—June 16, 19—

the shipment arrives before Monday, please send us by air

Mr. W. Ross Joyner   2   September 3, 19—

follow your specifications. The least expensive material

Griffin Brothers, Inc.—5 April 19—   2

It was a pleasure to work with Mr. Westman. He has a fine

Rollins & Rollins, Inc.
December 15, 19—
Page 2

the only way now open to us. When I talked with you on

ILLUSTRATION 63
Additional Styles Of Second-Page Headings

your magazine. I think it's only fair to tell you now that our modest ad brought results we consider spectacular. (¶) "We have already received 153 inquiries from business houses that our other advertising has never reached. Those inquiries have so far brought us nineteen good orders, and I know that more are on the way." (¶) A second Business-by-Mail issue will appear this August. Rates for that one issue are shown in the enclosed leaflet. (¶) The copy deadline is June 12, but it looks now as though most of the space will be gone long before then. So that you won't be disappointed, I'm enclosing a stamped AIR MAIL envelope for your use in mailing your ad. (¶) How about including a coupon in your ad to see what happens? Cordially yours, WHITTINGHAM PUBLICATIONS Craig G. Withers Advertising Manager Enclosures 2

(214 words)

Letter Confirming a Telegram. Many offices write a letter to confirm and repeat an outgoing telegram. Indent the quoted telegram. You will, of course, also enclose it in quotation marks.

Problem 47. (Form 5-47). This letter contains a quoted telegram. Type the letter in the block style with mixed punctuation.

Miss Loretta W. Stauffer   1473 Elmridge Avenue, N. W.   Washington, D. C. 20002 Dear Miss Stauffer: In making a final check this morning of the story you sent us, we discovered that you provided only captions for the illustrations. We sent you the following telegram: (¶) "Do you have signed releases for use of illustrations with your story? Rush copy for credit lines by air mail special delivery." (¶) We're sched-

uled to start page layout on Monday. Please let us hear from you at once, so that your material can be published as planned.   Cordially yours,   WHITTINGHAM PUBLICATIONS   Raymond Watson, Jr.   Editor

(76 words)

Personal-Business Letter. Style Letter 6 on the next page explains how to type a personal-business letter on plain paper. Study it carefully; then type the personal-business letters that follow (Problems 48, 49, and 50).

Use the semiblock style with mixed punctuation.

Problem 48. Type Style Letter 6 on a sheet of plain paper (8½ by 11). Use the home address and the writer's name given in the letter. Date your letter today.

Problem 49. Type the following letter on a sheet of plain paper. Follow the form of Style Letter 6. Type your own home address at the top of the letter and your own name at the bottom.

Sign the letter. (See page 153 for signature styles for women.)

Dr. Russell S. Grant   503 Fifth Avenue Des Moines, Iowa 50302   Dear Dr. Grant: This afternoon I had an interview with the Personnel Director of Triumph Insurance Company. As a result of that interview, I have accepted a position in the Accounts and Records Department. (¶) Miss Bolton, Personnel Director, showed me the exceedingly fine letter of recommendation that you wrote for me. I am convinced that your letter had a great deal to do with my employment, and I do want to tell you at once how grateful I am to you. (¶) During the first two or three months my work will be on an "on trial" basis. You may be sure that I'm going to do my best to make good.   Sincerely yours,

(108 words)

Typing Two-Page Letters. Letters 40, 41, and 42 are two-page letters. Type them in the style of Illustration 62—semiblock with mixed punctuation.

Use the letterheads in your Workbook for the first page of each letter. Use plain paper for the second page.

For Problem 40 use the second-page heading or reference line style shown in Illustration 62; for Problem 41, use the first style shown in Illustration 63; for Problem 42, use the second style shown in Illustration 63.

Problem 40. (Form 5-40)

Tollson Personnel Agency   20 Franklin Building   85 Madison Avenue New York, New York 10024 Gentlemen: Revere Stores will employ an advertising manager within the very near future. I'll outline in this letter the principal qualifications needed for the position. (¶) Only applicants with extensive retail store experience will be considered. The man we hire must combine a knowledge of advertising with a sound understanding of merchandising methods. He must be able to write and to supervise the writing of effective department store copy slanted to middle-income families. He must also be able to work intelligently and pleasantly with our merchandisers and with our individual store managers. (¶) The man we want is probably now employed by an independent store or by a small chain where future progress is uncertain—a man who is accustomed to responsibility but who can't hope for greater opportunity in his present position. (¶) Our present advertising manager is moving up to an executive position with Revere Stores. We want to replace him with a man who has qualities that will merit similar advancement in time. (¶) Although some newspaper experience will be helpful, it is not a "must." A New England background might be an asset, but it is, again, not necessary. Our selection will be made solely on ability. Ideally, the position will be filled by a man between thirty and forty. Promising applicants outside those age brackets, however, will be considered. (¶) The man we hire will have his office in Boston. We shall expect him to make occasional trips to many of our stores to help work out local advertising problems. Our present advertising manager has spent about ten per cent of his time outside his office. He has trained an office staff of four competent people to carry on in his absence. (¶) The salary for this position is open. We shall make it attractive to a competent and ambitious man. (¶) I am also writing about this position today to other employment agencies that have previously worked with us in securing personnel. We hope to interview at least a dozen applicants before we make a decision. (¶) In case you can refer qualified men to us, I'll appreciate your writing me at once to give me their names and backgrounds. Ask them, please, to apply promptly by letter—not by telephone and not in person. We shall acknowledge each letter and arrange interviews with promising applicants. (¶) Thank you for your help. I hope that you can find for us the ideal person for this position. Sincerely yours, REVERE STORES Keith F. Purdon   Personnel Manager

(405 words)

than good food. They want peace and quiet. They want elbow room. They insist upon a place that's pleasant. And ... according to the insurance companies ... the ladies outlive us by several years. (¶) Are you game to giving their system a try? If the ladies really have come up with a good idea, are you willing to cash in on it? (¶) Come around to the Men's Grill at The Fireside Lodge for lunch one day this week. Along with the best food in town ... along with fast service without fuss ... you'll find a masculine atmosphere of peace and quiet that's worth a million but that doesn't add a penny to your check. Cordially yours THE FIRESIDE LODGE President WWHartley/

(230 words)

Letters with Indented Quotations. When a business letter includes a long quotation or a quotation that the writer wants to emphasize, that material should be set off from the rest of the body. Notice how the quotation in Illustration 64 is indented to distinguish it from the other paragraphs.

A 5-space indention *from each margin* usually gives the best results. The letter in Illustration 64 was typed to a line length of 60 pica strokes for the regular paragraphs and to a line length of 50 pica strokes for the indented paragraphs.

Remember that quotation marks are required at the beginning and at the end of a quotation. When the quotation consists of more than one paragraph, there is a quotation mark at the beginning of each paragraph. Only the last paragraph has a quotation mark at the end.

Be particularly careful with vertical placement when the letter contains a quotation. If the quotation is fairly long, raise the starting point of the inside address. The body of the letter in Illustration 64 contains 209 words, and the first line of the inside address is typed on line 16.

Set a tabulator stop for the indented paragraphs to avoid thumb-spacing.

G. Garfield Moore, President
Leonard W. Brill, Editor-in-Chief

WHITTINGHAM
PUBLICATIONS

EDITORIAL OFFICES: 14 WEST 42ND STREET
NEW YORK, NEW YORK 10007

November 3, 19--

Mr. Walter B. Hoskins, Editor
Industrial Publishing Company
40 McFarland Building
Pittsburgh, Pennsylvania 15202

Dear Mr. Hoskins:

A forthcoming issue of MERCHANDISERS' REVIEW will be devoted to service industries. In addition to contributions by several well-known writers, it will also include staff-written articles that point out specific instances of unusual service plans.

May we have your permission to quote in that issue from the story, "Capital Ess Service," published in the October issue of COLD STEEL? Here are the paragraphs we have selected.

> "The use of control maps can be highly effective when properly planned and supervised. One Midwestern outfit, for example, found that a control map maintained at the office switchboard reduced by one-half the time consumed by its service men in going from one job to another.
>
> "This same dealer reports that the control map is the center of attention for office visitors. Customers are instantly impressed by the systematic way in which service calls are handled and routed. This dealer gives the control map a good share of the credit for an increase in business in a highly competitive field."

We shall, of course, make proper reference to the source of the quotation. If the reference is not made directly in the body of the article, it will be given in a footnote on the page containing the quotation.

Cordially yours,

WHITTINGHAM PUBLICATIONS

Louise J. Vollmer
Assistant Editor

typ

ILLUSTRATION 64

Letter Containing Quotation

Problem 46. (Form 5-46). The following letter has a two-paragraph quotation. Type it in the block style with mixed punctuation. Follow Illustration 64 as a model.

Mr. Thomas K. Nathan Holt, Latham & Cartwright 412 West Union Street Little Rock, Arkansas 72204 Dear Mr. Nathan: In a few days you'll get a copy of the Business-by-Mail issue of MERCHANDISERS' REVIEW that made advertising history when it was published. Please watch for it. (¶) This is the issue that set a new "fan mail" record for magazines in the Whittingham group. You may have read about the results. Here, for example, is what one advertiser wrote: (¶) "Until I invested in a small, column-width ad in your Business-by-Mail issue, I was highly skeptical about the pulling power of

Problem 41. (Form 5-41). This letter has a subject line and a postscript. Use the same indention for the subject line that you use for the paragraphs.

Mr. Henry D. Lansing, Manager   The Revere Store   80 Main Street   Portland, Maine 04102   Dear Henry: Subject: Trainee—Mr. Lester Fenwick   It was good to talk with you a few minutes ago on the telephone.   I am grateful for your unhesitating willingness to take another trainee under your wing for a few months. There isn't a store manager in our chain who can help him more than you can.   (¶) As I told you on the telephone, this young man, Mr. Lester Fenwick, will be ready to report for work on the first of next month. We shall have him stay at the State Hotel for a few days until he can find other living accommodations in Portland.   He is single.   (¶) You will find that he has some experience in dealing with the public.   While he was attending college, he worked part time with Destron Shoe Stores and with a small department store.   He has reinforced that experience with courses in merchandising. Unlike some young men, however, he makes no pretense of knowing it all.   I'm confident that you will find him eager to learn and quick to take advice.   (¶) Best of all, he has a good knowledge of accounting.   Please assign him some office duties while he is with you, so that he will become familiar with our methods.   Let him take over the daily register check for a while.   Please help him to get a grasp of the weekly and monthly reports.   (¶) I am glad to hear that he will be most useful to you now in the stock room.   He is by no means afraid of physical work, and I know no phase of our business that is more important than the proper checking, pricing, and stocking of merchandise.   (¶) Your suggestion that you then move him to one of the fast-turnover departments sounds fine to me. We want to see how he works with other personnel and how he meets customers.   He will also have a chance there to see the importance of ordering promptly to insure adequate stocks of fast-moving staple items.   (¶) He is in your hands.   We have made it perfectly clear to him that you are to be the sole judge of the assignments that will benefit him most.   He is to stay at any one job as long as you need him there and as long as you think best.   (¶) Please prepare the usual "Store Manager's Report on Trainee" at the end of each week and send it to Mr. Purdon, Personnel Manager.   I am asking Mr. Purdon to mail you a supply of those forms today.   Cordially yours,   REVERE STORES   Roger V. Woodland   Vice-President   *(Postscript)* Mr. Fenwick's salary will be paid directly to him by check from Boston.

(416 words)

Problem 42. (Form 5-42). This letter requires an enclosure notation.

Mr. Clark B. Hanson, President   Marvel Manufacturing Company   Fourth Street at Ohio Avenue   Wheeling, West Virginia 26005   Dear Mr. Hanson: Recently we ordered stocks of Marvel Ware to test your products in two of our stores.   I know you will be glad to hear that the results have been highly pleasing to us and that we are ready to make Marvel Ware a staple item in all Revere Stores.   (¶) You will find our

Problem 43. (Form 5-43). Type Style Letter 5, page 148. Use today's date instead of the date shown.

Start the first line of the inside address on the seventeenth line from the top of the sheet.

You will usually get best placement with the inverted letter by starting one line higher than you would start if you were using the semiblock style.

Problem 44. (Form 5-44). Note the third paragraph of this letter. A series of three periods is often used in sales letters in place of a comma or a dash. Here are the accepted ways of spacing.

```
surroundings ... the perfect

surroundings...the perfect

surroundings . . . the perfect
```

Follow the first method—solid periods with a space before the group and one space after the group—when you type this letter.

Mrs. Warren Lee Oster   3126 East Cypress Drive   New Orleans, Louisiana 70109   Dear Mrs. Oster   Congratulations on your election as President of Lafayette Garden Club for the coming year! Before the news appeared in yesterday's *Evening Herald,* you had probably already started to make plans for the meetings and special events of the next twelve months. (¶) I hope that The Fireside Lodge may have a part to play in those plans. Since we opened the distinctive Colony Room on the second floor last year, eight of your sister clubs have held functions here. Two clubs have arranged to have luncheon meetings with us regularly this season, and a third club has engaged the Colony Room for an Anniversary Banquet one evening next month. (¶) You'll find in the enclosed folder many of the reasons why The Fireside Lodge has become such

a popular meeting place for clubs ... why I believe it will appeal so strongly to all the members of Lafayette Garden Club. The comfortable and charming surroundings ... the perfect appointments ... the skilled service ... the astonishingly economical menus combine to help make each meeting here a success and a memorable event. (¶) Have you visited the Colony Room yourself? If not, please drop in to see me one day soon when you are nearby. I shall enjoy meeting you and showing you what many of our friends say is the most beautiful luncheon and banquet room in the South.   Sincerely yours   THE FIRESIDE LODGE   Manager   RFSullins/   Enclosure

(222 words)

Problem 45. (Form 5-45)

Mr. Roland G. Hunter, Manager   Hunter Marketing Services, Inc.   70 West Delta Street   New Orleans, Louisiana   70107   Dear Mr. Hunter   I know you won't quote me when you go home tonight, but I honestly wonder sometimes whether the ladies aren't just a bit smarter than the men. (¶) Take the matter of picking the right place for lunch. A good many of us men folks are content to slip into almost any place that's handy and gulp down the daily special. We let ourselves be pushed, shoved, and hurried. We endure the clatter of dishes, the potent odors of the kitchen, and the racket of noisy people ... and we get stomach ulcers. (¶) But some time watch the ladies pick a spot for lunch. They will carry an armload of bundles for blocks to find a restaurant that offers something more

Purchase Order No. 3047 with this letter. It calls for immediate shipment of stock to each store in the chain. This order is placed, however, subject to a few important conditions that I shall list here. If you are willing to meet those conditions, please write me at once to that effect and proceed to fill the order. In case you cannot meet one or more of the conditions, the order is void. (¶) I have, incidentally, gone over these conditions with your New England representative, Mr. Twyford. He agrees that none of them is likely to cause any difficulty. (¶) 1. You will ship within fourteen days of the date of our order. Cancel any item that you cannot ship; do not back-order. (¶) 2. You will ship prepaid—by the most economical means—directly to each individual store. You will bill us for transportation charges. (¶) 3. You will show our purchase order number on the outside of each carton or package. You will also mark the contents clearly on each carton or package. (¶) 4. You will mail all invoices to our Central Accounting Office here in Boston—never to individual stores. Each invoice must show our purchase order number, the date of shipment, and the Revere store to which shipment was made. The invoice must be mailed promptly—not later than two business days after the date of shipment. (¶) 5. You will replace defective merchandise or merchandise that has been damaged in transit if such merchandise is returned within four months after purchase. (¶) 6. You will accept this order and all future orders from us on terms of one per cent cash discount for payment in thirty days after invoice date. (¶) Because I know that your regular terms are 1/15 days, N/30, you are due some explanation about this last condition. We feel that it is a fair and reasonable one, but I do want you to understand why. (¶) A discount for payment in fifteen days doubtless encourages some of your customers to pay promptly invoices that they would otherwise hold until the first, the fifteenth, or even until the end of the following month. In the case of Revere Stores, however, all invoices—regardless of the discount—are automatically paid within two business days after our Central Accounting Office receives notice of the delivery of merchandise. (¶) Let's take an example. Assume that you make one shipment today to our store in Waterbury, Connecticut, and another to our store in Burlington, Vermont. The Waterbury shipment is delivered in six days; we get a receiving report in Boston on the ninth day; and your check is mailed not later than the eleventh day. The Burlington shipment, however, is in transit fourteen days; we get the receiving report on the eighteenth day; and your check is mailed by the twenty-first day. It seems to us just as fair to allow a discount for promptness on the second shipment as to allow it on the first. (¶) Please use the enclosed business reply envelope to let me know promptly whether you agree.

Sincerely yours,   REVERE STORES
Nelson H. Abbey   Purchasing Agent
(562 words)

Inverted Style. Style Letter 5, page 148, is typed in the inverted letter style. The body of the letter explains the style in detail.

You are to type the next three letters—Problems 43, 44, and 45—in the inverted letter style. Use open punctuation.

The
FIRESIDE LODGE

76 GASTON STREET • NEW ORLEANS, LOUISIANA   70105

17 January 19--

Miss Mildred N. Hughes
1485 Le Blanc Street
New Orleans, Louisiana   70108

Dear Miss Hughes

The style of this letter is called the inverted letter style.
Sometimes it is also referred to as the "hanging indention" style. The first line of each paragraph starts
at the left margin, but the remaining lines of the body
are indented and blocked. The usual indention is five
spaces.

You will need more time to type letters in this style than
to type them in the styles you have previously studied.
Some businessmen feel that the extra time is well spent
because the appearance of the letter gets attention.
The inverted style is used chiefly when a letter has an
unusual purpose or a special message. It is not recommended for routine correspondence.

After you have typed the first line of the body, reset the
margin for the indented lines. Set a tabulator stop
for the first line of each succeeding paragraph. When
you start a new paragraph, depress the margin release,
throw the carriage all the way across, and strike the
tabulator key.

You may use either mixed or open punctuation with this style.
You may either center the date or type it to end with
the right margin. The practice of the office in which
you work will determine whether the regular date style
or the military date style is used. Either is correct.

Sincerely yours

THE FIRESIDE LODGE

Manager

RFSullins/typ

Style Letter 5—Inverted With Open Punctuation
Line length: 6 inches. Words in body: 221

TYPING NUMBERS

Dates

1. Avoid adding *st, nd, rd,* or *th* to the number that represents the date of the month.

> June 1, 19— (*not* June 1st, 19—)
> Your letter of March 10 came.

2. In the military services the date is written in this style: 15 November 19—. Some persons and companies use this style, too.

3. When the date comes before the name of the month or when the name of the month is not given, follow this practice: (1) Spell out *first to ninth*; (2) type the contracted forms *10th to 31st.* Do not type a period after the contractions; they are not abbreviations.

> He is due on the first of May.
> Call us on the 25th of March.
> Be sure to be here on the second.

4. Never use diagonals in writing a date either in the date line or in the body of the letter. Write *all* the figures in the year date.

> August 18, 19—   July 9, 1966
> (*not* 8/18/—)   (*not* July 8, '66)

5. When a decade or a century is mentioned, spell out the words and capitalize them.

> I knew him in the Twenties.
> It is a Nineteenth Century novel.

6. Avoid dividing a date at the end of a line.

Amounts of Money

1. Omit .00 in writing even amounts.

> The price of $500 is low.
> (*not* $500.00)

2. If you are writing a sentence that has in it several amounts some of which include cents and others do not, then use .00 in the even amounts.

> These outfits sell for $57.85,
> $80.00, and $92.75, respectively.

3. Do not type a period after an amount in dollars when the amount comes in a sentence.

> Payment of $125 is now due.

4. In writing amounts of less than $1, follow this practice: (a) Spell out *one to nine*; (b) use figures from 10 to 99.

> The cost is eight cents a foot.
> The unit cost is 35 cents.

5. When a number is used as the first word of a compound adjective that expresses an amount, follow this practice: (a) Spell out the number if it can be written as one word without a hyphen; (b) write figures if the amount, when spelled out, is a hyphenated word.

> I gave him a five-dollar bill.
> A 75-cent charge is made.

6. Never begin a sentence with a number. Spell it out.

> Five hundred people came.

7. Use a comma in writing $1,000 and over.

> $2,785 $87,658 $327,495 $4,639,528

8. In writing large round numbers, you may use the word *million.*

> The cost was 75 million dollars.

9. Never divide a number at the end of a line.

Addresses

1. Spell out *one to nine.* Use figures for 10 and over.

> Nine Jackson Road
> 2875 Western Avenue

> *Note:* Do not use commas in writing numbers in addresses.

2. When two numbers are used, type a hyphen (not a dash) between them.

> 528-532 Grant Street (*not* 528—532)

3. The names of some streets are themselves numbers. To avoid confusing the street number with the street name, spell out the street name.

> 1482 Sixty-third Street

4. When one of the words *North, South, East, West* is used as a part of the street name, you may use figures both for the street number if it is 10 or above and for the street name.

> His address is 583 East 64th Street.

5. Write the ZIP Code number after the name of the state. Leave three spaces between the state name and the number.

> Cincinnati, Ohio   45233

		Use Of	How Typed	Illustration
Feet and Inches	' "	To represent *feet* and *inches*.	For *feet*, the apostrophe; for *inches*, quotation marks.	5' 7"
Long Division (marks for)	⌐	To indicate long division problem.	Type the right parenthesis mark and a line with the underscore (one space higher).	$\begin{array}{r} 15 \\ 462\,\overline{)6930} \end{array}$
Made Fractions	7/8	To type fractions not on keyboard.	Type keyboard figures with diagonal.	3/16 74/116
Minus (sign for)	–	To indicate subtraction.	Type hyphen with space before and space after.	41 – 17
Minutes and Seconds	' "	To represent *minutes* and *seconds*.	For *minutes*, use the apostrophe; for *seconds*, quotation marks.	17' 8"
Mixed Numbers	14 3/8	To represent a whole number and a fraction.	Use keyboard fraction with whole number. Or type whole number with made fraction.	$7\frac{1}{4}$ $9\frac{1}{2}$ 37 2/3 or 37-2/3
Multiplication (sign for)	x	To indicate *times*.	Type small x with space before and space after.	156 x 3 5/6
Number Sign	#	To represent *number* before a figure.	Shift of the 3 key	Five #316
Parentheses	( )	To enclose parenthetical matter.	Shift of 9 key (left) Shift of 0 key (right)	Mark Twain (Samuel Clemens), the famous humorist, was an American.
Per Cent Sign	%	To represent *per cent* (by the hundred).	Shift of 5 key	Deduct discounts of 5%, 15%, and 25%.
Plus (sign for)	+	To indicate addition.	Type hyphen, backspace, type apostrophe, backspace, turn paper up, and type apostrophe again. In technical matter, type hyphen, backspace, and type diagonal.	56 + 24 12 3/8 + 43 2/3
Pounds	#	To represent *pound* or *pounds* (*lb.* or *lbs.*) after a figure.	Shift of the 3 key; the number sign typed *after* the figure.	1#, 18#, and 326#
Short Division (marks for)	)‾	To indicate short division problem.	Type right parenthesis mark, followed by a line of underscores.	$\begin{array}{r} 6\,\overline{)46866} \\ 7811 \end{array}$
Under-score	—	To emphasize words. To show that words are to be italicized.	Shift of the 6 key. Do not underscore spaces or punctuation marks.	Order <u>now</u>.

One of the reasons that a young man who is starting his business 13
career does not always see the value of reading is that he is apt to be of a 28
thoroughly practical bent; he is not quick to see the worth of things that 43
do not seem to offer an immediate means of advancement. What that 56
young man should know and realize is that a properly directed course 70
of systematic reading will be of value not so much in helping him to 84
do better the work he now has in hand as in preparing him to do much 98
more important work. The young bank clerk whose duties are simple 111
and routine may ask what good it will do him to know the history and 125
provisions of the national bank law, for instance. Well, it will do him 139
little or no good if he intends always to be a bank clerk; it may do him 153
a great deal of good if he has ambitions to become a bank officer. 166

A beginner in business, therefore, should not search too closely for 180
evidence of a direct relation between the right kind of reading and 193
immediate advancement in his work. The relation is there all right, 207
but the young employee must have faith enough to do a great deal of 220
earnest work without expecting advances in salary or position to 233
follow with the same regularity with which credits are earned in school 247
or college. What the young businessman usually wants to know is how 261
he should specialize his reading so as to make it of distinct advantage 275
to him in the future. Generally speaking, he should read material that 289
will give him knowledge which will broaden his viewpoint. If his career 303
is in retailing, he should read everything he can get his hands on that 317
deals with the particular aspect of retailing in which he is engaged. The 332
young man who gets into the shoe manufacturing business, for 344
example, who will specialize his reading on leather, who will learn about 358
the various processes of tanning and different methods of manufacture 372
will not only be a better judge of shoes, but he will be better able to sell 387
them or suggest how they can be sold better. 396

The bank clerk who will master the history and development of the 409
banking system may not see the application of that knowledge to his 423
daily tasks; but if opportunity some day knocks at his door, he will be 437
much better prepared to accept the burden of greater responsibilities 451
and wider usefulness. You can take any field of business and apply 464
to it this principle of learning about the business or industry as a whole. 479
Thousands of people have thought about the branch of business in which 493
you are engaged, and some of them have written about what they have 506
learned. You ought to search out the books they have produced and 519
read them. In that way you will build a foundation of knowledge that 533
will enable you to make a contribution and thus advance yourself. 546

When you have occasion to write a business letter, you should have [13] clearly outlined in your mind or on paper all the facts bearing on the [27] subject and as much information as possible about the personality of the [41] man or woman to whom you are writing. Your letter should be written [55] to say clearly, completely, and briefly what you want to say and to say [69] it in a way that will make a favorable impression on the person to whom [83] you are writing. The most dangerous errors in a business letter are [97] undue familiarity, crude jokes, unnecessarily committing yourself or [111] your company to a price, a policy, or an adjustment, and, finally, an [125] unpleasant impression when your letter is read. Rarely is it necessary [139] to write a letter in such a way that the person at the other end will be [153] turned down or criticized. The occasions for such letters are infrequent, [168] and they should be written by one who holds a position of authority. [182]

The danger in familiarity lies in your uncertainty as to the mood [195] in which your letter will find the other man. There is nothing quite [209] so risky in a business letter as a joke, for the reason that you can never [224] guess just what the conditions will be when your letter is read. If you [238] are making a quotation to furnish an item at a certain price, you are [252] in a sense mortgaging the future. Word your quotation in such a way [266] that the person will be told clearly what the price is, but not so that [280] he can hold your letter for a long time and then come back after the [294] market has risen and claim your original figure. Always bearing in [307] mind the value of brevity in a business letter, you should never overlook [322] the chance, when writing to a customer, of bringing to his attention [336] some seasonable product. If you have a number of points which it is [350] important to bring to the attention of the person who will get the [363] letter, you can accomplish your purpose much better by devoting a [376] short paragraph to each point rather than by talking about two or more [390] points in one long paragraph. [396]

What you need to avoid above everything else is getting into a groove [410] in your letter writing by always beginning and ending with the same [423] phraseology. A man who gets frequent letters from you will get weary [437] of having every letter begin in the same way. Remember that a letter [451] is a conversation put into written form. Avoid all the old, outworn [464] expressions that are still to be found in entirely too many business letters. [479] Make your language simple, your wording clear, and your sentences [492] short. Above all, put yourself into the place of your correspondent [506] and give him the information he wants in a thoroughly human way. [519] The use of letters in business is growing all the time, and the demand [533] for people who can write letters that achieve their purpose is unlimited. [548]

In most businesses there are four kinds of activity that we may | 13
describe as the basic divisions of business. They are the producing | 27
division, the selling division, the financial division, and the accounting | 42
division. Although these terms may not apply exactly to the activities | 56
of every business, we shall find them, with some slight changes and | 69
in a more or less developed form, in every kind of business. Each of | 83
these divisions has its special part to play. The producing division | 97
turns out the article to be sold. The men and women who work in that | 111
division are called upon to apply the creative and technical skill they | 125
possess to the production of the article in the best possible form, at the | 140
lowest possible cost, and in the quickest possible time. When they | 153
achieve those results, it may be said that they have done their duty. | 167
Of course, in a trading business, such as a department store, there is | 181
no producing department. There is, however, a buying activity by | 194
which the articles to be sold are obtained. That buying activity may | 208
be said to correspond to production in a manufacturing business. | 221

When the finished article is placed in the sales or stock room to be | 235
sold, the sales department comes upon the scene. It is the duty of | 248
the sales executives and of the salesmen to sell the goods turned out | 262
by the manufacturing division. If the sales division can sell all the | 276
goods a company can make, nothing more can be asked of it. The | 289
financial division is charged with the duty of providing the funds | 302
needed to manufacture, sell, and advertise the product and to provide | 316
for the salaries and expenses of the sales department. While banks, | 330
bonds, and other sources of credit may be resorted to for funds, those | 344
funds must, in the long run, come from the customers to whom sales | 357
have been made. The function of the accounting division is to record | 371
all the transactions of the business and to tabulate and present these | 385
transactions to the management in the form of reports. Those reports | 399
largely determine the future activities of the business. The cost reports, | 414
for instance, indicate whether production costs are high, low, or normal; | 429
whether the investment in facilities for production is in correct proportion | 444
to sales as compared with previous periods; and whether particular | 457
departments of the business are falling below normal efficiency or are | 471
rising above it. Business statements and audit reports are, of course, | 485
a record of what has taken place in the past. They always include | 498
figures to show the wide variety of taxes which the business has paid | 512
during the period covered by the audit report or which are to be paid | 526
within the legal time after the close of the fiscal year. Such statements | 541
and reports aid management in charting the course for the future. | 554

No. 25

In training a new stenographer, the businessman gives her as great [13] a variety of work as conditions will permit. In her school training she [27] should have learned how to do billing and prepare statements of [40] account, type envelopes in the most efficient way, tabulate material [54] correctly and attractively, fill in business forms in the right manner, [68] type purchase orders and inventories, and do good work on the hundred [82] and one other aspects of applied typing. Such work is in addition to [96] letters, which make up the bulk of her daily work in the office. During [110] the first part of her employment and until she becomes accustomed to [124] her new surroundings, the work assigned will generally be of a more [137] or less routine nature. In many offices the first duty of the new [150] stenographer is the writing of brief letters and acknowledgments, doing [164] elementary filing, and carrying on work of a general character covering [178] the rudiments of office detail as those details are related to the [191] stenographic force. As the new stenographer improves in speed, more [205] technical work is given to her. That work is gradually increased in [219] volume and variety so that she can accustom herself to the handling [232] of complex details. In most offices it is to the interest of the business [247] to promote stenographers to the higher positions instead of employing [261] outsiders; work is assigned to prepare them for promotion. [273]

Ideals and standards are set by the business, and the work must be [286] done to conform to them. Before writing each letter, the stenographer [300] should look over her notes and lay out the letter accordingly. If the [314] notes are few, the message may be written on a short letterhead. [327] When there are many notes, the margins are, of course, narrowed. [340] One of the most important parts of your training is the setting up of [354] letters of different lengths to get the best possible appearance. [367]

One successful businessman says that he never scolds or finds fault [380] with a new stenographer, because scolding destroys the confidence that [394] the new employee should have in herself. Suggestions for improvement, [408] on the other hand, should always be welcomed by new employees who [421] really mean to become efficient workers. The thoughtful businessman [435] is keen to recognize progress, intelligence, and initiative. [447]

There are two factors about which every businessman is concerned. [460] First, he wants to make the working conditions for the employees just [474] as pleasant and agreeable as possible. Second, he keeps informed about [488] the progress and improvement that employees are making. He makes [501] employees understand that as they improve, they will get more money. [515] Efficient secretaries, correspondents, and workers of unusual ability do [529] constructive work; hence their salaries tend to go up steadily. [542]

Division Nine

Paragraph Typing A

Many of the words in these paragraphs are balanced-hand words.

1   The usual thing for us to do when we get sick is to go   11
to a doctor for the advice that his training and experience   23
entitle him to give us; but when many of us encounter other   35
problems, we turn for aid to anybody who is handy. The key   47
to the solution of any big problem is held by men and women   59
who understand such problems; if we take our own problem to   71
them, they may not have the solution ready for us, but they   83
do know how to go to work on the problem and get it solved.   95

2   It is usual for risk and profit to go hand in hand; if   11   106
a venture does not embody any risk, the profit to be got or   23   118
won from that venture is apt to be small. It is all right,   35   130
and for many of us it is also prudent, to make security the   47   142
goal of life; but it is also good to remember that security   59   154
may mean giving up the chance for any giant profit. Before   71   166
you envy the man who took a big risk and won, try to decide   83   178
whether you would have been willing to take that same risk.   95   190

3   A man or woman who wishes to own antique furniture may   11   201
pay a big price for an antique chair and then refuse to sit   23   213
in the chair or allow the chair to be used. The chair thus   35   225
becomes an ornament; the person who owns it does so for the   47   237
reason that he or she may thus earn the envy of friends who   59   249
do not own such a chair. There are also some men and women   71   261
who make the same use of their brains; they do display them   83   273
now and then, but they never permit them to be put to work.   95   285

Paragraph Typing B

Each of these paragraphs contains all the letters of the alphabet.

Words

1 The foundation of good human relations is friendliness | 11

and good will. You think quite correctly about business if | 23

you view it as a series of transactions to be carried on in | 35

the spirit of friendliness. There are some people who seem | 47

to score just about zero in friendliness. Having any deals | 59

with them chills the blood. They resent any questions that | 71

you ask; they show by their manner and by the expression on | 83

their faces that they do not desire to be agreeable to you. | 95

2 Everyday experience demonstrates that approval is more | 11   106

effective in getting results than is censure. A person who | 23   118

is always being censured can easily become dejected and may | 35   130

get to feel like quitting. The business executive who goes | 47   142

out of his way to give praise when it is merited is sure to | 59   154

create a fine working spirit in his organization. He knows | 71   166

and realizes that sincere praise warms the spirit and gives | 83   178

a person the best kind of incentive to jump in and produce. | 95   190

3 We should realize that thousands of individuals remain | 11   201

employees rather than become executives because they cannot | 23   213

or will not sacrifice their personal ease or desires to the | 35   225

acquisition of the skills and resources that equip them for | 47   237

major responsibilities. Too many employees in business are | 59   249

concerned with security. They jog along day after day, and | 71   261

they do not use the experience they have secured to develop | 83   273

initiative; then they wonder why they do not win promotion. | 95   285

Paragraph Typing C

These paragraphs contain many figures, symbols, and capital letters.

1   The following members were present at the meeting held at the office of Nickel, Foster & Brooks on Monday, July 5: George A. Clemson, Randall Kirby Smithson, Barton Zwirlein, Daniel Elson Youngman, Walter J. Quinn, Harrison I. Xintas, Karl Oscar Lambert, Peter Viverette, and John W. Schwemmer. Henry C. Poor, Executive Secretary of the County Historical Society, presented copies of his report to all the members. The current assets of the Society were shown to be $47,635.

2   Statistics show that in a recent year we had more than 650,000 building fires in the United States. Of this total 40% (260,000) took place in homes. About 8½% (55,250) were in shops and stores. Fires in plants and factories made up 6½% (42,250) of the total. In the year there were fires in 58,000 apartments (9%). In garages and filling stations we had 26,000 fires (4% of the total). Restaurants and hotels to the number of 32,500 (5% of the total) had severe fires.

3   North Dakota, the "Sioux State," is in the center of a far-flung wheat belt. The territorial motto was nine words from a speech by Daniel Webster--Liberty and Union, Now and Forever, One and Inseparable. When North Dakota was made a state in 1889, that motto was continued. In long ago times the state was the abode of various Indian tribes. A statue of Sacajawea, the heroic Indian girl who acted as the guide for the Lewis and Clark Expedition, was put up in Bismarck.

Division Nine—Legal Typing

The papers typed in a law office fall, broadly speaking, into three classes: (1) documents that are entirely in typewritten form, such as Wills, Affidavits, and Agreements covering special situations; (2) printed forms that are filled in, such as the forms used for Mortgages and Leases; and (3) typewritten papers that are prepared in connection with various aspects of litigation or court procedure.

Legal paper that is 8½ inches wide by 13 inches deep is often used. Such paper has a double vertical rule 1½ inches from the left edge of the sheet and a single vertical rule ½ inch from the right edge. The typing is done within these vertical rules. Two spaces are left between the double vertical rule and the beginning of the typed lines.

Double-spacing is the general rule in typing legal documents. Leave a top margin of six double line spaces (two inches) and a bottom margin of three double line spaces (1 inch) on each sheet. When the document consists of more than one sheet, the sheets should be numbered by centering the proper figure (2, 3, 4, etc.) one-half inch from the bottom of the sheet.

If ruled legal paper is available, use it in typing Problems 1 and 2. Make carbons as directed by your instructor. If you are not supplied with legal paper, your instructor may ask you to rule sheets of paper.

Problem 1. Type the following AFFIDAVIT. Double-space. Use a 10-space paragraph indention. Fill in the current year date wherever 19 - - occurs. Type the three rules and *Notary Public* as shown in Illustration 102. Leave two double spaces for each of the signatures.

Note: The expression *t/a* means *trading as.*

AFFIDAVIT

WE, GEORGE H. LINDSTROM and MARY E. LINDSTROM, his wife, HEREBY CERTIFY that we are the owners of the property on the south side of Amster-

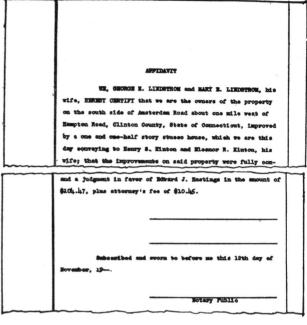

ILLUSTRATION 102
Affidavit

dam Road about one mile west of Hampton Road, Clinton County, State of Connecticut, improved by a one and one-half story stucco house, which we are this day conveying to Henry S. Kinton and Eleanor R. Kinton, his wife; that the improvements on said property were fully completed in January, 19--, and that we have been occupying the said premises as a residence since the latter part of February, 19--; that all the materials used in the construction of said improvements were supplied by Fred S. Alexander, t/a Clinton Lumber Company, the full amount for such materials being represented by the mortgage from the affiants to said Fred S. Alexander dated January 10, 19--, which mortgage is being released in connection with the transfer of the property to Henry S. Kinton and

Eleanor R. Kinton, his wife; that all the labor in the erection of the improvements on said property was performed by the said George H. Lindstrom and his brother, Henry C. Lindstrom; that there are no mechanics' liens upon said property and that the affiants have not received any notice of any intention to file such liens; that there are no conditional sales or chattel mortgages or any claims or liens of any nature whatsoever, disclosed or undisclosed, upon any of the fixtures or equipment on the property or in the improvements thereon; that the affiants have a clear and undisputed title to the said improvements and all the fixtures therein; and that the only liens upon said property are the mortgage above referred to and a judgment in favor of Edward J. Hastings in the amount of $104.47, plus attorney's fee of $10.45.

Subscribed and sworn to before me this 12th day of November, 19--.

Notary Public

Problem 2. Type this AGREEMENT. Double-space your work. Use a 10-space paragraph indention. Fill in the current year date wherever 19 - - occurs. Type two lines with (SEAL) for the signatures. See Illustration 103, page 260.

AGREEMENT

THESE ARTICLES OF AGREEMENT made this first day of June, 19--, by and between Frederick C. Calhoun of the City of Evansville, County of Vanderburgh, State of Indiana, party of the first part, and John W. Selden of the City of Columbus, County of Franklin, State of Ohio, party of the second part:

WITNESSETH, that the parties to this agreement, in consideration of payments to be made as hereinafter stated, stipulate and agree as follows:

THE PARTY OF THE FIRST PART agrees, subject to the reservations hereinafter named, to sell to the party of the second part five thousand (5,000) tons of coal in such quantities as the party of the second part may require for use at his factory situated in Columbus, Ohio, from the date hereof until the thirty-first day of December, 19--, at the rate of Nine Dollars and Sixty-five Cents ($9.65) a ton, said coal to be delivered by the party of the first part to the said factory of the party of the second part.

THE PARTY OF THE SECOND PART agrees to buy from the party of the first part all the coal needed for use in said factory from the date hereof until the thirty-first day of December, 19--, and to pay the said party of the first part the rates above mentioned for all coal used under these Articles of Agreement, said amount to be due and payable on the fifteenth day of each month for all coal delivered during the immediately preceding calendar month.

IT IS FURTHER MUTUALLY AGREED that the said party of the first part shall not be held responsible for failure to deliver coal to the party of the second part during unusual delays in transportation resulting from strikes, severe storms, or other causes beyond the control of the party of the first part. In case of stoppage of his mines caused by a strike among his miners or other employees, the party of the first part is to be released from all obligation to furnish coal to the party of the second part during such suspension.

IT IS FURTHER AGREED that the party of the first part will, if required, use his best endeavors to purchase some other corresponding grade of coal and furnish the same to the party of the second part at the lowest market price at which it can be obtained by the party of the first part; or the party of the second part may, at his option, secure his supply of coal elsewhere during such suspension.

WITNESS our hands and seals on the day and year first above written.

ILLUSTRATION 103
Typed Rules For Signatures

Problem 3. Type this DEED OF TRUST. Double-space your work. Type one rule with (SEAL) for the signature of Mr. Shelton. Type *two* rules, beginning at the left margin, for the signatures of witnesses. Use the current year date.

DEED OF TRUST

WHEREAS, it is my intention and desire to create a trust for the purpose of erecting, maintaining, and operating a Nurses' Home for the Provident Hospital, Portland, Oregon, I do hereby declare this the following trust.

KNOW YE, that in pursuance of such intention, I, Frederick Walter Shelton of Portland, Oregon, in the Year of our Lord One Thousand Nine Hundred and   , have nominated, appointed, and declared and by these presents do nominate, appoint, and declare The Community Fund, Inc., of Portland, Oregon, to be my trustee of the sum of Four Hundred Thousand Dollars ($400,000), which said sum is this day paid and delivered by me to the said The Community Fund, Inc., in trust nevertheless for the purposes following: the construction, maintenance, and operation of a Nurses' Home for the Provident Hospital at Portland, Oregon; the said trustee or its successor in trust to have and to hold the said sum of money for the purpose above mentioned and for no other or different purpose or purposes and to account to me in writing of all its actings and doings in respect of the said trust hereby created, and of the sum so delivered to it, at such reasonable time or times as it shall be requested in writing so to do.

The said The Community Fund, Inc., trustee, is hereby authorized and empowered to use the said money for the full execution of the trust, following out the purpose herein set forth, without let or hindrance from anyone, exercising its own best judgment and discretion for the advancement of the purpose herein set forth.

If, for any cause, the said trust shall not be fully executed or shall fail or become inoperative, then the balance of the aforesaid sum of money, if any remains after payment of all expenses and charges of said trust, shall be returned to me, the said Frederick Walter Shelton.

This trust shall become operative and binding immediately upon its acceptance by The Community Fund, Inc., trustee.

IN WITNESS WHEREOF, I have hereunto set my hand and seal this 14th day of February, A. D., 19--.

Problem 4. Study this General Power of Attorney. Detach Form 9-4 from your Workbook and fill it in. The date of the paper is September 25 of *this* year. Fill in all year dates accordingly.

General Power of Attorney   KNOW ALL MEN BY THESE PRESENTS

THAT I, Frederick West Kenton, of the City of Cumberland, County of
Allegany, State of Maryland,
do hereby constitute and appoint Henry Lester Green, of the City of Frederick,
County of Frederick, State of Maryland,
to be my agent and attorney for me and in my name to sell or otherwise
dispose of, for value, all my capital stock in the Allen Tool and Machine Company, a corporation formed and doing business under and by virtue of the laws
of the State of Delaware, said capital stock which I own consisting of Two
Thousand (2,000) Shares.

GIVING AND GRANTING unto the said agent and attorney the full power and authority
in and about the premises; with power to use all means and processes in law for the full and effectual
execution of the business herein described; and in my name to make and execute due acquit-
tance and discharge , and in and about the premises to appear for and represent me before
any governor, judge, justice, officer, or minister of the law whatsoever, in any court of judicature,
and there on my behalf to institute, answer, defend, and reply unto all actions, causes, matters,
and things whatsoever relating to the premises. Also to submit any matter in dispute respecting the
premises to arbitration or otherwise; with full power to make and substitute, for the purpose aforesaid,
one or more attorneys and the same again at pleasure revoke. And generally to say, do, act, transact,
determine, accomplish, and finish all matters and things whatsoever relating to the premises as fully,
amply, and effectually, to all intents and purposes, as I , if present, ought or might personally
do, although the matter should require more special authority than is herein conferred; I ratify-
ing and confirming all and whatsoever said agent or attorney or his substitute shall lawfully
do or cause to be done, in and about the premises, by virtue of these presents.

IN WITNESS WHEREOF, I have hereunto set my hand and seal this
twenty-fifth day of September   in the year of our Lord One Thousand Nine Hundred
and_____.

Signed, sealed, and delivered
in the presence of

_____(SEAL)

_____   _____(SEAL)

State of Maryland, County of Allegany , to wit:
BE IT REMEMBERED That on this twenty-fifth day of September One
Thousand Nine Hundred and_____personally appeared before me the subscriber, a
Notary Public in and for the State and County aforesaid,
Frederick West Kenton and acknowledged the foregoing instrument of writing to be his act.

_____

Problem 5. Study this Lease (Landlord and Tenant's Agreement). Detach Form 9-5 from your Workbook and fill it in. The Lease is executed on November 27 of *this* year to begin on January 1 of *next* year. Fill in the year dates accordingly.

Landlord and Tenant's Agreement

THIS AGREEMENT, Made this __twenty-seventh__ day of __November__ ,
19____, between _____ George Wesley Morton _____, Landlord ,
and _____ Frederick Clayton Andrews _____ Tenant ;

WITNESSETH, That the said Landlord hereby rents to the said Tenant __the eight-room__ __cottage located at 1765 North Fulton Street in the City of Columbus, Ohio,__ for the term of __twelve months__ beginning on the __first__ day of __January__ , _____, and ending on the __thirty-first__ day of __December__ , _____ , at __One Hundred__ __and Ten Dollars ($110)__ a __month__ payable __monthly in advance on the first__ __day of each month.__

And the said Tenant hereby covenants with the said Landlord to pay the rent as aforesaid, keep the premises in good order, and surrender the peaceable and quiet possession of the same at the end of the said term, in as good condition as when received (natural wear and decay of the property and unavoidable accidents excepted) and, further, that the said Tenant will not do, suffer, or permit anything to be done in or about the premises that will contravene the policy of insurance against loss by fire; nor use or permit the use of the premises for purposes other than those of a __dwelling__ , and will not at any time assign this agreement or sublet the property thus let, or any portion thereof, without the consent in writing of the said Landlord or __his__ representatives; and further, that whatever alterations or repairs the said Tenant shall be permitted to make shall be done at __his__ own expense.

IT IS FURTHER AGREED that if the rent shall be __fifteen (15)__ days in arrears, the Landlord shall have the right to distrain for the same and to re-enter and take possession; and if the Tenant shall violate any of the foregoing covenants on his part herein made, the Landlord shall have the right without formal notice to re-enter and take possession; and if the property shall be destroyed or rendered untenantable by fire or unavoidable accident, the tenancy hereby created shall be thereby terminated, and all liability for rent hereunder shall cease upon payment proportionately to the day of fire or unavoidable accident.

AND IT IS ALSO FURTHER AGREED that this agreement, with all its provisions and covenants, shall continue in force from term to term after the expiration of the term above mentioned, provided, however, that the parties hereto, or either of them, may and can terminate the same at the end of the term above mentioned, or at the end of any __month__ thereafter, by giving at least __sixty (60)__ days' previous notice thereof in writing.

IN TESTIMONY WHEREOF, the said parties have hereunto subscribed their names and affixed their seals the day and year first above written.
in the presence of

_____(SEAL)

_____(SEAL)

State of __Ohio__ , County of __Franklin__ , ss.

This day before me, a __Notary Public__ in and for said County, personally came __George Wesley Morton and Frederick Clayton Andrews__ , the parties to the foregoing Lease and acknowledged the signing thereof to be their voluntary act.

WITNESS my hand and official seal this __twenty-seventh__ day of __November__ , 19____.

_____
Notary Public

Problem 6. Type the DEMURRER exactly as shown on this page and on page 264. Use ruled legal paper, if available, or rule two sheets of 8½ by 11 plain paper.

GEORGE PRESTON 1417 Hanover Street Baltimore, Maryland 21210	) :) :	
Plaintiff	) :	IN THE
vs.	) :	
HENRY MAYNARD and MARTHA MAYNARD, his wife 4208 West Lanvale Street Baltimore, Maryland 21212	) :) :)	
and	) :	COURT OF COMMON PLEAS
THE MAYOR AND CITY COUNCIL OF BALTIMORE (Municipal Corporation)	) :) :	
Defendants	)	

* * * * * * * * * * * * *

DEMURRER

TO THE HONORABLE, THE JUDGE OF SAID COURT:

Now comes one of the above-named Defendants, the Mayor and City Council of Baltimore, a municipal corporation, by Frederick W. Mayne, City Solicitor, and Henry C. Higgins, Assistant City Solicitor, and demurs for the Declaration in the above-entitled case as particularized by a Bill of Particulars heretofore filed by the Plaintiff at the demand of the Defendant, the Mayor and City Council of Baltimore, and for reasons therefor states:

1. That the Declaration as particularized is bad in substance and insufficient in law.

2. That the Declaration as particularized alleges no facts sufficient to show negligence on the part of the Defendant, the Mayor and City Council of Baltimore.

3. That the condition of the sidewalk described in the Declaration as particularized does not constitute action-able negligence on the part of the Defendant.

_____
Frederick W. Mayne
City Solicitor

_____
Henry C. Higgins
Assistant City Solicitor

Attorneys for the Mayor and City Council of Baltimore, a municipal corporation, Defendant

STATE OF MARYLAND,
                              TO WIT:
CITY OF BALTIMORE,

I HEREBY CERTIFY, That on this eighteenth day of September, 19 , before me, the subscriber, a Notary Public of the State of Maryland, in and for the City aforesaid, per-sonally appeared Frederick W. Mayne, City Solicitor, and made oath in due form of law that the foregoing Demurrer is not filed for the purpose of delay.

AS WITNESS my hand and Notarial Seal.

_____
Notary Public

Problem 7. Double-space; 10-space paragraph indentions. Type parenthesis marks and colons as in Problem 6. Leave two double spaces below the line Respectfully submitted,. Type a rule for the signature.

MARGARET E. PUTNAM

686 North Green Street

Baltimore, Maryland   21208

<table>
<tr><td>Plaintiff</td><td>IN THE</td></tr>
<tr><td>vs.</td><td></td></tr>
</table>

JOHN'P. WANAMAKER and

HELEN WANAMAKER, his wife

615 East Raynor Avenue

<table>
<tr><td>Baltimore, Maryland   21204</td><td>COURT OF</td></tr>
<tr><td>and</td><td>COMMON</td></tr>
<tr><td>THE MAYOR AND CITY COUNCIL OF</td><td>PLEAS</td></tr>
<tr><td>BALTIMORE (Municipal Corporation)</td><td></td></tr>
<tr><td>Defendants</td><td></td></tr>
</table>

* * * * * * * * * * *

MOTION FOR DIRECTED VERDICT

Mayor and City Council of Baltimore, Defendant, requests that the Jury be directed to return a verdict in its favor for the following reasons.

1. That there is no evidence in this case legally sufficient to entitle the Plaintiff to recover against it, and their verdict must be for the Mayor and City Council of Baltimore.

2. That there is no evidence in this case legally sufficient to prove any negligence on the part of the Mayor and City Council of Baltimore for which it is responsible; and, therefore, the Plaintiff is not entitled to recover against the Mayor and City Council of Baltimore.

3. That there is no evidence in this case legally sufficient to prove that Defendant, the Mayor and City Council of Baltimore, had any notice, either actual or constructive, of the defect mentioned in the evidence at the time and place where the accident happened in time

to have the same repaired prior to the happening of the accident mentioned in the testimony; and, therefore, the verdict of the Jury must be in favor of the Defendant, the Mayor and City Council of Baltimore.

4. That the undisputed evidence shows that the Plaintiff, Margaret E. Putnam, was guilty of negligence which directly contributed to the happening of the accident; and that, therefore, the verdict of the Jury must be for the Mayor and City Council of Baltimore.

5. That the undisputed evidence shows that the Plaintiff, Margaret E. Putnam, saw or by the exercise of reasonable care could have seen the defect which is alleged to have caused the injuries complained of in time to have avoided her being injured thereby, and by her failure to see said defect the Plaintiff directly contributed to the injuries and accident complained of; and, therefore, the verdict of the Jury must be for the Mayor and City Council of Baltimore.

6. That the Plaintiff has failed to show by preponderance of evidence that the defect in the cellar door existed prior to the accident; and, therefore, the verdict of the Jury must be for the Mayor and City Council of Baltimore.

Respectfully submitted,

_____

Allen W. Weldon
Assistant City Solicitor

Indorsements (sometimes spelled *Endorsements*). Legal forms and documents are often filed vertically. A "backing sheet" is usually prepared. It is a sheet of heavy paper long enough so that the upper part may be folded down over the sheet or sheets which make up the legal document. The packet, consisting of the backing sheet and the typed or filled-in sheet or sheets, is then stapled at the top.

Before the stapling is done, however, the indorsement must be prepared. That indorsement may be a form printed on the back of the backing sheet in such a way that it appears at the front of the folded document. Sometimes, however, it is necessary to prepare the entire indorsement. It consists of the title of the document and other identifying information.

Problem 8. Study the following indorsements. Detach Form 9-8 from your Workbook. In the indorsement forms for the MORTGAGE (left) and for the LEASE OF APARTMENT (center), fill in the typed material in the first two illustrations. In the blank form at the right type all the copy shown in the illustration at the right. Use the current year date.

MORTGAGE FROM MAURICE C. GLYNDON, Mortgagor. TO HORACE C. WEST, Mortgagee BLOCK NO. Received for Record................, 19........, at..........o'clock..........M. Same day recorded in Liber.............No...........Folio...........&c., ... Records of .... and examined per ...., Clerk, Cost of Record, $............................	**LEASE OF APARTMENT** FROM WORTHINGTON REALTY COMPANY TO HENRY F. ALLENBY October 14, 19--	COURT OF COMMON PLEAS Sacramento, California - - - - - - - - - - - - - - Burton W. Ryerson, Plaintiff vs. Charles W. Patterson, Defendant - - - - - - - - - - - - - - SUMMONS AND COMPLAINT = = = = = = = = = = = = = = Hilton, Guthrie & Langdon Attorneys for Plaintiff 765 Mercantile Building Sacramento, California - - - - - - - - - - - - - - To James W. Alexander, Esq. Attorney for Defendant - - - - - - - - - - - - - - Due and timely service of a copy of the within Complaint is hereby admitted this 25th day of August, 19 . Attorney for Defendant

The stenographer in a business office is mainly concerned with reproducing, in a different form, material that is given to her; that is, she takes dictation and transcribes that dictation on the typewriter. In some offices the dictation is given to a dictating machine, and the operator reproduces that dictation in the form of typewriting. The great majority of secretaries in business come from the ranks of stenographers. Through their training and experience, coupled with inherent ability, they have developed skills and personal traits which make them, to some extent at least, creative workers.

If you are aiming at a secretarial position, you need first to assure yourself that you can take dictation accurately and reproduce it correctly in the form of a typewritten transcript. Shorthand is really only a means to an end. The same observation applies to all other methods of recording dictation. When a businessman dictates a letter, he is not thinking about the rate at which he is dictating. Some men dictate slowly; others dictate rapidly. When the subject with which the letter deals is of an important nature, most men will dictate fairly slowly because they have to think and choose their words carefully. If the subject is of a more or less routine nature, their dictation will probably be given at a rapid rate. The stenographer must have reserve speed, so that she can record dictation under varying conditions. She should have something up her sleeve, so to speak, for emergencies.

Be sure that the businessman is not at all concerned with your shorthand; he is concerned entirely with the typewritten transcript. It is the typewritten pages which you will put before your employer that come under his eye. It is on the basis of your transcribed work that he judges your ability. Skill in shorthand and speed and accuracy in typewriting have to go hand in hand.

Secretaries, as we have said, are chosen from the ranks of competent young men and women who, as stenographers, have shown that they are good transcribers. The ability to reproduce dictation in the form of correctly transcribed letters depends largely on the knowledge of language and spelling which the stenographer has. Let us assume that you have sufficient speed to take dictation correctly. Let us also assume that you know how to set up letters neatly and attractively on the page. You can readily see that there is still another element which enters into the situation. The good stenographer is the one who has a thorough understanding of the mechanical aspects of the language. Unless she has mastered spelling, punctuation, and grammar, she lacks the foundation on which to build a successful career as a secretary.

The word counts in the right margin: 12, 26, 41, 55, 68, 81, 94, 108, 119, 133, 148, 162, 176, 190, 203, 217, 231, 245, 260, 274, 288, 300, 312, 326, 340, 354, 368, 375, 389, 402, 416, 430, 444, 459, 472, 486, 500, 513, 527, 541